Essential Strategic Management

From modernism to pragmatism

Paul Joyce and Adrian Woods

Butterworth-Heinemann
Linacre House, Jordan Hill, Oxford OX2 8DP
A division of Reed Educational and Professional Publishing Ltd

℞ A member of the Reed Elsevier plc group

OXFORD   BOSTON   JOHANNESBURG
MELBOURNE   NEW DELHI   SINGAPORE

First published 1996
Reprinted 1997

British Library Cataloguing in Publication Data
Joyce, Paul
   Essential strategic management: from modernism to
   pragmatism
   1 Strategic planning
   I Title   II Woods, Adrian
   658.4'012

Coventry University

ISBN 0 7506 2383 7

Typeset by Avocet Typeset, Brill, Aylesbury, Buckinghamshire
Printed and bound in Great Britain by Hartnolls Ltd, Bodmin, Cornwall

ESSENTIAL STRATEGIC MANAGEMENT

Contents

Preface

The writing of this book started with the idea that strategic management could be introduced to students of management clearly and concisely. As the work got underway it was realized that this had to be done without implying that strategic management was itself simple, static or uniformly the same everywhere.

Strategic management may be provisionally defined as a process through which an organization thinks about its future and then acts accordingly. This may involve attempts to predict the future on the basis of quantitative techniques; it may involve attempts to design grand plans to control the organization, in detail and for many years ahead. But quantitative-based prediction and detailed planning are merely forms which strategic management has taken. These forms should not be mistaken for the general notions contained in strategic management, namely, that organizations should think about the future, develop intentions and act purposefully to achieve them.

Conceived as concerned for the future, it would be difficult to imagine any manager objecting to strategic management in principle. If senior managers were to concentrate only on present problems and co-ordinate only day-to-day operations, they would seem to many people to be very short-sighted. We expect chief executives and their management teams to be carrying out an intellectual role, charting strategic directions and plotting ways for their organizations to get there. We would be surprised if they regarded the future as totally unknowable and relied on blind luck and total guesswork to make key decisions. Paradoxically, doubts about planning strategically for the future and implementing strategy in a top-down manner built up in the 1980s and early

1990s, just as the numbers of students of strategic management in the United States and Europe were expanding. By the early 1990s the subject of strategic management appeared to be a very diverse, complex and dynamic one, with sharp disagreements about how to approach it, the proper role of senior managers in relation to strategic management and the topics and disciplines which should be covered when studying it. In sum, it appeared a very confusing field of study.

Because it has been written at a time marked by rapid development of ideas, complex views about complex problems and strongly divergent advice about the correct approach to strategic management, the book also sets out to reform the chaotic picture of the state of thinking on strategic management. It has been written to provide an introduction to the essential topics in strategic management, including: the strategy process and analytical concepts, environmental analysis, evaluating company perform-ance, strategies for businesses in market contexts, international management, ethics and strategy, and managing strategic change. We have offered a view of three main classes of approach to strategic management – modernism, postmodernism and new modernism – which we think dispels some of the chaotic appear-ance of this field. We have set out to offer a more ordered consideration and, at times, integrated account of the different ideas about strategies, internationalization, ethics and the management of change, rather than try to smash them all into a simple unified view of the field of strategic management. The book does not make the field of strategic management any less dynamic, complex or diverse, but it does provide an intellectual map to help the student of strategic management find their way around.

This book will be useful to postgraduate students of management and final year undergraduates on business courses. It complements and should be read alongside the standard academic textbooks on this subject. It will also be useful to managers looking for a deeper understanding of strategic management in an organizational world which is seen by many as becoming increasingly turbulent and dynamic.

There are three key features of this book we would like to emphasize in this preface. First, it offers a fairly conceptual and theoretical analysis of strategic management. This is achieved in part by explaining how strategic management thinking and approaches have developed historically. For those readers just starting out on a study of strategic management this will provide you with the concepts, language, frameworks and empirical research findings you need to evolve your own intellectual position in relation to strategic management. Even those who have some knowledge of the field already will find our intentional tracking of some of the main developments in a chronological way helpful. For this has been done partly to build up the accretions and layers of insight and thinking which each theoretical development adds to the field. But it is also a warning that the student of strategic management has to be ready to evaluate and reconceptualize new contributions to strategic management as the field continues to move and evolve.

The emphasis on a conceptual and theoretical approach is not an inessential luxury in the study of strategic management; it is important in enabling students of strategic management to get beneath the confusing welter of ideas and opinions which lie on the surface of the strategic management field. It is also essential for the development of the conceptual flexibility which effective strategic managers use in diagnosing and assessing situations. This is the same as, or closely related to, the conceptual flexibility that some education courses foster by using case studies of strategic management problems to develop analytical and creative decision-making capabilities. At its best and at all levels, studying strategic management is not about learning the concepts and techniques and applying them mechanically to cases in a way which produces 'pat answers'. Likewise, at its best, doing strategic management is more than taking 'to-do' lists from books and doing them – or telling others to do them.

Second, this book provides a critical introduction to the analytical techniques and tools of strategic management. In our experience, it is necessary to provide students with help in understanding the way in which the 'intellectual apparatus' employed in strategic analysis partly determines the results obtained. This is not to say that strategic management is fatally arbitrary. Any, and every, strategic analysis is bound to contain some degree of subjectivity. But analyses not only need to be as objective as possible, they also need to be suitable and acceptable. On the latter point, however, it is increasingly unlikely that others can be persuaded to accept the 'facts' presented on the basis of the use of a strategic management technique without discussion of, and agreement to, the assumptions underlying the technique used.

Third, and returning to a point made above, the book acknowledges the dissension, apparent fragmentation, and confusion which currently characterizes the field of strategic management. We no longer have even a close approach to a consensus about the benefits of 'grand strategic planning'. Many people have written expressing disappointment with the meagre results of traditional strategic planning. It is fairly clear that influential theorists of strategic management are against the formal strategic planning of the 1960s and early 1970s. This is because they doubt the ability of senior managers to analyse strategic situations, and doubt their ability to formulate and implement strategy in any effective way. They certainly reject the notion of strategic planning as a rational and linear process with discrete and successive phases. But critics of strategic planning are often less than convincing in their suggestions of how senior managers should think and act if strategic planning is not valid. Their remarks seem to point to a very indirect and peripheral role for senior managers in strategic thinking.

Our own view is that there is a central role for senior managers in strategic management and that it is unwise to give into the temptation of wishing away the internal tensions of strategic management. Some of the anti-strategic planners seem to us to be doing this by suggesting that strategic learning should replace strategic planning and that top managers should voluntarily step down from the role of strategic formulator. But this thinking can make little sense to top managers. They will not, indeed cannot, for long step down from the responsibility of formulating strategies and making plans. The tensions internal to strategic planning – which concern the limits of knowledge and the limits of control over organizational members – have to be faced. Strategic management practice has to be evolved and along with it a new culture of top management has to be developed, which confronts the limits and does not just wish them away.

Consequently, this book is also implicitly concerned with the development of strategic management practice and theory. We agree with the anti-strategic planning perspective that the old grand planning form is not valid, but unlike that perspective we see that the best hope for the managers of organizations is to evolve new forms of strategic planning. We would also underline the way in which the well-known anti-strategic planning theorists – notably Mintzberg and Stacey – have at times theorized strategic change in ways which could be subsumed within a 'reformed' strategic planning. The outline of a new form of strategic management, based in part on ideas such as those of Quinn and of Hamel and Prahalad, is emerging. Some of its ingredients seem to us to consist of:

- a culture of strategic experimentation imbued with a spirit of pragmatism
- attention to strategic issue agendas
- greater use of long-term orientations centred on resource-based strategies
- the design of strategy processes with greater stakeholder involvement
- more ethically driven management.

We do not think the new strategic management is yet fully apparent; there are, for example, still inadequacies relating to the theorization of how organizations involve as many people as possible in strategy formulation as a way of dealing with the need to gain commitment. The stakeholder model, which we consider in the book, suggests some ways forward on this, but its feasibility is yet to be proven. There are also inadequacies in the theorization of how organizations experiment with new corporate identities. The current temptation is to reduce this to a discussion of cultural change; but, insofar as this is seen in terms of 'rolling out' a culture designed at the top of the organization, this is far from convincing.

As to the future, we expect strategic management practice and theory to continue evolving, for example as a result of the increasing influence of global competitive forces and the growing environmental concerns.

Paul Joyce and Adrian Woods

Acknowledgements

We both appreciated the support and help we have received along the way in the writing of this book.

Colleagues at the University of North London and Brunel University have inevitably contributed to the development of our ideas through discussions and working together on strategic management courses. We would especially like to thank Nick Winstanley and John Goodfellow at the Business School of the University of North London and the staff of the Department of Management Studies at Brunel University.

Our thanks also go to Marianne and Robert Young in Horetown, Wexford, for the comment – and conversation.

We wish to express thanks to Catriona Gordon at Butterworth-Heinemann, who was a valued source of encouragement and support from beginning to end.

Finally, we record the usual but genuine appreciation of our families: Theresa, Thomas, Caitlin and Patrick; and Mary, Anthony and William; and of course our parents, Albert and Rita, and Ted and Joan.

1

Themes and issues

Introduction

Many people in recent years criticized the notion of strategic planning as it had emerged from the 1960s: the tendency was to question whether those in charge of strategic management were really able to direct and plan the future. In part the criticisms were a realistic appreciation of the failures of strategic planning. But there was also an anti-intellectualism element in the criticisms, even though the critics could be both very intellectual in their style of critique and very concerned to offer their own intellectual analysis of the limits of strategic planning. This anti-intellectualism had two major manifestations. First, it distrusted the use of intellectual work to understand and have foresight about the future. Second, it was unimpressed by the work of the business schools that had propagated confidence in strategic planning by teaching the intellectual ideas that underpinned this early form of strategic management.

In this first chapter we will begin by observing the different orientations to the future that writers on strategic management have adopted. We are inclined to see the attitude to the future as the most basic attitude of all in strategic management, and we believe that the different postures towards knowing the future assume a major importance in demarcating different schools of strategic management.

We will also explore, albeit briefly, the possibility of there being a systematic knowledge of strategic management which managers can study formally and thereby increase their effectiveness. All strands of opinion in strategic management seem to value the results of conceptualization of strategy processes and strategy but, as will be seen, there are considerable differences of opinion about how different theories may be substantiated and what counts as empirical substantiation.

The importance of a future orientation

Many years ago Peter Drucker (1968) suggested that managers had no choice but to anticipate the future and try to shape it. This suggestion, when stated baldly, may seem patently obvious. Management that only worries about the tasks immediately facing it is likely to be ignoring the decisions that are critical for the future prosperity and survival of the organization. This is by no means an academic point. Many newly started businesses will not survive to see their tenth birthday. The average life expectancy of a business appears to be less than that of a human being in the western world. The future survival of a business is, then, far from assured.

Many owner-managed businesses need to plan for the future direction of their business when the owner retires – or to plan for the disposal of the business. Big firms have to plan for the renewal of the top management team, as Burton the UK retailer has found difficult more than once. Then there is the need to think about investing for the future – in new products, new markets and new businesses. This takes considerable forethought. Big companies launching new ventures may find it takes five to ten years before profitability is achieved. Companies have to think ahead when their current businesses are peaking, or the technology looks like moving on. Do they keep on doing what they are doing for as long as they can, or should they already be planning for a move out of their present commitments? The one certain thing about business is that it is dynamic, and it always has been. Knowing this, how can any responsible management fail to look ahead and attempt to outguess the twisting and turning of market forces and the opportunities and threats that are thereby posed?

Of course, thinking about the future is very difficult for managers. Ask any owner of a business to predict future trends, just one year ahead, in their firm's order book, output, sales, profitability or investment and many will express much uncertainty. The last twenty years have been very turbulent, or, as the pundits of strategic management put it, full of 'discontinuities'. Lengthening the time horizon to five or ten years does not reduce the uncertainties of predictions, and yet this is how long it takes many firms to make long-term investments, develop capabilities and embed structural changes in their organization.

Not all things are equally unpredictable. For example, the birth rate over the last year can be projected forward to give good forecasts of the size of the population of five-year-olds in five years' time. Other predictions are more tricky and there are famous examples of overly pessimistic assessments in the postwar period. In the 1950s IBM, for example, underestimated the growth of demand for computer capacity. It is difficult accurately to estimate not only demand, but also development times and development costs. These are obviously critical in developing completely accurate forecasts of the costs and revenues to be expected from strategic investments.

But must there be total certainty and total accuracy to make a strategic interest in the future either desirable or possible? No serious management expert could argue that anticipating the future could be based on totally certain predictions. But this does not mean that managers must give up trying to anticipate the future; nor does it necessitate that they rely on pure 'hunches' or ungrounded 'visions'. However, because managers must settle for educated guesses about the future, any plans they make for shaping their destiny must build in the possibility for revisions and experimentation, and they must at times be prepared to admit to mistaken foresight and resort to salvaging a mistaken plan.

Doing the right thing, doing the thing right

An interest in the future is, we are insisting, the real bottom line of strategic thinking. Many definitions are attempted of strategic thinking, but if they miss out this point they are, in our view, flawed. Once this point is grasped it becomes evident why Ansoff, one of the greatest thinkers on strategic management, anchors his distinction between strategic and operational management in what is essentially a time difference. Ansoff (1987) defines strategic management as concerned with the problem of optimizing the *potential* return on investment, whilst operational management concerns the *realization* of the optimum return on investment.

The two different moments of management – the strategic and the operational – are associated with different activities. Strategic management activities may be centred on, for example, developing and launching new products or services, entry to, or exit from, markets, the design and implementation of new competitive strategies, and so on. These activities, as it were, define the profit potential of a business. Operating management transforms this potential into actual results in terms of profits. It does this through the management and maintenance of the basic activities of the enterprise – acquiring inputs, producing goods or services, and of course marketing the goods or services. Obviously, operational management is seeking the greatest possible efficiency and productivity in the use of resources to meet needs catered for through the market mechanism.

There is a need for both strategy and operational effectiveness. Ansoff and McDonnell (1990, p. xvii)), quoting Peter Drucker, suggest that 'strategic activity insures that the firm "does the right thing," while operating activity makes sure that the thing is done right'. The importance of paying attention to both seems to have been obscured in recent years as firms often lost sight of the need for strategy, getting caught up in one or more of the waves of organizational reform that focuses on operational effectiveness, e.g. just-in-time, total quality management and business process re-engineering.

The strategic and the operational spheres of management do not merely coexist in the well-run organization. They impact on each other. Or, to put it better, they are *inputs* to each other.

The way in which strategy is an input to operational management has without doubt received more attention than the way in which operational management can impact on strategy. In the 1950s when, in the US, 'long-range planning' was emerging, strategy was seen as directing operational management (Ansoff and McDonnell, 1990). Planning was informed by forecasts of company performance based on extrapolations of past experiences of growth; it was then, or so it seemed, a simple matter to set the goals, budgets, profit plans and programmes which were implemented by the operating units. Long-range planning was succeeded by 'strategic planning', which, according to Ansoff and McDonnell, was invented in the 1960s. At this time, they claim 'it was clear that it was both undesirable and dangerous to plan the firm's future on the basis of extrapolation of past trends' (1990, p. 247). So, firms made forecasts that took account of threats and opportunities and did not just extrapolate the trends of the past. Despite this key difference in the approach to forecasting, strategic planning still determined operating goals and budgets which had to be implemented by operating units, although it also initiated strategic programmes and projects (see Figure 1.1)

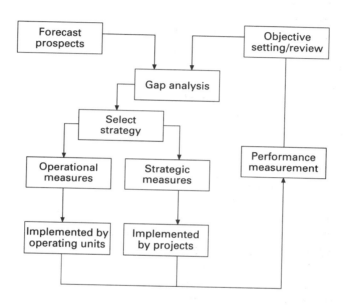

Figure 1.1   *Strategic planning*

Improvements in operational effectiveness, such as major increases in productivity, can enable firms to improve the price, quality, etc. of their products or services and this can have a big impact in their existing markets. Sometimes existing markets are saturated and such improvements in productivity cannot be translated into market impact. On these occasions, the increased operational effectiveness triggers a strategic issue: what should the firm do with the excess capacity that improvements in operational effectiveness have created? If big improvements in productivity are possible through techniques such as re-engineering – and there have been many such claims – then substantial scope for strategic moves open up. Companies can, for example, enhance their position in existing markets or even enter new ones; and, thus, increases in operational effectiveness can lead to firms seizing major new market opportunities (Johansson, McHugh, Pendlebury and Wheeler, 1993, p. 20).

Doing anything

In the 1980s theoretical attacks on strategic planning gained increasing respectability and supporters of old-style strategic planning were on the defensive (Mintzberg, 1990). Criticizms had surfaced regarding the feasibility of formal strategic planning in the 1970s, but they came to the attention of many people through the ideas of Peters and Waterman (1982) in the United States, Ohmae (1982) in Japan, and Stacey (1991) in the UK.

Peters and Waterman, in many different ways, were against *thinking* about the future. They railed against the overemphasis on analytic tools and the over-reliance on the analysis which preceded action. They put the emphasis instead on *doing*. They sloganized this view in their advice to have a 'bias for action'. They castigated 'paralysis by analysis' and argued for more experimentation and more implementation. They downgraded the concept of strategy to 'a damn good idea for knocking the socks off the competition' (Peters and Waterman, 1982, p. 30). They suggested that setting strategic directions – 'pathfinding' – was aesthetic and intuitive. Selecting the right idea for strategic direction was ascribed ultimately to 'taste'. They were against the belief in the use of business analysis to find *the* right answer. In summary, analysis was useful as a small element of the overall picture, but the business schools had overemphasized it. The attack was clearly directed at the formal strategic planning.

> What we are against is wrong-headed analysis, analysis that is too complex to be useful and too unwieldy to be flexible, analysis that strives to be too precise (especially at the wrong time) about the inherently unknowable – such as detailed market forecasts when end use of new product is still hazy ... and especially analysis done to line operators by control oriented, hands-off staffs.
>
> Peters and Waterman, 1982, p. 31

Ohmae similarly attacked the planning staff and their planning techniques and argued the need to put the emphasis back on executive leadership. It was suggested that successful businesses did not have elaborate and formally rational planning processes, or large numbers of corporate planners. They had dynamic leaders with good strategic sense, intuition and creativity.

Stacey (1991) followed Peters and Waterman in attacking the

rational approach to strategic management. He was sceptical of the prospects for foresight in business situations where innovation was the issue. He characterized existing models of managing and organizing as assuming 'that it is possible to say something useful about the long-term future' (Stacey, 1991, p. 129) and offered his own approach to strategy based on chaos theory. When the future is unknowable, he suggested that firms cannot be proactive and must learn as the future unfolds. 'It is impossible to establish in advance the future direction of an innovative business' (1991, p. 303). In place of strategic plans, he advocated creative interaction with other organizations and people in the environment. The role of top managers was to enable key groups of managers to engage in coherent behaviour which could spontaneously cope with the new and unknowable.

Whatever caveats and provisos were noted by such writers on strategic management, the main message was clear enough. Firms should forget about trying to think about the future and plan for it. Top managers were to put their faith in intrapreneurship by lower level managers who could be motivated to thrive on chaos and act spontaneously.

Doing something with foresight

It is, we think, rather unhelpful to suggest either that the future is unknowable or that there can be complete certainty about what it will be. For a start, the future is obviously partly the product of what businesses try to make it. Prediction can, for example, be a self-fulfilling prophecy. Businesses can also work to make their preferred image of the future come true. In addition and a point which has received some attention, it may be important to consider the possibility of there being degrees of uncertainty, and the possibility that the things that are especially uncertain about the future may vary.

Ansoff and McDonnell (1990), in a useful contribution, have suggested that future threats and opportunities may become progressively clearer and more concrete in some situations. At the outset the information may be so vague in fact that firms may just have a *sense* of a threat or opportunity, but be unable to specify exactly the nature of it. Over time information accumulates – or is accumulated – until a comprehensive understanding of the threat/opportunity and a feasible response is achieved. They suggest five stages might form this progressive growth of knowledge.

1 Management only senses the impending occurrence of a threat or opportunity.
2 Management identifies the source of the threat or opportunity.
3 Management knows the nature, timing and seriousness of the threat or opportunity.
4 Management knows how to respond (action programmes, budgets and timing).
5 Management understands the situation well enough to predict the costs and profit that will be the probable result of the response.

It may seem logical for a firm's management to wait until it has progressed through all the stages before it makes up its mind what to do about a threat or opportunity. But sometimes the management will launch a response when it has only partial knowledge but not the complete information it needs for what we might call a formally rational decision. For example, people were thinking about the potential of solid state physics in the 1940s long before it became a commercial reality. The pioneering firms in this new industry did not wait for complete knowledge of the costs and profit potential, they began product development and were well entrenched as industry leaders by the time more cautious firms were ready to take the plunge. This pioneering approach seems to have been the case of Fairchild, which was a leader in the development of integrated circuits. Jantsch reports that: 'Integrated circuits were recognised by Fairchild as a breakthrough of such far-reaching consequences that a "Make them, then sell them" attitude was adopted during the development without much trouble being taken with quantitative assessments of the impact or even with formal market research at that stage' (Jantsch, 1967, p. 89).

Firms can begin their response to new opportunities (or threats) in a variety of ways even when they have only just begun to understand the source and nature of them. Ansoff and McDonnell (1990, p. 390) suggest, for example, that they can:

1 acquire necessary technological, production and marketing skills
2 launch new product development
3 develop sources of supply

Whilst the farsighted firms may begin to respond when the information is still vague, it is likely that their behaviour becomes more and more focused as knowledge accumulates. By the time knowledge of possible responses is developed, the entrepreneurial firms will have been working for some time on developing their response. In situations where firms *must* and do start their response when knowledge is very vague, or risk being too late to enter a new industry, then firms can be said to be managing by weak signals.

Hamel and Prahalad (1994) also argue that the importance of acting with foresight, well ahead of complete knowledge, is critical to industry leaders. 'Industry foresight gives a company the potential to get to the future first and stake out a leadership position' (Hamel and Prahalad, 1994, p. 73). Cues and weak signals are there for everyone to read; they deny that the future is unknowable. Foresight, they say, is easier with respect to what will happen, even though its timing and the route to it are very difficult to determine. Foresight is not easy: it involves considerable intellectual energy. Even when a company has developed foresight, a lot of learning by doing is then necessary.

Like Ansoff and McDonnell, Hamel and Prahalad suggest that there is a lot to be done before a market-based competitive response is launched. Senior managers must, for example, establish a sense of purpose and set about building key competences. This can take decades, as shown by the example of the video cassette recorder (VCR) industry, where three companies – Philips, Sony and Matsushita (JVC) – took about twenty years to produce a VCR for the consumer market. The battle to be industry leader finally took place in the 1970s, when Matsushita became the industry leader, and it retained this title into the early 1990s. Hamel and Prahalad make two interesting points about the race to 'invent' the VCR market. First, the race was a marathon and was not won until the 'last mad scramble for the finish line'. Second, those who were near the finishing line at the end were all in at the race from the beginning. The big message is that strategy encompasses developing industry foresight and developing competences and coalitions with other companies; and it is a big mistake to see strategy as only concerned with the last stage of competition for market share.

Strategic management – an evolving and context dependent practice

It is not just ideas about strategic management which change. Strategic management itself is an evolving practice. John Harvey-Jones (1987), for example, refers to the 'planning era' in strategic management as having 'occurred some time ago' and as having 'been discredited' (1987, p. 8). His pen portrait of the way in which planning was carried out during this period suggests that the practice had severe limitations:

> In many large organizations planning became the job and responsibility of an increasingly specialized planning department, who were divorced from the everyday business and sought to apply theoretical measures of a quantified type to the complexities of business decisions.
>
> All too often in those days one was faced with plans produced by the staff that seemed somewhat remote or at variance with one's own experience of the actual behaviour of the market in which one was operating. But another and even more worrying variant of the same problem arose when the plans laid would have been helpful in a business sense, but were not followed because of the illusive lack of commitment in a decentralized organization.
>
> Harvey-Jones, 1987, p. 8

Amongst large US companies with multiple strategic business units (i.e. divisions, profit centres and any other parts of large organizations which have their own individual strategies) there have been shifts in the organization and activities of strategic management in recent years. Based on recent survey work (Pekar and Abraham, 1995), we can suggest that sophisticated approaches to strategic management practices by such large US companies do not bear out images of remote corporate planners totally preoccupied with specialist techniques for evaluating competitive situations and industry structures and making overly precise predictions of long-range futures. Instead, it seems that these corporations do the following.

- form teams of planners and line managers that focus on major opportunities and strategic issues
- evaluate trade-offs between short-term and long-term financial results

- prepare creative strategies to improve the competitive position of SBUs
- plan resource allocation relatively rigorously and in detail
- experiment with strategic alliances and partnerships and other novel strategic options
- have senior managers who get involved in new 'beachhead' investments.

The actual content of strategic management practices will vary from place to place, over time and between different kinds of organizations. As Mockler (1995) has put it, 'management in business is context-specific' (1995, p. 6). So we should not expect the preceding list to be much of a guide to the nature of strategic management practices in, say, a small owner-managed firm or a large not-for-profit public services organization in the UK.

Recognition that context matters can lead people to adopt a contingency theory perspective. They may, for example, expect that the strategic management practices actually occurring will be contingent on the context, or, that the most effective practices will vary according to the context.

We can illustrate the contingency theory approach using the work of Ansoff and McDonnell (1990). They claim that there are at least seven distinct modes of strategic behaviour and 'each is optimal under different conditions' (Ansoff and McDonnell, 1990, p. 475). According to them, 'strategic learning' behaviour is appropriate to a context characterized by low predictability, high novelty and high complexity. This mode of strategic behaviour is described as involving a progressive commitment process, in which decisions are designed to keep open as many options as possible and to foster strategic learning. Planning and implementation are not sequential but parallel. In contrast, when the context is highly predictable and low on complexity and novelty, they recommend an 'ad hoc management' mode of strategic behaviour. This is where strategic issues are handled one at a time as they come to the attention of management.

How do you know it is the right thing?

The general strategic management process (which will be discussed in more detail in Chapter 3) has been variously characterized. It can be seen as a set of sequential steps, for example:

1 the study of environmental trends;
2 assessing the internal capabilities of the organization;
3 confirming and amending corporate objectives and target;
4 identifying strengths, weaknesses, opportunities and threats;
5 identifying potential strategic actions;
6 evaluating strategic options;
7 implementing them.

Knowledge and research to back up the validity of any particular statement of the overall strategy process is limited. In consequence, some people advocate empirical research to model more specific strategic decisions in specific situations and then to, eventually, base more general process models on the accumulated research findings on them. This is a plea for 'micro contingency research' (Mockler, 1995).

Micro contingency research begins with the study of real expert strategic planners and focuses on the strategic management decision process in a specific area (e.g. a multinational's decision to introduce a new product into one of its national markets). The research models the real reasoning processes of expert planners and then creates expanded and more complex models through development work (by, for example, working with other expert planners and incorporating macro contingency research). The result can be to develop micro contingency models of individual manager-based strategy processes. These are normative models in the sense that they aim at addressing managers' needs. They are empirically based in that the starting point is the study of the actual thinking processes of real strategic planners.

The implication behind this line of argument is that knowledge of strategic management is still in its infancy and that theories and models will have to be patiently built up over a long period of time. In such a view, arguments should be settled on the basis of *valid* evidence.

> To be valid, a descriptive observation must meet a single test: it must be an accurate observation of reality. A prescription must pass a much more rigorous test: it must offer evidence that use of the prescription will enable an organization to meet the objective by which it judges its success.
>
> Ansoff, 1991, p. 81

Some arguments in strategic management can stem from the failure of people to be clear about whether they are speaking descriptively or prescriptively. So, when theorists are arguing about formal strategic planning as against emergent strategies that result from informal learning, are they arguing about which one is actually used, or are they arguing about which one would produce the best results if it was actually used? Ansoff (1991), for example, has complained that Mintzberg, a critic of formal strategic planning, 'converts descriptions into prescriptions without offering any evidence that they will bring success to organizations using them' (Ansoff, 1991, p. 81).

There have been studies which attempted to determine whether or not strategic planning improved company performance. In evaluating such studies there will be issues around the quality of the research and the generalizability of the research findings (see Figure 1.2).

Figure 1.2　*Does strategic planning work?*

Greenley (1989) reviewed nine previous studies which had looked at manufacturing firms in the USA and the UK. He reported that five of them had found a relationship between the use of strategic planning and performance; the other four did not find such a relationship.

One of the studies he reviewed, by Karger and Malik, involved a sample of ninety companies. They made a comparison of those companies that were planners with a group comprising nonplanners. Comparisons were made in terms of variables such as sales value, sales per share, earnings per share, operating margin and net income. Out of thirteen variables examined, six were significantly different ($P < 0.05$). This suggested that planning did lead to a better company performance.

Another study, by Kudla, involved a sample of 328 companies and used a control group of nonplanners. The study compared the level of shareholders' earnings before and after the introduction of strategic planning. It was concluded that strategic planning had a negligible effect on shareholders' earnings. This finding was taken as evidence that there was no relationship between strategic planning and company performance.

True to the spirit of scientific argument, Greenley then proceeded to assess the methodological rigour of the studies. He made use of five criteria to evaluate the credibility of the methods used.

1 Was a representative sample used?
2 Was the sample reasonably large (over thirty companies)?
3 Did the research design involve a control group?
4 Were measurements made before and after strategic planning was initiated?
5 Were differences tested for statistical significance?

Greenley concluded that the studies were not particularly rigorous, and made a number of specific criticisms of the studies, pointing out failures to measure potentially important factors, the inference of causality from correlations, deficiencies in operationalizing key concepts (e.g. formality of planning), and so on. He was careful to say, however, that the inconclusive nature of the assessment of the relationship between strategic planning and performance applied to manufacturing companies. So, Greenley, in effect, was stating that the results could not be generalized to firms outside manufacturing.

Not everybody is convinced by scientific research. Not everybody thinks it is worth basing arguments on it. Ansoff (1991), has levelled 对准 this latter charge at Mintzberg, when he wrote: 'Mintzberg seems oblivious to the need for evidence to support his descriptive statements' (Ansoff, 1991, p. 81). The reply was very robust. Mintzberg (1991, p. 83), making a passing reference to 'great gobs of wonderfully scientific statistics', suggested that the whole literature trying to assess the impact of planning 'never proved anything'. His own defence of strategic learning was on this occasion based on the story of Honda's breakthrough in the USA which is said to have occurred by mistake.

The lesson of this particular exchange between two leading thinkers on strategy – Ansoff and Mintzberg – is that some arguments about strategic management are difficult to settle because people have different views of what counts as evidence. We think a concern for scientific evidence is important, but we recognize its limitations. Research looking at what happened in the past – or what worked in the past – may not be applicable to newly emerging and novel situations. When this is the case, the truth may have to be established by practical experiments. Then the companies must learn by doing.

Present versus the future

One further difficulty in thinking about, and shaping, the future is the requirement for managers to pay attention to the day-to-day problems *as well* as thinking about the long-range future. If they spend insufficient time on the present, profits and survival may be imperilled and there will be no future for their business. If they spend too much time thinking about the present, they will suffer from short-termism and a lack of foresight. Hamel and Prahalad (1994, p. 47) offer the opinion 'that managers are spending too much time managing the present and not enough creating the future'. They suggest that uncertainty about the future is far higher than it need be – because companies do not engage in sufficient thinking about the future.

Is the formal study of strategic management desirable?

As we noted earlier in this chapter, doubts about the work of business schools has been voiced in recent years. This has been underpinned by an anti-intellectualism which sees business schools as stifling creative and intuitive instincts. Ohmae (1982), reflecting on the Japanese scene, was worried that the intuitive strategists were losing ground to the rationalist strategic planners.

> Often – especially in Japan, where there is no business school – these outstanding strategists have had little or no formal business education, at least at the college level ... But they have an intuitive grasp of the basic elements of strategy. They have an idiosyncratic mode of thinking in which company, customers and competition merge in a dynamic interaction out of which a comprehensive set of objectives and plans for action eventually crystallises.
>
> Ohmae, 1982, p. 2

Ohmae's opinions have found favour with some western commentators, such as Coulson-Thomas who suggests (1992, p. 233) that 'many western business schools and consultants encourage the "analysis of problems to the death"' and accepts Ohmae's argument that 'many of the more intuitive and pragmatic approaches of Japanese strategists' are more effective.

The criticisms levelled against business schools are not only that they overemphasize analysis, at the expense of action; there are criticisms that they are out of date, irrelevant, too academic and too preoccupied with knowledge for its own sake. These criticisms have some validity, but there is an element of scapegoating and a real danger of throwing out the baby with the bath water. The 1980s mood was to suggest that thinking and planning were the causes of the problems of poor competitiveness. Implicitly there was an accusation that business leaders lacked the will and leadership qualities which could radically transform the business scene. It was almost as if there was a belief that everyone could instantly decide to become innovative, dynamic and competitive. All they had to do was simply do it. Peters and Waterman offered eight easy rules for action.

This 1980s mood has passed. People are again writing about the need for persistence and a long-term view of strategic change. Perhaps it is now time to reconstruct the role of formal study in strategic management, one that places thinking alongside doing. If so, the business schools, as important providers of formal education, will need to consider how they develop the capability for approaching the future with foresight, how they help managers acquire the knowledge, concepts and techniques which they can use to form educated guesses about the future, and how the skills and technologies needed for long-term management of effective strategic change can be taught.

Formal study in business schools will only be one method by which managers can be developed to carry out their responsibilities for the future, but they are an important symbol of the need for the intellectual development of managers. The glorification of 'intuitive' managers, visionaries and spontaneous responses to complex, dynamic and diverse situations needs to be ended, even whilst recognizing the business schools' preoccupation with the analytical aspect of strategy.

Outline of the rest of the book

In this first chapter we have introduced what we see as some of the key themes and issues of strategic management. We have selected those we think are of more than momentary significance and which are likely to be of enduring imporance in the debates of how to manage strategically. We have also introduced some of the concepts and some of the language of strategic management. In the rest of the book we develop the themes and issues, elaborate and add to the concepts, bring in empirical data where we think it is helpful, and attempt to draw together the development of thinking in specific areas of strategic management. (The structure of the book is illustrated in Figure 1.3.)

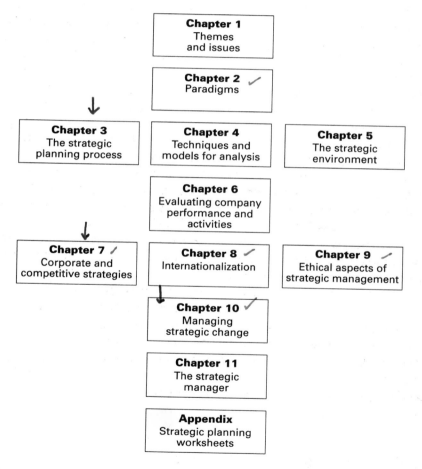

Figure 1.3 *The structure of the book*

In this first chapter we have emphasized the diversity of perspectives – paradigms – on strategic management. This is taken up systematically and in more detail in Chapter 2 where we mainly outline three perspectives on strategic management – modernism, postmodernism and new modernism. Just as in the present chapter we have emphasized how strategic management is essentially concerned with thinking about and shaping the future, these three paradigms can be read as grounded in different attitudes about how to achieve this. We would sum this up by saying that modernists get to the future through programmed innovation, postmodernists (at least in strategic management) want to discover the future in the spontaneous and 'uncontrolled' actions of lower level managers and employees and new modernists recognize that experimentation has to complement foresight. We put this typology of three paradigms forward because, first, we think it works. The second reason we have presented it here is that we have found it useful in addressing the complexity of strategic management thinking. We do not, however, claim that those writers whom we have associated with the different paradigms would accept the labels we have attached.

In this first chapter we have also acknowledged the strong foundations of strategic management in the analytical and rational ethos so vigorously attacked by the anti-strategic planners. This is an authentic foundation for strategic management, no matter how much its limitations have been exposed in recent years. Consequently, Chapters 3, 4 and 5 have a strongly rationalist character and are intended to represent the continuing contribution of the rational model of strategic planning. However, in each case we have introduced issues and concepts which begin to stretch the technocratic form of the planning process and to encompass the developments in thinking of more recent years.

Chapter 3 begins with a look at the planning process conceived in a very technocratic form, but it quickly moves on to look at strategic issue management and the identification of strategic issues. This concern with strategic issues has become more popular, perhaps as confidence in modernist conceptions of programmed innovation began to fragment under the impact of increasing environmental turbulence (in part created by the growth of global competition). This chapter also notes the importance of contingency views of strategic planning and briefly overviews organizational aspects of the strategy process.

Chapter 4 is perhaps the most 'rational-analytic' chapter of the whole book. It reviews some of the major techniques and tools of strategic planning. The anti-strategic planners are right to argue that the use of conceptual techniques are sometimes seen (falsely) as the whole of strategic planning. This is a wrong view – there is much more to strategic management than a facility for using analytical techniques. Such techniques cannot guarantee that the planner has arrived at the right answer. No matter how much time and effort is put into an analysis before taking strategic action, there is intrinsically always some uncertainty about whether the analysis will prove true. However, techniques can be useful analytical tools when used by skilled and farsighted managers. Thus, we attempt to turn them from being 'techniques' into useful 'tools' by stressing the way they relate to the strategy process and pointing out some of their limitations. We have also been keen to include those techniques/tools which are relevant to some of the newer thinking on strategic management. The Appendix provides a set of resources in the form of planning worksheets to support the use of these techniques and tools.

If people at times seek to reduce strategic management to the application of analytical techniques, they sometimes seek to reduce it down even more by concentrating on conceptual techniques for diagnosing the competitive environment of the firm's industry. In Chapter 5 we have set out to extend the conceptions of the business environment beyond the competitive forces which define an industry structure and which were such a feature of strategic thinking about competition in the 1980s. In particular, we examine post-industrialism and the emergence of strategic alliances and networks. These both contribute to more recent ways of thinking about business environments and both, in different ways, challenge the notion that all firms have to do is think about positioning themselves in their industry in terms of lower cost and differentiation. We do not suggest that the competitive structures of industries no longer matter, only that there is much more to the business environment. In this way, we think this chapter reflects the greater diversity of thinking in the 1990s.

In Chapter 6 we cover a number of important topics in strategic management, including analysing financial statements, accounting ratios analysis, creative accounting, the difference between profit and cash flows, and the use of value chains to evaluate activity. We use this chapter to consider and problematize many of the naive analytical versions of approaches to strategic planning. These naive versions take a surface level view of how company performance may be evaluated and take at face value the usefulness of the most popular measures using accounting ratios and data contained in financial statements. We also seek to reflect the growing interest within strategic management in moving away from seemingly 'hard' and apparently precise evaluations based on accounting data towards 'soft' and more pragmatic interest in 'value metrics', based ultimately on customer value criteria. For example, the value chain approach to looking at costs cannot be done properly without determining the perception of value by customers; for judgements of value to customers influence the analysis of activities, including what activities matter, how far activities are disaggregated and how they are categorized within the analysis.

If Chapters 3, 4, 5 and 6 together develop a comprehensive understanding of the analytical aspects of the strategy process, the next three chapters concentrate on the search for strategic effectiveness. In Chapter 7 we cover the popular topics of corporate and competitive strategy: acquisitions and corporate strategies, Porter's generic strategies, innovation, competence-based strategy, strategic networks and alliances and business process re-engineering. Some of the themes of Chapter 7 have already been introduced in this first chapter, including the diversity and complexity of thinking on strategy, the distinction between strategic and operational management and the possibility of knowing the future (raised particularly by adherents to competence-based strategy). This chapter shows the inherently dynamic nature of the search for strategic effectiveness, for example, in the way that portfolio management techniques have fallen out of favour and competence-based strategies are enjoying a period of growing influence.

We sense that the dynamism in the search for strategic effectiveness has been powerfully influenced by two principal forces since the 1960s. First, there is the economic force represented by the trends to globalization, which are partly evident in the growth of globalization strategies and the emergence of strategic alliances. Second, there is the social force represented by growing cultural changes, which have produced stronger societal expectations about the social responsibility of business and demands that it approaches strategic and operational issues more ethically. Consequently, we have devoted Chapter 8 to the theme of internationalization of business, probing in particular how businesses have sought strategically effective ways of internationalizing. The chapter explores major theories in the internationalization literature, including Levitt's modernity model and Ansoff and McDonnell's progressive commitment model. We also review theories of global re-engineering and look at the organizational and cultural aspects of the design of global businesses. We have not concerned ourselves with the complementary issue of how local industries and firms defend themselves against internationalization, which is an important topic but would have added considerably to the length of this chapter.

In Chapter 9 we have looked at the search for strategic effectiveness in relation to ethics. We trace, to some extent, a parallel course here to that in our discussion of the overall evolution of strategic management paradigms. First, we explore the social responsiveness model, which is modelled on a strategic planning view of matching the business to its environment. Next, we look at an approach which is very focused on the ethical relations between corporate leaders and their lower level managers and employees; this approach is concerned with creating the right kind of corporate climate for the intrapreneurial activity advocated by the postmodernist-style anti-strategic planner theorists. Finally, we look at the stakeholder model, an approach which opens up strategic formulation to a coalition of stakeholders. This last view has a certain kind of kinship to those theories which stress the emergence of network organizations and strategic alliances; both the stakeholder model and strategic network/alliance theories envisage the blurring of organizational boundaries and the sharing of decisions with wider 'communities' beyond the legal definition of the enterprise. We also look briefly at two areas which represent an overlap between the economic and social forces which we sense have been partly responsible for the dynamism of the search for strategic effectiveness. These are the ethics of international business and intercompany ethics.

In Chapter 10 we address the issue of managing strategic change. Again we reflect in the contents of this chapter the themes and issues which are explored throughout the book. In this case we have structured the chapter around the strategic planning (modernist) view of managing strategic change and alternatives to it. So, the chapter begins with viewing strategic change as merely a matter of implementing strategy which has already been determined. This is the model which has been attacked by the postmodernist school of strategic management. For example, they object to the way that implementation is neglected, because all the attention is lavished on rational methods of analysis within the strategy formulation phase.

They also suggest that the linear sequence – strategy formulation followed by implementation – fails to motivate and engage those who have to do the implementing. These and other objections lead to their rejection of the simple equation of strategic change with strategic implementation. The chapter proceeds then to look at a problem-solving model (based on Peters and Waterman) which focuses on social change and intrapreneurship and a political model (based on the work of Mintzberg). We tentatively offer the view that these different approaches can be brought together and integrated.

In the final chapter – Chapter 11 – we are again reflecting the dynamic and complex nature of strategic management thinking, but this time as reflected in prescriptions for the role of senior manager, that is, the personal agents of the strategic management process. So, we are again dealing with the different paradigms and with the overall issue of whether people can anticipate and shape the future. We explore different conceptions of the role of senior manager – the technocratic leader (modernist), the transforming leader (postmodernist), the passive-learner leader (also postmodernist) and the pragmatic leader (new modernist). This diversity of conceptions is brought together by us to suggest the profile of the all-round strategic manager, which we think can be supported by some empirical work on effective senior managers. We conclude with a discussion of an issue raised in Chapter 1: the formal development of strategic managers.

Key points

1 Strategic management is essentially concerned with thinking about and shaping the future of organizations. Whilst a wide variety of definitions of strategy and strategic management exist, to the extent that they overlook the concern for anticipating the future they are unsatisfactory.

2 The current state of strategic management – theory and practice – has followed twenty to thirty years of development, with corporate approaches having passed through earlier forms such as long-range planning and strategic planning. The increasing rate of change facing firms, competitive rivalry and turbulence are strong candidates for explaining the development of planning and the current

complexity of strategic management. We sense that the dynamism of the search for strategic effectiveness in the last twenty or so years is partly explained by major economic forces (globalization) and social forces (societal expectations about social responsibility and the ethical duties of business).

3 Arguments about strategic management are no longer easily settled by scientific evidence, with its concern for validity, the quality of evidence and generalizability. Some people are not convinced by such scientific evidence. And there are clear limitations in using scientific findings about the past to explain strategic management in emerging and novel situations. Companies then have to use practical experiments to determine the truth about the effectiveness of strategic practices and learn by doing.

4 The work of business schools has been the scapegoat for problems of poor competitiveness. The 1980s passion for glorifying 'intuitive' managers, visionaries and spontaneous responses to complex, dynamic and diverse situations is no longer acceptable. The intellectual development of strategic managers can be assisted by formal study and the business schools have an important role to play in that.

References

Ansoff, I. (1987) *Corporate Strategy* (Penguin).

Ansoff, I. (1994) 'Round 2: Response to Henry Mintzberg' in De Wit, B. and Meyer, R. *Strategy: Process, Content, Context* (West Publishing).

Ansoff, I. and McDonnell, E. (1990) *Implanting Strategic Management* (Prentice Hall).

Coulson-Thomas, C. (1992) *Transforming the Company* (Kogan Page).

Drucker, P. F. (1968) *The Practice of Management* (Pan).

Greenley, G.E. (1989) 'Does Strategic Planning Improve Company Performance?' in Asch, D. and Bowman, C. (editors) *Readings in Strategic Management* (Macmillan).

Hamel, G. and Prahalad, C.K. (1994) *Competing for the Future* (Harvard Business School Books).

Harvey-Jones, J. (1987) 'Introduction' in Ansoff, I. *Corporate Strategy* (Penguin).

Jantsch, E. (1967) *Technological Forecasting in Perspective* (OECD).

Johansson, H.J., McHugh. P., Pendlebury, A.J. and Wheeler, W.A. (1993) *Business Process Reengineering* (John Wiley and Sons).

Mintzberg, H. (1990) 'Round 1: Reconsidering the Basic Premises of Strategic Management' in De Wit, B. and Meyer, R. (1994) *Strategy: Process, Content, Context* (West Publishing).

Mintzberg, H. (1991) 'Round 3: Learning 1, Planning 0; Reply to Igor Ansoff' in De Wit, B. and Meyer, R. (1994) *Strategy: Process, Content, Context* (West Publishing).

Mockler, R.J. (1995) 'Strategic Management: The Beginning of a New Era' in Hussey, D.E. (editor) *Rethinking Strategic Management* (John Wiley and Sons).

Ohmae, K. (1982) *The Mind of the Strategist* (McGraw-Hill).

Pekar, P. and Abraham, S. (1995) 'Is Strategic Management Living Up to Its Promise?', *Long Range Planning*, Vol. 28, No. 5, pp. 32–44.

Peters, T. and Waterman, R.H. (1982) *In Search of Excellence* (Harper Collins).

Stacey, R. (1991) *The Chaos Frontier* (Butterworth-Heinemann).

2

Paradigms

= parodigme

Introduction

In this chapter we will be outlining some major ways of thinking about strategic management processes. We will present them as paradigms – theoretical 'mindsets' – within which theorists tend to *work* intellectually. This is necessary to achieve a clearer understanding of the intellectual contributions which have been made in recent years and which, at first sight, suggest a chaotic melange of ideas and insights. 'After almost 40 years of develoment and theory building, the field of strategic management is, today more than ever, characterized by contrasting and sometimes competing paradigms' (Hamel and Heene, 1994, p. 1). These contributions are not so much chaotic as evidence of the contradictory evolution of thinking, in which ideas are developed in counterpoint to existing ideas, or in attempts to unite existing opposing ideas. There is not a simple historical evolution of these paradigms, although the timing of works by Ansoff, Peters and Waterman, Mintzberg, Quinn, Stacey, and Hamel and Prahalad does suggest to us that the paradigms of intellectual thought are connected to general developments in the business world. Moreover, it is important to appreciate that the different paradigms, insofar as we have been able to piece together a coherent picture of them, do not replace so much as coexist in tension with each other. The paradigm we associate closely with the early work of Ansoff, which we call a modernist approach, continues to be very important today, some three decades after his ideas were presented.

One thing needs to be said by way of introduction. Anyone

standing back and looking at the landmark works can hardly fail to notice the parallels that exist between the fashions in thought about strategic management and those to be observed in philosophy and public life generally. The confidence and the certainties of the 1960s gave way to a more fragmented and diverse set of outlooks in the 1980s and 1990s. Beneath this transition can be seen, fundamentally, a shift of ideas about progress and change – usually referred to in strategic management as the issue of innovation. Thus three of the paradigms presented here – modernist, postmodernist and new modernist – rest on different attitudes to successful change by organizations.

Before we explore the three paradigms and some of the associated research, we will place the theorization of strategic management in context and clarify what we understand by the term 'paradigm'. By the end of this chapter we will have shown that the development of the theory of strategic management has produced a diversity of approaches on offer today. We make clear which of these we think are more useful and why. It will be apparent, we believe, that those approaches that stress the role of the senior manager as a thinker about the future are more useful than those that reduce the role of the senior manager to a passive, reactive one. As Hamel and Prahalad (1994, p. 46) suggest, the world's industry leaders are engaged in a race to the future – the first stage of this means a 'competition to imagine the future'.

Two fundamental assumptions

Most practitioners and most of those who write about strategic management, make two assumptions about top management that are fundamental.

- It has some ability (possibly quite small) to plan and act rationally.
- It can use this ability to improve organizational performance.

Both these assumptions are accepted in this book. We are, therefore, interested in those theoretical paradigms that explore the role of intellectual processes in planning, organizing and improving private, public and voluntary sector organizations.

Not all approaches to strategic management described in the literature are within the scope of this book. For instance, Whittington (1993) outlines what he calls the Evolutionary perspective, which says that the best businesses are selected by the competitive forces of the market. He says that Evolutionist theorists doubt the capacity of organizations to achieve deliberate adaptation *to* the environment: they assume a Darwinian model of selection *by* the environment and see the idea of managerial strategy as an expensive and dangerous delusion. He sums up one of the main practical implications of the perspective as follows: 'The construction of grand long-term strategies may be so much vain distraction; managers would do much better to get down to the modest business of making sure that what they do now is done as efficiently as possible' (Whittington, 1993, p. 22).

Pre-modern

There was strategic thinking in pre-modern times (Machiavelli). What form it took within economic organizations is difficult to imagine. For instance, whilst goods were made and exchanged in medieval times, it is hard to imagine the scope of strategic management in the context of the church doctrine of 'just price' (Postan, 1972, p. 255). In the English medieval towns there were associations of burgesses and guilds to regulate industrial and commercial activities. These ensured the maintenance of a monopoly by the existing mercantile and industrial trades- or craftspeople; they had elaborate rules to ensure that individuals did not get more than their fair share of business or take unfair advantage of others. Today's tolerance of 'dog eat dog' business practice would have been out of place then.

Even a cursory exploration of the genealogy of the present business system shows that powerful normative codes from the past have been handed down to the present. Max Weber (1930) charted the subtle but momentous shifts in religious life that created space for entrepreneurial action. Medieval thought had seen profit-seeking behaviour as unworthy and contemptible; later nonconformist religious thought took a different line. 'With the consciousness of standing in the fullness of God's grace and being visibly blessed by Him, the bourgeois business man, as long as he remained within the bounds of formal correctness, as long as his moral conduct was spotless and the use to which he put his wealth was not objectionable, could follow his pecuniary interests as he would and feel that he was fulfilling a duty in so doing' (Weber, 1930, p. 177). In nineteenth-century Britain, the modern period, many nonconformists did well in business; and, not wishing to succumb to the dangers of the wealth they were accumulating, many of them engaged in philanthropic giving and providing above-average conditions to their employees (Taylor, 1980, p. 14). Strikingly, the descendants of these ideas are now found within strategic management texts as issues of 'social responsibility' and 'business ethics'; they are the vestiges of that religious frame of reference, still often anchored in Judaic-Christian values.

Modernist, postmodernist and new modernist paradigms

The theoretical paradigms of strategic management which emerged over the last thirty years in Europe and the United States reflected the prevailing cultural, economic and political conditions. It is often not appreciated how specific are the values embedded in the western world's version of strategic management. A comprehensive treatment of strategic management would have to include a discussion of nonwestern management approaches to strategy. For example, the role of Confucian thought in Asiatic societies has led to important differences in management and organizational structures. For a detailed treatment of this see Stewart Clegg's *Modern Organisations* (1990).

Corporate business leaders such as, say, Alfred Sloan and Lee Iacocca in the United States and Arnold Weinstock in the United Kingdom, showed that businesses could be managed strategically. There was also a degree of confidence in strategic management capabilities with respect to governmental power (e.g. Keynesianism in Europe) and global conflicts and politics (hence the roles of the United Nations and NATO). But, without doubt, theoretical paradigms have also been created by the rise of business and management studies within business schools and by the 1980s phenomenon of the management 'guru' (most powerfully exemplified by Tom Peters).

Paradigms, in the sense used here, provide a means of interpreting and understanding organizational life and performance; they also provide a theory or perspective on how best to carry out strategic management. It is important to bear in mind that a paradigm has this dual function – both a means of interpreting the situation and a basis for action. This reflects a distinction encountered in the previous chapter in terms of the difference between the validity tests for observations and for prescriptions (Ansoff, 1991). Of course, there can be a certain interdependence between these functions: interpretation of, and understanding, a situation is essential for diagnosis which precedes effective strategic action, and strategic action based on a theoretical paradigm helps to shape future situations which then are reinterpreted and understood.

A paradigm of strategic management may accurately describe what managers tend to do in practice. But only if it provides an effective way of thinking and acting. The argument here is a simple one: the successful use of a paradigm leads to its continued use; failure will prompt the search and trial of new ways of doing strategic management.

Not everyone subscribes to this view of paradigms or theories. Some observers of the corporate scene believe that managements' talk about formal strategic planning can be mere rhetoric. For instance, a popular (modernist) paradigm of strategic management assumes that top managers need to develop mission statements, goals and visions of the future. Coulson-Thomas (1992) claims that most company chairmen see the function of the company board as providing precisely these things. 'Seven out of ten describe the function of the board in terms of establishing policy, objectives, strategy or vision, and monitoring and reviewing the extent of their achievement. The implementation of strategy is usually undertaken by a management team that is accountable to the board' (Coulson-Thomas, 1992, p. 38).

Obviously, where management fails to implement agreed strategies, then there is a situation in which talk of formal strategic planning can be mere rhetoric. Strategic management is then a mere intellectual process which does not affect realities (Barnard, 1938).

But, more controversially, it can be argued that *successful* forms of strategic control can be obscured by the rhetoric of formal strategic planning. That is, there is an important difference between the failure of implementation of a strategic plan and a situation in which implementation is never seriously contemplated by successful organizations; in the latter case, strategic planning is a myth rather than a failure. Thus, Stacey (1991) has claimed: 'managers in successful companies do not actually use the framework of missions, visions, and plans in the real strategic development and control of their business' (Stacey, 1991, p. 14). Nor did he think that top managers are visionaries in the way they think they are. Managers he talked to could only supply general statements (e.g. about being bigger), or could only list current aspirations. He could not equate what managers said with 'relatively constant pictures of some future state which qualifies them as a vision'. He could not see in their answers 'overarching goals which provide the guiding principle for long periods'. Stacey suggested that managers and observers reconstruct events to explain what has happened as in accord with this model (1991, p. 12) and dismissed formal strategic planning as a ritual. In other words, Stacey saw the formal strategic planning process as a misleading myth.

It might seem relatively simple to use research to clarify what really goes on in organizations and what works. Renowned theorists seem to agree that there is in existence a practice of *a priori* strategic planning, in which analysis is followed by implementation. Ansoff (1994) claims that *a priori* strategy formulation is in widespread use, especially where managers are in environments in which they are not sure about the future. Mintzberg (1994a) agrees that there is widespread use of such strategy formulation, even though he regards this as a problem. There is certainly survey evidence to back up the widespread existence of both annual strategic planning and written business plans in the United States (see, for example, Baker, Addams and Davis, 1993). And there is evidence suggesting that the prescription of formal strategic planning is valid: Pearce, Robbins and Robinson (1987) found that completeness and commitment to strategic planning correlates with effective organizational performance (see Figure 2.1).

Figure 2.1 *Formal planning – Pearce, Robbins and Robinson (1987)*

In 1983 Pearce and his colleagues studied ninety-seven small US manufacturing firms. They explored the relationships between the formality of strategic planning, the grand strategy being pursued and the performance of the firm. Their evidence was collected by means of a postal survey of chief executives. The response rate was 16 per cent.

Formality was measured using a scale consisting of six items gauging the development of strategic planning within firms. These items referred to: the existence of short-range profit plans, the acceptance of the final plans, the presence of a person or group to co-ordinate a company-wide strategic planning effort, a climate in the company supporting the planning effort, a formal statement by top management of what business the company is in or wants to be in, and the use of plans to judge managerial performance. Pearce and his colleagues say that the scale enabled systematic comparisons of firms in terms of completeness of, commitment to and utilization of their strategic planning activities. (This scale, therefore, provides a measure of the importance or seriousness of strategic management and arguably it is a simplification to describe this as 'formality'.)

Firms were classified as having one of the following grand strategies: stability, internal growth, external acquisition or retrenchment. This is a fairly familiar way of classifying generic strategies. Most of those surveyed identified themselves as having a stability strategy or internal growth strategy.

Performance was measured using subjective evaluations of: return on assets, return on sales, sales growth and overall performance. (They were able to check these subjective evaluations against data supplied by about forty of the firms; the subjective evaluations checked out reasonably well.)

Planning formality was consistently linked to performance but there was no correlation between the grand strategy and performance. Pearce, Robbins and Robinson concluded: 'Increased emphasis on formal strategic planning activities appeared to be an effective method of achieving improved financial performance for this sample of ninety-seven small manufacturing firms' (Pearce *et al.*, 1987, p. 132).

But some research work contradicts a link between strategic planning and organizational performance (Greenley, 1989). And some work provides a more complex picture of the nature of effective strategic management: Quinn's (1991) study of a small number of organizations suggested that managers did act logically but were not acting in line with the usual picture of good strategic management.

Perhaps some of the discrepancies in the empirical evidence are a function of managers saying one thing and doing another; but perhaps those who are better at formal strategic planning, even if it is not perfectly executed, are also better at other methods of strategic management. In any event, we need to bear in mind the subjective biases of research that mean many organizations with mediocre or moderately effective planning and varying levels of performance might be seen by different observers as evidence confirming the truth, or the myth, of the efficacy of formal planning.

How is the usefulness of a paradigm of strategic management to be judged? If managers use a paradigm it must have some use and we might assume that the usefulness might be measured in terms of organizational success (e.g. profitability). However, usefulness in relation to business performance is only one of the dimensions that may be relevant. Organizations are not only systems for getting things done; they are also systems of social relationships. Perhaps the language and discourse of a paradigm of strategic management sometimes has a usefulness in relation to the system of social relationships. This usefulness may be seen as partisan, as in the case of a paradigm that meets top management's ideological needs for an account of its necessary importance (Knights and Morgan, 1991).

On the other hand, the paradigm may, in part, be an attempt to provide an effective model for the social relationships, one that enables an optimum level of co-operation. For example, Barnard (1983), a major figure in the early history of management theory and for a time the President of the New Jersey Bell Telephone Company, assigned responsibility for abstract, generalizing, prospective, long-run decisions to top management. He also said that inherent organizational difficulties were created by making the executive responsible for deciding on the general purposes of the organization, whilst those at lower levels, at the base of the organization, made the detailed decisions about action in the concrete conditions they faced. Those at the top needed to understand the concrete conditions and specific decisions being made at the base and those at the lower levels needed to be indoctrinated in the general purposes in order to ensure cohesiveness and coherence. In a judgement which continues to ring down through generations of strategic management studies, he considered that up-and-down-the-line co-ordination of decisions was essential and that its absence reduced top management's decisions to intellectual processes in an organizational vacuum. Of course, this is not to decry intellectual processes by those at the top. But it is critical that they are not insulated from operational realities by what Barnard called layers of misunderstanding.

We will certainly see shortly that different paradigms provide for very different relationships between top management and those at lower levels and provide different answers for the inherent difficulty of linking intellectual processes and the realities.

Finally, we should acknowledge here the culturally specific nature of business in Europe and the United States, which certainly places limits on the relevance of the theoretical paradigms considered in this chapter. This is a point made by Whittington (1993, p. 30): '"Strategy" has strong connotations of free-will and self-control, but many cultures prefer to interpret events less as the product of deliberate human action and more as the result of God, fate, luck or history' (Boyacigiller and Adler 1991).

We have found it convenient to describe each of the three paradigms discussed below using the following six dimensions.

1 The role of the top management
2 The nature of successful change
3 Expectations about others at lower levels
4 Attitude to planning
5 Attitude to chance events
6 Organizational requirements.

The modernist paradigm

Arguably the modernist paradigm was *the* paradigm of the 1960s and early 1970s. It is well exemplified by Ansoff's book *Corporate Strategy* (1968) which concentrated on strategy formulation as a process of analysing information in order to make a decision about the business the private firm should be in. It is still the basic approach taught in the business schools, where the concern is to train managers in how to provide analytical justification for strategic decisions (Peters and Waterman, 1982, p. 29). The aspiring strategic manager is taught to deploy techniques, many of which seem to involve listing, classifying, rating and evaluating.

Modernist dimensions

The role of the top management

Modernist thinkers see strategic management as the province of the decision-making elite within the corporation, that is, the chairman, the board members, etc. and the specialist planning staff that advise them. These top decision makers, guided by their analytical tools and measurements, determine the new strategic moves. They carry out rigorous (analytical) assessments of their situation and choices and undertake, ideally, quantitative forecasts of the organization's environment.

The nature of successful change

In essence, change is managed and controlled by the strategic plan, which is the fruit of analysis and choice by the strategic decision makers; by means of the plan the organization is adapted to its environment to ensure continued growth. The tone of the approach is that decision makers are confident that they can determine the organization's destiny: the corporate future is programmable because the future and the environment are knowable and organizational change is controllable. The top managers reconfigure policies, strategies, budgets, organizational structures, etc. and, providing these are then carried through operationally, produce growing and healthy businesses.

Expectations about others at lower levels

Planning and execution are separated. Therefore, the main implementation problem is securing the commitment of others to the changes the strategists devise. 'The planners must determine who in the organization must be committed to the change and to actually carrying it out for the change actually to take place' (Beckhard and Harris, 1987, p. 91). Whilst modernists are prone to underestimate the importance of implementation, pouring a lot of effort into making the right analysis and choice, they can be sensitive to the motivational aspects and the internal politics of securing commitment. As Barnard (1938) argued long ago, efficiency in a fundamental sense is concerned with efficiency relative to securing the necessary personal contributions to the organization. And this contribution is not bought by money alone – even if the organization could afford it. He just doubted that people could be sufficiently motivated by financial rewards to contribute enough effort to a co-operative system, by which he meant a business organization, such that it would be efficient and durable over an extended period.

Attitude to planning

In the modernist paradigm, planning is the core activity. It is conceptualized as a set of logically sequenced activities. For example, Ansoff's method had four basic steps: establish objectives, estimate the 'gap' between the current position and the objectives, propose courses of action (strategy) and accept a course of action which closes the gap. These basic steps were elaborated by Ansoff into a complex decision flow with decision rules (an algorithm). The whole process of decision making is presented as programmable.

However, as Ansoff made clear, the reality of strategic management moves the decision making into a more complex process than first appears from the algorithms. For a start, establishing objectives is not without its difficulties. There is not in reality a single objective, but a vector of objectives and there are conflicts between the various objectives. Different circumstances require different balances to be struck between objectives: 'For example, a profitable firm which has good growth prospects, but is a captive of a single customer, very likely needs emphasis on flexibility' (Ansoff, 1968, p. 67).

The conflicts between short-term and long-term performance, and between performance and flexibility, require careful consideration. Ansoff recommended the use of return on investment (ROI) to evaluate different product-market entries; decision makers had to balance forecasts of this against long-term growth (which requires investments in respect of periods beyond the planning horizon, i.e. investments in periods in which profitability forecasts are unreliable) and also against the requirement to invest for flexibility.

Planning to close the gap between the current position and established objectives involves selecting courses of action on the basis of the future benefits that are expected. However, some of the alternative courses of action open to the firm may not be immediately obvious. There are also difficulties in the accurate forecast of the benefits likely to be obtained. Ansoff said that 'attempts to compute cash flows for long-lived projects are frustrated by the rapid decrease in reliability of data for long-term forecasts' (1968, p. 27).

He estimated that reasonably reliable profitability forecasts were limited to periods of between three and ten years. (But he was writing in the 1960s at the end of a long period of economic upswing.) The calculation of benefits from a particular product-market entry might have to be very approximate: strategists might have to base their calculations on the general performance characteristics of the industry.

The unidirectional movement from establishing goals to analysis of the business environment is only assumed in the simplest of presentations of modernist ideas of strategic management. During the process of formulating a strategy, decision makers may get extra information and thus need to re-examine decisions and even their goals and objectives. Modernist strategic planning only assumes complete planning in one go and at one point in time as an abstract proposition. In practice, the modernists assume some recycling of the planning process. Ansoff argued, for instance, that information and decision rules are developed and refined over time. 'This gives the appearance of solving the problem several times over, but with successively more precise results' (1968, p. 32).

Attitude to chance events

Planning obviously implies that firms can know the future, providing they make some effort to analyse and diagnose it. Study and analysis enables what would have been chance events to be anticipated and assessed for their threats and opportunities. But limits to what is knowable are accepted. Ansoff recognized the possibility of unforeseeable events with major impacts on firms. He pointed to the invention of the transistor as an example, which was catastrophic for some firms and a market breakthrough for other companies. This was part of the reason he stressed flexibility as one of a vector of objectives of the firm. This flexibility was, he believed, to be achieved through diversified product-market investments and liquidity of resources.

Implicitly, modernist planning is seeking to beat the danger of stagnation. Without the plan, modernist managers fear that work on operational issues will exclude strategic ones: the managers will continue to maintain the organization as it is but will not seize the chances (opportunities) open to it and may find itself suffering as a result of threats to which they have been blind.

Organizational requirements

These tend to be underplayed in the modernist paradigm. The structure of the organization is seen as probably being functional or divisionalized, but in any case viewed merely as a formal configuration of roles which should provide operational efficiency suited to the chosen strategy. Thus operational decision making is subsidiary to strategic decision making. In addition, the modernist paradigm is likely to see the organization as a repository of various competences which can be exploited by the chosen strategy. (The relationship between organizational structure and the development and exploitation of the organizational competences is rarely considered: the analytical approach splits structure and competence.)

In summary, modernist thinking on strategic management believes that those at the top of the organization have, or could get, the knowledge to achieve improvements in future performance and will use this to innovate.

The postmodernist paradigm

It is tempting to see Peters and Waterman (1982) as pioneering the postmodernist paradigm in strategic management. However, their writing defies tidy classification and in some respects – such as their ideas about the importance of firms developing a consensus based around shared values and the desirability of deliberate experimentation – they do not fit the postmodernist perspective with its emphasis on diversity and preference for emotional rather than intentional responses. Nevertheless, they played a critical role in establishing a postmodernist paradigm, not least because of their call for top managers to empower front line managers to take the initiative. Their astonishingly successful book marked a recognition that the old strategic management paradigm was not working.

The postmodernist style of thinking about strategic management is to be found also in some work by Mintzberg (which also defies completely unambiguous classification as postmodernist) and, perhaps most self-consciously, in Stacey's work.

This paradigm rejects the positivist science notion of being able to predict the future and it is also suspicious of the efforts of top managers in dictating strategy. It places organizational members lower down the organization in the driving seat of strategy.

Postmodernist dimensions

The role of the top management

The postmodernist style thinkers see top management and the formal institutions of strategic decision making as, at best, creating the context in which spontaneous action by others at lower levels can occur and then ensuring successes are backed (Stacey, 1991, p. 54). The strategic pattern is discoverable by top management; they do not have the capacity to invent or make an original pattern themselves. Consequently, the top managers discover – make sense retrospectively – of action produced spontaneously by others. The ex post facto discovery of strategies which developed inadvertently and without the conscious intention of senior management has been emphasized by Mintzberg (1994b):

> Some of the most important strategies in organizations emerge without the intention or sometimes even the awareness of top managers. Fully exploiting these strategies, though, often requires that they be recognized and then broadened in their impact … It is obviously the responsibility of managers to discover and anoint these strategies.
>
> Mintzberg, 1994b, p. 113

The senior management have the task of selecting, after the fact, from among 'experiments' naturally going on in the organization. 'Those that succeed and are in accord with management's purposes are labelled after the fact ("retrospective sense making") as harbingers of the new strategic direction' (Peters and Waterman, 1982, p. 108). So strategic management is essentially a matter of backing, or perhaps copying, the patterns which have occurred 'naturally'.

The nature of successful change

Responding to change is the core activity in postmodernist strategic management because it provides the means of *discovering* a strategic direction. A common-sense postmodernism of strategic management sees change as simply 'chaotic' . This means that what is happening has no pattern at all and there are no prospects of anticipating and planning for the future. The only successful mode of decision making in this case is to react as things happen. Responses are essentially improvised on the spot and spontaneous. In postmodernism's most antirational form, these responses must be intuitive (Stacey, 1991, p. 51). Mintzberg (1994b) identifies people who are able to 'see' discontinuities coming and claims that they create strategies in intuitive ways. He calls them visionaries.

In contrast to common-sense postmodernism there is another more esoteric postmodernism of strategic management. Change is still unpredictable, but, as in Stacey's work, chaos is defined as containing a hidden pattern. He did stress that strategic direction is dependent on chance and talked of the need for spontaneity. Yet his insistence that there is a pattern in chaos allowed him, in effect, to argue the possibility of creative learning. His emphasis on the importance of the political power of those at the top also allows for the two qualities – the chance factors and the hidden pattern – to be reconciled. The top managers, in the end, transmute both spontaneity and learning into strategy. Whether it is backing the successes of spontaneous action (linked to chance) or the successes of experimental action (linked to learning), the ultimate decision rests with the top managers (Stacey, 1991, p. 56).

Mintzberg also has actually two different views about the nature of successful responses to change (discontinuity). One is emergent and the other deliberate. The emergent response involves pattern recognition and discovery. For Mintzberg, as for Stacey, there is a pattern to be found amidst the behaviour. He says 'a strategy can be emergent, meaning that a convergent pattern has formed among the different actions taken by the organization one at a time' (Mintzberg, 1994b, p. 111). Since he also claims emergent strategies can develop inadvertently and without the conscious intention of top management, this implies almost a random and accidental coming together of the pattern. On the other hand, he also sees the possibility of action being experimental and contributing to emergent strategies. 'We try things and those experiments that work converge gradually into viable patterns that become strategies' (1994b, p. 111). So, inadvertent actions and experiments both contribute to emergent strategies. This suggests that Mintzberg envisages the raw material of emergent patterns as a cocktail of human behaviour containing unintended and random actions and experimental actions. He suggests at one point that planners should snoop around places to look for patterns 'amid the noise of failed experiments, seemingly random activities and messy learning' (1994b, p. 113).

Essentially, Mintzberg is arguing that discontinuities require novel strategies – new strategic moves – and that these cannot be innovated by strategic programming; the new moves have to be learnt, partly through discovering patterns, partly through trying things. In effect, Mintzberg, again like Stacey, places considerable importance on learning, which can either be learning in the sense of discovery or learning through trying things (experimentation). He also suggests that viable strategies contain both emergent and deliberate qualities. In the end, the classification of Mintzberg as a postmodernist is ambiguous. He is postmodernist if we pay attention to his remarks about how strategies may be emergent and if we have regard to his ideas that top managers must discover inadvertently produced patterns. We can also read another Mintzberg in his suggestions that strategies can be deliberate and that there can be a learning process based on experimenting. This other reading of Mintzberg does not, however, suggest he is an old-style modernist. He believes that strategic planning could not learn – it could only programme change based on known strategies. We would say that he is also a new modernist.

Expectations about others at lower levels

The postmodernist conception of strategic management expects, and wants, a lot of diversity, difference and spontaneity to be found lower down in the organization.

> People in a company will be more prone to detect open-ended change when they are different from each other ... The beginning of strategic control, the creative response to open-ended change, therefore lies in spontaneity and difference.
>
> Stacey, 1991, p. 51

This may be contrasted with Peters and Waterman's assumption of the importance of shared values in successful companies. In contrast, Stacey notes the importance of conflict as well as difference. Innovation when it takes on the form of discovery thrives on difference and thus conflict. Innovation, in any case, threatens vested interests. 'Despite the techniques available for promoting consensus, we observe continuing differences of view, and conflict in companies which are actively doing new things, because without difference and conflict new things are impossible' (Stacey, 1991, p. 13).

Attitude to planning

Proactive planning is impossible. Chance events and the feedback effects of the organization on the environment see to that. 'While certain repetitive patterns, such as seasons, may be predictable, the forecasting of discontinuities is virtually impossible' (Mintzberg, 1994b, p. 110). Postmodernists substitute real-time spontaneity and improvization for planning. Mintzberg says that strategic thinking involves intuition and creativity; strategies cannot be developed on a schedule.

Attitude to chance events

Postmodernists emphasize the way in which strategic direction is at the mercy of chance factors. (This is the essence of chaos.) They also recommend some internal chaos to cope with unpredictable trading environments (see Figure 2.2 on *In Search of Excellence*). The pragmatics of strategic innovations are often discussed in terms of avoiding polar states (stagnation/ossification and chaos/disintegration). Indeed, Stacey sees organizations as *tending* towards these conditions as equilibrium states.

> Both of the equilibrium states, disintegration and ossification, are incapable of dealing with rapid change. Organizations at or near to these equilibrium states can effectively do little that is new – the one because it is hidebound by complex structures and formal rules, the other because there is no cooperation across units. In the extreme, both are states of organizational death.
>
> Stacey, 1991, p. 96

Figure 2.2 *In Search of Excellence – Peters and Waterman (1982)*

Peters and Waterman's famous book, *In Search of Excellence* (1982), was based on their research into sixty-two big US companies, selected because they were regarded as innovative and excellent by business people, consultants, academics and other informed people. (Public data on financial performance showed that thirty-six had proved to be successful over a twenty-year period.) Structured interviews were carried out in some of these in 1979–80 and the literature (spanning a twenty-five-year period) on all of them was reviewed.

Eight features of the excellent companies were identified.

Excellent companies:

- had a bias for action
- were close (listened) to their customers
- fostered leaders and entrepreneurs throughout the organization
- valued individual employees
- had leaders who were both hands-on in their style and value driven
- tended to stick to businesses they knew
- had simple and lean structures
- combined autonomy down on the shop floor with tight commitment to the company's core values.

Interestingly, these excellent companies 'allowed some chaos in return for quick action and regular experimentation' (Peters and Waterman, 1982, p. 13). At Digital, it was said by one manager that the level of chaos meant that, 'Damn few people know who they work for' (p. 16).

Peters and Waterman did not claim that excellent companies studied by them would stay culturally innovative. They did say of one of their excellent companies, General Motors, that it was likely to survive the troubles it was experiencing better than others in the industry.

These polar states may not be seen as *equally* disastrous. Peters and Waterman (1982, p. 145) quote Karl Weick as saying 'chaotic action is preferable to orderly inaction'. Mintzberg (1994b, p. 108) suggests that strategies 'must be free to appear at any time and at any place in the organization, typically though messy processes of informal learning'. This preference for some internal chaos or messiness – unpredictability and a breaking down of the hierarchical codes – is motivated by a desire to escape the stagnation of the formal institutions of strategic management. Implicitly, this is an argument for encouraging as many as possible to take advantage of chance events (or take remedial action in the case of threatening events).

Organizational requirements

The postmodernist paradigm tends to be antistructure. Peters and Waterman certainly thought structures were not the solution to contemporary business ills. Postmodernists distrust the straightjacket of central and formal control. Organizations should provide the space or territory which is conducive to spontaneity and this is essentially in the informal arenas of organizational life. Mintzberg (1994b), for example, argues against formalized strategic planning and expresses the need to loosen up strategy-making processes. Stacey (1991) suggests that organizations may set up meetings and committees to deal with strategic management, but that these are unfavourable settings for strategic processes. Strategic issues are instead progressed in informal and spontaneous processes (Stacey, 1991, pp. 253–4). And, of course, the organization is required to tolerate diversity within it.

Arguably, a 'simple' postmodernist paradigm would encourage spontaneity in the belief that following intuition will produce the right result. Again, as a simple form, the postmodernist paradigm has lost all confidence in the formal institutions and in top management and has no confidence in the notion of progress through rational-purposive action.

New modernist paradigm

The old modernism of strategic management has been criticized by work which is by no means postmodernist. The work of Quinn (1991) is one example, which we will be considering in some detail. He studied the dynamics of strategic change in ten major firms. Whilst seeing top managers as purposeful and proactive, he came to the conclusion that firms did not use the rational-analytical systems recommended in the specialist planning literature. Like the modernists, he did see the top management team as the prime architects of strategic developments, but he assumed that top management have only a limited capacity to foresee what is required and to impose the required change.

Hamel and Prahalad (1994) followed Quinn in accepting that foresight is limited; they argued that senior executives must ensure that their organizations have foresight, but they suggested that organizations may not have much knowledge initially of when and how they will achieve their strategic intentions. The important point is that, whilst limited, industry foresight is possible. It is also a key aspect of competition between businesses to become industry leaders. This, according to Hamel and Prahalad, is a competition for 'intellectual leadership'. Moreover, they consider that foresight demands a significant expenditure of intellectual energy, which top managers have to focus, presumably, in part, so as to establish a sense of purpose.

The work of Ansoff and McDonnell (1990) also offers criticisms of the modernist assumptions of strategic planning from a position which is clearly not a postmodernist one. They have developed an approach which shows two major breaks with Ansoff's early work. First, they introduce the importance of strategic diagnosis so as to take account of the turbulence of the environment. This turbulence can vary but reaches a state at the upper end of the scale when the environment is discontinuous and unpredictable. Second, they have developed detailed analyses of the phenomenon of organizational resistance to change because they saw it as a fundamental problem requiring attention. In other words, they were no longer assuming that the environment was knowable or the organization controllable.

So new modernist strategic management resembles the modernist paradigm in its positing of strategic management as a rational and intellectual process, but it recognizes that there are significant limits on knowing and controlling. It is, therefore, by definition more modest than modernist strategic planning. The spirit of new modernism is probably best captured in Mintzberg's (1987) metaphor of strategic management as a 'craft'. This metaphor conjures up a picture of strategic management as a skilled activity in which the strategy is shaped by the strategist who knows or learns how to work with the strategic situation. Crafting a strategy implies working *with* the situation whereas the old modernism entailed an assertion or imposition of strategy *on* the situation.

Strategic moves in the new modernist paradigm are essentially guided by foresight but are experimental and opportunistic, enabling a strategy to emerge, in contrast to the programmed innovations of modernist strategic management and the discoveries of postmodernist approaches (Mintzberg, 1994b).

New modernist dimensions

The role of the top management

Top managers develop industry foresight, quietly construct strategies, nurture developments, experiment with strategic directions and at times wait for the opportune moment. Quinn argued that strategies emerged as top managers handled events calling for

urgent decisions in the context of limited knowledge and understanding.

> Recognizing this, top executives usually consciously tried to deal
> with precipitating events in an incremental fashion. Early commit-
> ments were kept broadly formative, tentative and subject to later
> review.

Quinn, 1991, p. 99

Hamel and Prahalad emphasize, similarly, that organizations get to
the future through a process of successive approximations.

The nature of successful change

Successful change is not the result of rigid planning systems. Nor
can a capacity to manage change successfully be inferred from the
mere fact of a business plan (see Figure 2.3 on the study by Baker,
Addams and Davis). Successful change is about learning from
experiments. Hamel and Prahalad have suggested that 'the relative
merits of specific routes [to achieve strategic intentions] emerges
only as one moves forward' (1994, p. 215). Even after an organization has developed industry foresight, there is still much uncertainty. Consequently, 'Having exhausted what can be deduced analyti-
cally about the future, a firm must learn by doing' (1994, p. 126).
This learning by doing includes testing out what customers want by
experimenting with product and service concepts. Hamel and
Prahalad refer to fast-paced experiments in testing out customer
requirements as 'expeditionary marketing'.

Figure 2.3 *Business planning in small firms*

Baker, Addams and Davis (1993) were interested in strategic planning and the extent and benefits of written business plans. They studied a sample of 194 American firms that had sales of between
$100,000 and $25 million in 1984 and that had showed a sales
increase between 1987 and 1988.

Baker and his colleagues found that nearly nine out of ten of the
companies surveyed did perform strategic planning. Most of these
firms prepared written plans and most did their strategic planning at
least annually.

Most of the firms that had written business plans felt that these
were successful; but when the most profitable firms were compared

with the least profitable ones, both groups were equally prone to have a business plan. In the case of strategic planning, all firms in the most profitable group did such planning, but some in the least profitable group did not.

The researchers concluded that the:

> study suggests a significant association between strategic planning and profitability. However, the use of business plans was not found to be significantly associated with profitability.
>
> Baker *et al.*, 1993, p. 87

Expectations about others at lower levels

A new modernist does not expect others in the organization simply to play the role of implementers of the strategic direction set by the top manager. They expect others to have their own agendas. They are also, unlike their modernist counterparts, reluctant to set a strategy and then think about the skills of those involved in implementing it. This may mean that plans are changed to take account of the people concerned – and this may occur incrementally as knowledge of the people builds up. In consequence, as Quinn explains, the top executive acts opportunistically:

> He then frequently has to bring in, train, or test new people for substantial periods before he can staff key posts with confidence. During this testing period he may substantially modify his original concept of the reorganization, as he evaluates individuals' potentials, their performance in specific roles, their personal drives, and their relationships with other team members.
>
> Quinn, 1991, p. 101

Attitude to planning

In the new modernist paradigm planning is not rigid but is based on foresight and experimentation. This combination of foresight and experimentation is a good definition of planning as an emergent process. Strategies emerge in response to events which require urgent decisions. Full details of the plan (as far as it has been conceptualized) are vague initially because of limited knowledge. They may also be kept vague and fluid in order to mobilize organizational commitment – or avoid resistance.

Attitude to chance events

By definition, a precipitating event, which presses the new modernist strategist into a decision that helps their strategy emerge, has something of the character of a chance event. The decision on how to handle the event must be made urgently and in that sense is unforeseen. (Or, alternatively, the new modernist has to wait for the right moment or event.) This is the essentially opportunistic nature of the strategy. (A pure modernist seeks out the events which constitute opportunities and threats; the new modernist is confronted by, or has to wait for, an event and seeks to seize any opportunities it offers and to handle any threats it poses.) So, chance and strategy formulation are combined in new modernist planning with its special character as incrementalist decision making. In a sense, rigid planning of a modernist kind is made into incrementalist planning by the fact that a strategy is formed and implemented through chance events. Thus, Quinn insists, incrementalism 'is a purposeful, effective, proactive management technique for improving and integrating both the analytical and behavioral aspects of strategy formulation' (1991, p. 98). New modernist planning is also incrementalist because of the experimental approach to learning which is needed to build on the industry foresight.

Organizational requirements

The new modernist top manager always assumes that the organization will have to be developed in order to realize a new strategy. This has two dimensions. First, organizational members need to be aware, accepting and committed to the strategy. Mintzberg (1994b) suggests that strategic planning (actually the modernist version of it) was a calculating style of management. What was needed was a committing style:

> Managers with a committing style engage people in a journey. They lead in such a way that everyone on the journey helps shape its course. As a result, enthusiasm inevitably builds along the way.
>
> Mintzberg, 1994b, p. 109

Hamel and Prahalad have stressed a moral interpretation of how leaders achieve this readiness and commitment. They have suggested three particular responsibilities for top management in this area: top managers must establish a sense of purpose, identify key capability building challenges and help employees understand their role in the pursuit of industry leadership. In contrast, a more political interpretation of the top managers' role may be suggested. According to this view, the top manager will be circumspect about what he or she has in mind, recognizing that explicit plans may arouse resistance or make it difficult to negotiate a new strategic direction. The political tactics of building this readiness will involve deploying incentives and persuasion to motivate commitment. The content of these tactics are difficult to specify, especially as many of the incentives are tied to the size and structure of the organization (Barnard, 1938).

The second dimension of achieving organizational readiness is the development of the capabilities or competences needed – or more broadly the resources. Hamel and Prahalad have stressed that this is a long-term and critical aspect of getting an organization into a position to become an industry leader. They have also suggested that strategic alliances with other companies can be used to learn specific skills needed for competence acquisition.

Summing up, we see that top managers proceed incrementally because of limited knowledge and understanding; they do this by testing, and experimenting with, courses of action and organizational shifts. They also proceed incrementally with blending and shaping the strategy because of the need to build awareness, acceptance and commitment. 'Successful executives link together and bring order to a series of strategic processes and decisions spanning years' (Quinn, 1991, p. 104).

The three paradigms are summarized in Table 2.1.

The roots of diversity

In the early 1980s Peters and Waterman wrote: 'Perhaps the time has come to change our ways' (Peters and Waterman, 1982, p. 3). This call for a change struck a chord. In the 1980s, managers and students of management turned in their millions to the writings of Peters and other management gurus; it has been suggested that this was linked to the 'increasingly turbulent change in the business world and the disillusionment with the excessive trend to analysis and rigid hierarchies' (Stacey, 1991, p. 115).

The economic times were difficult for strategic planning. The oil

Table 2.1 *The three paradigms*

Dimensions	Modernist	Postmodernist	New modernist
Top management role	Decision-making élite	Back successful initiatives by lower level managers	Responsible for intellectual leadership
Successful change	Programmable	Discoverable	Based on foresight and experiment
Expectations about those at lower levels	To be committed to proposals and to implement strategic plan	To show diversity, difference and spontaneity (empowerment)	To have their own agendas – but agendas which can be included
Attitude to planning	Planning is core activity	Proactive planning is impossible	Planning is emergent
Attitude to chance events	Need to plan for flexibility	Require chaotic action in response	Chance events can be opportunities
Organizational requirements	Operational management to be shaped by strategy	Anti-hierarchy culture – support for informality	Organizational readiness – commitment and competence – which have to be developed

price shocks of the 1970s and the return of mass unemployment in the 1980s provided the context of the loss of confidence in quantitative forecasting. Forecasting errors became larger and more frequent in the face of chronic instability in the business environment. Change felt chaotic. Stagnation was also evident in the 1970s and 1980s as US and British companies woke up to the competitive strength of the Japanese (Taylor, 1973).

As the economic world became more 'messy', modernist planning faltered. Some blamed its mechanical approach and use of quantitative methods. Coulson-Thomas (1992, p. 66) says that there was a general reaction against 'many of the analytical approaches to strategy formulation that were used in many companies during the 1970s'. Others point to the failure on the change front. Mintzberg (1994b) claims that it was the formalization of strategic planning which had gone too far and that innovation has never been institutionalized. Management experts were probably saying much the same thing when they proclaimed that the only way to innovate was to experiment (Peters and Austin, 1985, p. 117). In a sense, modernist strategic planning had simply not been able to keep up with the movement of the business environment.

But postmodernism was never likely to replace modernist strategic planning. It could show up the problems of modernist thinking but was not equipped to provide an ideology for strategic action. Perhaps that is why the new vision championed by the gurus of chaos – the aspirations to be customer driven, to be more flexible and responsive, to compete on the quality of their products and services and to empower their lower level managers and employees – has not been able to realize itself in practice. Surveys suggest a big gap exists between the aspirations and the reality. Many managers are disillusioned with being asked to do more with less and without being equipped or empowered to cope with the new demands on them (the problem of the lean, flat structure); quality is said to be largely a matter of rhetoric; and economic recession forced short-term responses at odds with long-term relationships (Coulson-Thomas, 1992, p. 64). Postmodernist strategic change obviously was not successfully mobilized. The failure to implement this new vision has been attributed to:

- the absence of action programmes to realize the strategy
- roles and responsibilities not allocated
- success measures not identified
- target achievement levels not determined (Coulson-Thomas, 1992, p. 67).

The list looks like a strikingly modernist list of measures!

The question remains, however, how can firms cope with change? The search for the key to innovation continues. Will new modernism provide the answer?

With hindsight, it might be claimed that seeds of the new paradigms were already contained in the modernist school of thought. It only took the chaotic or messier conditions to bring about their flowering. For example, modernism long ago conceded the need for some flexibility because of chance events, but postmodernist approaches to strategic management brought the impact of ignorance and unforeseeable events to centre stage. Modernist thought also recognized the emergent nature of knowledge and the refining of decisions, as well as the motivational aspects and internal political influences on decisions; but it was only in new modernist thinking that these were seen as crucial for the experience of strategic management.

Key points

1 The modernist paradigm places top managers in the position of the intellectual élite who will tell or persuade the rest of their organization to implement the strategy they have chosen. It could be accused of oversimplifying organizational realities. It has certainly been seen as suspect in the last ten years or so.

2 The modernism paradigm portrays change as programmable. In contrast, both the postmodernists (extolling discovery) and new modernists (extolling experimentation) seem better adjusted to the turbulence that followed the 1960s. The essential analytical distinction which we can make between postmodernists and new modernists is between their respective support for discoveries which strategic decision makers study and back and experiments which the decision makers engineer or enable. In practice, this distinction may be blurred.

3 There is evidence, as we have seen, that formal planning of strategy pays off. The simplistic and unskilled use of a modernist approach, however, may have reached the limits of its effectiveness. There is also the argument (see above), that postmodernist businesses may be difficult to develop, because they have to be brought about by modernist planning.

4 The new modernist approach extends the effectiveness of rational planning by accommodating the defects of modernist thinking. It deals more plausibly with chance and unpredictability and with the need to gain commitment. It is more flexible than modernism as it does not lead to a 'locking' in of strategy as the environment and experience changes, while at the same time being more optimistic about planning than postmodernism is. Simply put, senior managers who reflect and think about the future, and act upon these reflections, will be more successful than those who do not.

References

Ansoff, I. (1968) *Corporate Strategy* (Penguin).

Ansoff, I. (1994) 'Round 2: Response to Henry Mintzberg' in De Wit, B. and Meyer, R. (editors) Strategy: *Process, Content, Context* (West Publishing).

Ansoff, I. and McDonnell, E. (1990) *Implanting Strategic Management* (Prentice Hall)

Baker, W.H., Addams, H.L. and Davis, B. (1993) 'Business Planning in Successful Small Firms', *Long Range Planning*, Vol. 26, No. 6, pp. 82–8.

Barnard, C.I. (1938) *The Functions of the Executive* (Harvard University Press).

Beckhard, R. and Harris, R.T. (1987) *Organizational Transitions* (Addison-Wesley).

Clegg, S.R. (1990) *Modern Organisations: Organisation Studies in the Postmodern World* (Sage).

Coulson-Thomas, C. (1992) *Transforming the Company* (Kogan Page).

Greenley, G. E. (1989) 'Does Strategic Planning Improve Company Performance?' in Asch, D. and Bowman, C. (editors) *Readings in Strategic Management* (Macmillan).

Hamel, G. and Heene, A. (1994) 'Introduction: Competing Paradigms in Strategic Management' in Hamel, G. and Heene, A. (editors) *Competence-based Competition* (Wiley).

Hamel, G. and Prahalad, C.K. (1994) *Competing for the Future* (Harvard Business School Press).

Knights, D. and Morgan, G. (1991) 'Corporate Strategy, Organisations and Subjectivity', *Organisational Studies*, Vol. 12, No. 2, pp. 251–73.

Mintzberg, H. (1987) 'Crafting Strategy', *Harvard Business Review*, July–August, pp. 65–75.

Mintzberg, H. (1994) 'Round 3: Learning 1, Planning 0; Reply to Igor Ansoff' in De Wit, B. and Meyer, R. (editors) *Strategy: Process, Content, Context* (West Publishing).

Mintzberg, H. (1994) 'The Fall and Rise of Strategic Planning', *Harvard Business Review*, January–February, Vol. 72, No. 1, pp. 107–14.

Pearce, J.A., Robbins, D.K. and Robinson, R.B. (1987) 'The Impact of Grand Strategy and Planning Formality on Financial Performance', *Strategic Management Journal*, Vol. 8, pp. 125–34.

Peters, T. and Austin, N. (1985) *A Passion for Excellence* (Fontana).

Peters, T.J. and Waterman, R.H. (1982) *In Search of Excellence* (Harper Collins).

Postan, M.M. (1972) *The Medieval Economy and Society* (Penguin).

Quinn, J.B. (1991) 'Strategic Change: "Logical Incrementalism"' in Mintzberg, H. and Quinn, J.B. (editors) *The Strategy Process* (Prentice Hall).

Stacey, R. (1991) *The Chaos Frontier* (Butterworth-Heinemann).

Taylor, A. (editor) (1973) *Perspectives on US–Japan Economic Relations* (Ballinger).
Taylor, I. (1980) *The Edwardian Lady* (Michael Joseph).
Weber, M. (1930) *The Protestant Ethic and the Spirit of Capitalism* (Unwin).
Whittington, R. (1993) *What is Strategy – and Does it Matter?* (Routledge).

3

The strategic planning process

Introduction

A strategic planning process is not the same as the set of techniques that are to be found described in many strategic management textbooks. A strategic planning process may make use of these techniques, but is not reducible to them. Particular models of the overall strategy process are often advocated (see Ansoff and McDonnell, 1990), but it is arguable whether or not general models of strategic management can yet be scientifically established. Mockler, for example, has stated 'that general overall strategic management thought processes are simply too complex to be accurately replicated, given the limited existing knowledge of them' (1995, p. 12).

A strategic planning process, according to Dyson (1990, p. 3), 'is a management process involving consultation, negotiation and analysis which is aimed at ensuring effective strategic decision making'. The analytical component of this, which is the chief focus of this chapter, can be seen as involving analysis and choices. It can be seen as issue based, when the concern is to identify and resolve the key strategic issues.

The point of this chapter is to encourage a perspective in which the design of the process is treated as being as important, if not more important, than the selection of techniques.

We will introduce three key ideas: first, the idea that the process should be seen as concerned with the identification and resolution of strategic issues; second, the idea that the design of a strategic planning process should really be considered from a contingency theory perspective; and third, the idea that issues are generated by both uncertainties and discontinuities stemming from the environment and from an organization's strategic experimentation.

We will also look at the organizational aspects of the design of the strategic planning process.

Technocratic strategic planning

The technocratic approach to strategic management – also known as the rationalist school – is said to be loosely based on military thinking:

> The first task of the strategist is to describe, understand, and analyse the environment. The second stage – the key task for the senior executives in the firm as it is for the senior generals of the army – is to determine strategy in the light of that analysis. The third phase is that of implementation.
>
> Kay, 1993, p. 336

This seems logical enough, but we do not want to support a technocratic approach that appears to lead to an overemphasis on analytical technique and accounting ratios to the detriment of study, experimentation and reasoning and at the expense of inquisitiveness, intuition and creativity. In the terms of the previous chapter, the old modernism – with its overemphasis on analytical techniques, etc. – needs to be reformed, taking into account some of the concerns of the postmodernist perspective, by being more intuitive and creative, but without completely rejecting thinking about the future.

The process of strategic management conceptualized as a linear sequence of analysis, choice and implementation has been thoroughly disputed by Quinn's incrementalist theory of strategic management (see Chapter 2). It has also been contested by Pettigrew and Whipp's model of strategic change, which sees knowing the competitive environment and strategic management (mobilizing and managing resources for change) as continuous and simultaneous processes (see Chapter 10).

It is evident that there is a gap between the clarity, simplicity and technical logicality of the linear model of the strategy process as depicted in many textbooks and the more informal and more complex appearance of strategy processes in real situations. Mockler (1995), commenting on strategy as found in business practices, has pointed out that:

- the strategy formulation process is not always explicit
- strategy and its process of formulation varies from situation to situation
- clear distinctions between strategy formulation and implementation are not always evident
- strategies are not always written down
- the role of strategy is not always the same.

Whilst few practical experiences may correspond to the fixed linear sequence, it does have the merit of being easily communicated and thus appears to have a form that is appropriate for training managers for strategic management. It is quite likely that some teachers of strategic management would be indifferent to this justification: reality is just not like that, they might say.

Our objection to the usual formulation of the linear process is based on quite different grounds. For, in reality, we suspect many managers do, from time to time, make use of a linear strategy process. As Kay (1993, p. 336) has remarked:

> the rationalist process achieves the curious conjunction of being both dominant and disparaged. Few firms, or their advisers, approach the strategy process in any different way. But most senior managers are also critical of the rationalist approach.

Our concern is that formulating the strategy process as analysis, choice and implementation, which is the formulation which many people first encounter, is so rooted in the technocratic assumptions of the modernist paradigm discussed in Chapter 2 that the overall conception of the strategic planning process gets off to a bad start. At its worst, this formulation leads to wooden thinking with little reasoning and little creativity. Under its influence managers can work through strategic analysis and strategic choice in a way that suggests they see the process as nothing more than a set of analytical techniques strung together. They can find great difficulty in moving from listing and classifying of data to a clear definition of the strategic issues and concrete ideas about how to tackle implementation. In formal terms, we are suggesting that there is a need to rethink the detail of the strategic planning process.

Strategic issue management

In recent years there has been growing interest in conceptualizing the strategy process as the management of strategic issues. Ohmae (1982), in his work on strategic thinking, stressed the analytical importance of pinpointing 'the critical issue in the situation' (1982, p. 15). Bryson (1988) claimed that identifying strategic issues is the heart of the strategic planning process. The focus on issues informs Argenti's definition of corporate planning as a systematic procedure for identifying a small number of top key issues (see Figure 3.1). Nutt and Backoff (1992, p. 121) recently added their voices to calls for strategic issues to guide the search for strategy.

Figure 3.1   *Argenti and hunting for elephants*

According to Argenti (1989), who had assisted a number of companies with corporate planning, most companies have major strategic issues which they have not yet handled. But how are such issues to be identified? Argenti has claimed that:

- many but not all strategic issues are bad news
- some strategic issues may not be affecting current organizational results but will impact in the future
- only about half the strategic issues are in the marketing area.

Argenti referred to corporate planning as an elephant hunt, that is, a process of looking for strategic elephants – major strategic issues – in the organizational undergrowth.

It would be useful at this point to have a formal definition of a strategic issue. One definition, which is linked with more traditional views of the planning process as guided by formal objectives, is that it is 'a forthcoming development, either inside or outside of the organization, which is likely to have an important impact on the ability of the enterprise to meet its objectives' (Ansoff and McDonnell, 1990,

p. 369). A more inclusive definition by Bryson suggests that strategic issues are issues affecting 'the organization's mandates, mission and values, product or service level and mix, clients, users or payers, cost, financing, or management' (Bryson, 1988, p. 56). But it should also be added that this more inclusive definition is supported by two assumptions: (a) that strategic issues have to be dealt with 'expeditiously and effectively if the organization is to survive and prosper' and (b) that a failure to respond will result in 'undesirable results from a threat, a missed opportunity, or both' (1988, p. 56). So, the second definition differs from the first mainly by widening concern to issues that impact on the ability of an organization to meet its aims (i.e. mandate, missions and values, etc.) and on other things (i.e. service, clients, financing, management, etc.).

Both formal definitions share an appreciation that a strategic issue exists where the organization's survival and prosperity are at stake. But Bryson's definition has a supporting assumption that action in response to strategic issues must be expeditious. The urgency of the required action may vary and this has implications for the process used to resolve the strategic issues. Urgent action to deal with strategic issues may be delayable so that they it can be planned within the next regular planning cycle, but immediate action may need to be planned and taken in a nonroutine way (see Ansoff and McDonnell, 1990, p. 376).

We have taken something from both these definitions to arrive at our own definition, outlined in Figure 3.2.

Figure 3.2   *Definition of a strategic issue*

A strategic issue is something which causes concern because of its expected impact on the aims of the organization (expressed as goals, mandates, mission, values, etc.) and which requires urgent action if the organization is to survive and prosper.

Interest in conceptualizing the strategy process as strategic issue management may be linked to a growing body of theorizing which sees reality as turbulent (Ansoff and McDonnell, 1990) and as posing contradictory or paradoxical issue tensions (Nutt and Backoff, 1992, pp. 128–30) and thus explains the extreme importance of properly diagnosing the environment and/or analysing the specific nature of the strategic issues confronting organizations. Interestingly, Ansoff (1968, p. 18) had long ago defined strategic decisions as those made in regard to the relationship between the firm and its environment, which presumably could be represented to a large degree as a set of opportunities and threats. So, perhaps it has been the reconceptualization of the environment – from a context made up of separate opportunities and threats to a turbulent and discontinuous environment, or a context composed of contradictory forces – that has led some to rethink the strategy process? For them it is no longer simply an analytical and goal-directed decision-making process; it has become a problem-solving process of strategic issue management.

Back in the world of strategic management practice there is a pragmatic argument for focusing on strategic issues. Smith (1994, p. 40) points out that issue-based planning stands more chance of succeeding than objectives-based planning: ' ... plans which are tied to recognised issues tend to be implemented and obviously we need to accept that something is of concern before we can be activated to set adequate and comfortable objectives'.

The issue-based strategy process can still make use of many of the analytical techniques developed and popularised over the last thirty years.

An issue-based strategic planning process

It could be argued that each attempt to formulate a strategy provides an opportunity for a unique design of the strategy process and a unique selection, blending and sequencing of the many techniques available into that process. But writers on strategic management are more likely to offer a particular process which they feel produces the best results. The following eight-step model is loosely based on one model of strategic issue analysis (Ansoff and McDonnell, 1990, p. 372), and is illustrated in Figure 3.3.

Step   Purpose
Step 1   Trend analysis
Step 2   Environmental and resource analysis
Step 3   Target setting
Step 4   SWOT analysis

Step 5   Identification of strategic issue(s)
Step 6   Formulation of strategic actions
Step 7   Evaluation of proposed actions
Step 8   Planning implementation

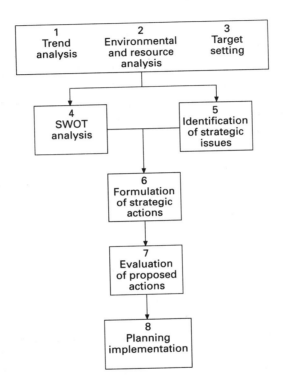

Figure 3.3   *An issue-based strategic planning process*

Trend analysis (step 1) can look at a range of trends relating to the organization (e.g. products made or services provided, management style and practices, organization and communication structures, technology, customer behaviour, etc.). It can look at trends in the performance of the organization (e.g. profitability, social responsiveness). It is also possible to look at environmental trends in step 1, but we have included this under step 2, which covers environmental and resource analysis. The environmental analysis looks at trends and events, with the latter including future discontinuities. Resource analysis can look at the different kinds of resources currently being used by the organization and can be informative in terms of internal strengths and weaknesses. Target setting by private firms may involve determining quantified profitability objectives for, say, the next five years; but there are other kinds of targets based on qualitative statements of desired future states, which may be appropriate for some types of organizations.

Sometimes managers skip the early steps – steps 1 to 3 – and begin strategic planning with a SWOT analysis, which is a widely used technique to carry out a situational assessment focused on the strengths and weaknesses of the organization and the opportunities and threats of its environment. (It is described in Chapter 4.) But steps 1 to 3 function, at least in part, as an important intellectual preparation for the SWOT analysis and for the identification of the key strategic issues. They are very useful for 'flushing out' important facts and considerations which may be overlooked if the process begins with a situational assessment. The results of these early steps do not have to be input in a mechanical way into later steps. The strategic analyst can easily keep the results in mind when carrying out the later steps.

The methods for identifying strategic issues is a relatively neglected topic in strategic management. We will look at some methods shortly and we note just a few key points here. First, how many strategic issues should be, or can be, identified? Argenti (1989, p. 17) suggests that the top issues number about six – 'the half-dozen that every organization must get right if it is to prosper over the next few years'. Second, it is easy to confuse operational problems and strategic issues and it is important to be clear that strategic issues are identified in terms of their consequences for the organizations' overall aims or mission. Third, an important question to be considered in resolving the key strategic issues is the question of causal relationships between issues. Nutt and Backoff (1992) have provided advice on how precedence between issues may be determined, so that those issues which cause or influence other issues can be dealt with as a matter of priority. Fourth, for pragmatic reasons, the strategy process needs to concentrate on the highest priority issue, which therefore provides the focus for the search for strategy.

The formulation of strategic action is usually seen as drawing on the results of a situational assessment (strengths, weaknesses, opportunities and threats). Thus, there is the familiar textbook pronouncement that strategies should be formulated which take advantage of strengths and opportunities, correct weaknesses and minimize threats. But it also involves problem solving because strategy formulation should produce strategies which are designed to resolve the strategic issues. Successful issue resolution is a fusion of the known and the novel. For, on the basis of the known situation and the known issues, the formulation of action requires an element of creativity – new ideas for strategic action.

Evaluation of proposals for strategic action are usually done against a set of criteria such as acceptability, feasibility and suitability. Each of these criteria can be operationalized in various ways. For example, acceptability can be operationalized by assessing whether the expected level of profitability (e.g. return on investment, ROI) resulting from a proposed strategy meets some predetermined acceptability threshold. Ansoff (1968), however, suggests that this level should be adjusted for riskier decisions. So, a company would set higher thresholds for profitability where the risks of a proposed course of action are judged to be relatively high. According to Rappaport (1991), companies almost invariably evaluate strategic plans in terms of accounting ratios such as return on investment, return on equity, or earnings per share. But the selection of such ratios, even assuming that they can be predicted reliably, is complex. Ansoff (1968), for example, warned that the earnings per share ratio might be inadequate as a measure of internal efficiency because it can conceal a failure to invest long term. Consequently, evaluating strategy proposals on the basis of earnings per share could foster short-termism.

Another important criterion that can be used to evaluate strategy proposals is timeliness, which may be seen as an aspect of the other ones, but is important enough to identify separately. Ansoff and McDonnell (1990) say that assessing the future impact of trends requires attention to be paid to the timing of the impact. Logically, therefore, the analyst has to be concerned at the evaluation stage with the urgency of strategic issues and the timeliness of strategic action to resolve them.

Planning implementation is a complex business and different aspects get emphasized from different perspectives. For some writers it is a matter of developing operational policies and objectives (production, marketing, finance, HRM and IT). Others emphasize the criticality of managing the response of customers to the planned changes, or planning to get a critical mass of support in the organization through strategies to engineer commitment. At the very least, planning the implementation of strategic action needs to take account of the power of stakeholders and the acquisition and mobilization of necessary resources.

Recent developments in the design of strategic-planning processes

The circumstances of the last twenty-five years seem to have been putting an unhurried and highly formalized planning process under pressure. Ansoff and McDonnell (1990) suggest that the speed and novelty of issues impacting on organizations is one of the reasons making the splitting of strategic issue analysis from the annual strategic planning cycle desirable in some situations. Where this is so, where issues are impacting quickly and the organization cannot delay responding to them, the organization manages strategic issues in 'real time', with continuous surveillance, frequent updating of the issue agenda and special organization to manage strategic action. In some cases, organizations may have both the annual strategic planning cycle and strategic issue management systems; in some cases, they may do away with the strategic planning cycle and just have the strategic issue management system.

Another view, with similar underlying concerns, is to be found in Nutt and Backoff's (1992) observations about strategy process recycling. The whole process, they say, may be carried out every two to ten years, whereas issue agendas may be revised as often as every three months, although it may be longer in less volatile environments.

The conclusion we draw from these views is that strategic issues are so fundamental to the strategic management process that formal strategic planning processes that do not enable them to be dealt with as they emerge have to be short-circuited, supplemented or abandoned.

The discussion so far suggests, possibly, that the need for strategic issue management will produce a more short-term and reactive approach to strategy. However, in the previous chapter, in outlining the new modernist paradigm, it became obvious that strategic managers face two major sources of uncertainty:

- uncertainties caused by the environment (precipitating events)
- uncertainties about how to get to the future (experimentation).

So, an organization's issue agenda may be formed by both the environment and its own experimental moves to achieve its strategic intent, which in turn is based on some long-term industry foresight. This implies that strategic issue management may not be driven by short-term or reactive thinking, but this depends on how effectively the organization establishes industry foresight and strategic intent (see Figure 3.4).

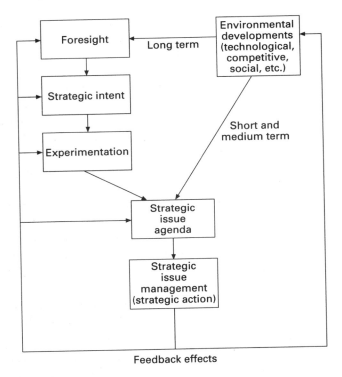

Figure 3.4   *A revised issue-based strategic planning process*

Identifying strategic issues

Identification of strategic issues is at the heart of the overall strategic planning process. It is important, therefore, to look in detail at the various options for identifying the key strategic issues. There are undoubtedly many options which can be pursued, but we will briefly review:

- gap analysis
- SWOT analysis
- vision of success approach
- direct approach.

Gap analysis

As we noted in the previous chapter, Ansoff (1968, p. 33) suggested that the overall process of strategy formulation had four simple steps: (1) objectives were set; (2) an estimate was made of the difference (the gap) between the current position of the firm and the objectives; (3) courses of action were identified; and (4) the course of action that substantially closes the gap was accepted. Ansoff, writing over twenty years later with McDonnell, respecified this analysis as a comparison of performance objectives with *forecasted* performance trends, a comparison which they saw as forming a part of the annual planning cycle (Ansoff and McDonnell, 1990, p. 374). The comparison identifies what they term as the 'objectives gap'. The next step is to carry out a diagnosis which detects the causes of the gap. Some of these causes may take the form of problems in operational effectiveness (inefficiencies) or problems in the implementation of the organization's strategy, but others were what Ansoff and McDonnell recognized as strategic issues – these were causes due to general threats and weaknesses.

Gap analysis is also associated with the name of Argenti (1989). He recommends that corporate planning teams establish corporate objectives at the outset of the strategy process and then quantify them into targets. He then recommends that the team forecasts likely performance for a suitable planning period (normally five years) 'in order to compare the target with the forecast to reveal the Gap' (Argenti, 1989, p. 41). He strongly champions the use of gap analysis, believing that a number of strategic issues will always be found in the process of doing the analysis, as well as revealing to the team what kind of strategy is needed, how urgent it is and how big the strategic task is. (He also believed, however, that strategic issues will also be found during internal and external appraisals of the company, which he suggests should follow the gap analysis.)

It is evident that Ansoff's original method identifies the gap on the basis of the company's current performance, whereas his later method and that of Argenti as well, uses a forecast of the company performance. Moreover, while the gap can be seen as the first order statement of the strategic issue, this should be further diagnosed to arrive at the strategic issues which cause the gap; that is, the causes of the gap are a better definition of the strategic issues, rather than the gap itself. However, it must be borne in mind that some causes of the gap will require operational and not strategic measures and so not all causes of the gap are strategic issues.

The use of forecasting in conjunction with gap analysis may be seen as problematic; for forecasting has itself been criticized (see, for example, Stacey's 1991 comments on quantitative investment appraisal in the next chapter). Argenti has argued that the criticism is not fatal for the use of forecasting and has provided the following advice on how to carry out forecasting properly.

> Many corporate planners dispensed with gap analysis after the oil crisis of 1973 because they felt that it had become impossible to make accurate long-term forecasts. In my view, it has never been possible to make an accurate long-term forecast and the correct approach is to admit that you cannot do this and to show explicitly how gross the errors might be. So in my system the team is very strongly recommended to make these forecasts and boldly and deliberately to display the errors.
>
> Argenti, 1989, pp. 42–3

SWOT analysis

The use of SWOT analysis to identify strategic issues can be justified on the basis of a proposition that the key strategic issues emerge from the fit, or tension, between an organization and its environment, rather than the gap between its goals and actual or projected performance. This is consistent with those definitions of strategic management which see it as the management of the relationship between the organization and its environment (Ansoff, 1968, p. 18; Kay, 1993, p. 335). The technique itself involves, essentially speaking, listing the opportunities and threats of the environment and the strengths and weaknesses of the organization.

The strategic issues may be identified by taking each of the listed items separately and considering whether action by the organization is required if it is to prosper. This approach is implied in the following statement by Ansoff and McDonnell (1989, p. 369).

An issue may be welcome: an opportunity to be grasped in the environment, or an internal strength which can be exploited to advantage. Or it can be unwelcome: an external threat, or an internal weakness which imperils continuing success, even survival of the enterprise.

Alternatively, the strategic issues may be identified by considering the interaction of opportunities/threats and strengths/weaknesses. So, for example, an organization could have recognized the existence of an interesting opportunity, but judge that it cannot exploit it because of specific weaknesses; this would be a strategic issue if it was judged to have a major impact on the firm's future prosperity, or indeed, if it was considered to be significant in terms of the firm attaining its corporate objectives. This approach can be seen in Smith's (1994) recommendation of a cross-tabulation of opportunities and threats and strengths and weaknesses as one way to identify issues (see Figure 3.5).

	Opportunities	Threats
Strengths	Can you exploit the opportunities using strengths?	Can strengths be used to face or avoid threats?
Weaknesses	Can opportunities be used to correct weaknesses?	Can threats that test weaknesses be handled?

Figure 3.5 *Cross-tabulating opportunities and threats by strengths and weaknesses. Source: Based on Smith (1994), p. 41*

The vision of success approach

This is 'where the organization develops a "best" or "ideal" picture of itself in the future as it successfully fulfills its mission' (Bryson, 1988, p. 58). The vision of success statements are formulated in qualitative terms and may be based on values identified by the top management team. Bryson suggests that, 'All that is needed here is a one-page idealized scenario of the future' (1988, p. 149). After this the approach could be somewhat akin to gap analysis in that the organization, having spelt out a desired future state, then identifies the gaps between this and the organization's current state. The strategic issues are thus defined by the organization's concerns about moving from where it is currently to its vision of success.

The direct approach

In this method, issues are identified without first establishing objectives or visions of success. One example of this kind of approach is to be seen in the abstraction process described by Ohmae (1982). This, like the use of vision statements, may be seen as more subjective than the use of a gap or SWOT analysis. It starts from management's perceptions of problems in competing with other firms. The process involves the following three steps:

1 classifying the different respects in which a company is at a disadvantage compared to its competitors (using brainstorming or opinion polls)
2 grouping these phenomena into problems (e.g. personnel, cost and strategic problems)
3 looking for the crucial issue that each group of problems poses.

Ohmae, himself, advocates, after the use of the abstraction process, that issues are further analysed (broken down and down) in an issue diagram until the final items are amenable to action (see Figure 3.6).

The abstraction process may seem unsystematic, subjective and unsophisticated, but it has three major advantages which matter in a pragmatic world. First, it is not necessary for people to share the same objectives, nor share the same vision, in order for them to agree what the key issues are, or how to resolve them. So, pragmatically, it may be better in some cases to accept that there is little consensus around aims and instead get on directly with resolving the strategic issues. Second, the abstraction process is built on the perceptions of managers who know a great deal about the organization and its situation. Argenti (1989, p. 26) claims that the chief executive and his colleagues 'know more about their company than anyone else in the world' and suggest that 'a plan based on the knowledge of these top men will have firm foundations'. Third, because it is based on management perceptions, the diagnosis of the problems and issues will be owned by those who have the clout to tackle the key strategic issues.

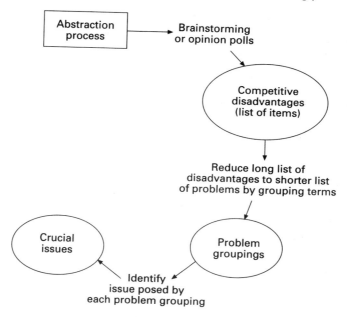

Figure 3.6 *Ohmae's abstraction process. Source: Based on Ohmae (1982)*

This last argument about the pragmatism of the abstraction process indicates the need for chief executives to adopt a participative style when managing the strategy process. This can be achieved by polling the views of all managers, but it certainly suggests that strategy formulation cannot be the province of just the chief executive. Argenti (1989) has said, for example, that the planning group should comprise the chief executive and his closest colleagues:

> The chief executive must lead the team. Today, however, when the team style of management has largely replaced the autocrat, it is essential that he discusses matters of such moment with his closest colleagues. I cannot imagine a modern system of corporate planning in which their full participation is not a central feature ... He must obtain the approval of his colleagues for almost everything he does ... A corporate planning system that failed to place this participative feature at its heart would be useless in today's managerial milieu ...
>
> Argenti, 1989, p. 26

However, while an individual chief executive may need to enlist other managers for the strategy process, the top managers may still have the power to initiate strategic change even when problems are not generally apparent:

> It is especially important to recognize the pressures that derive from the personal 'gut' feelings of top leaders. Often there are no salient external pressures – recent and projected short-term market performance is satisfactory; no significant internal pressures – staff morale is high and systems are operating smoothly; yet the top leader senses the need for a major change in corporate orientation, values, or culture. Pressures for change from the chief executive are no less legitimate than from anywhere else, although they probably have different consequences in terms of initial support for change.
>
> Beckhard and Harris, 1987, p. 44

So, there are the four different approaches to identifying strategic issues. The selection of an approach could well be contingent on situational factors, but we would hazard the guess that in many contemporary organizations a pragmatic approach is necessary to some significant degree.

A contingency view of process and techniques

We can take the Ansoff and McDonnell based model of the strategy process and associate with each stage the various techniques and models we will review in Chapter 4. As far as it goes, this seems to put techniques in their place, as tools to help with an issue identification and resolution process.

However, this does overlook the implications of a contingency theory of strategic management processes, which would require that the steps in the process and the selection of techniques are designed to fit contingent factors such as size, sector, market conditions, technology and so on. There is little discussion of this in most strategic management books. Perhaps this should not be considered surprising. Organizations are nowadays expected to devise and update strategies to ensure success in a way that appears not to have been expected years ago. The whole distinction between strategic and operational management was quite novel for many organizations even in the 1970s. Perhaps it is natural, therefore, that people still approach the question of strategic management processes as if there was one universally best way of fashioning the strategy process. Much research still needs to be done to ground a contingency approach in empirically verified evidence. All we can do here is make the case for a contingency approach by considering the problems that are experienced when attempts are made to apply private sector strategy processes to public sector organizations.

Argenti (1989) has observed that setting corporate objectives and targets seems to require more time for nonprofit making organizations and is more prone to failure. He has stated: 'Deciding corporate objectives for non-profit making organizations is the last unconquered peak in the study of management' (Argenti, 1989, p. xiv).

He is so committed to his method of making corporate strategy that he favours closing down or reforming nonprofit organizations which cannot define their corporate objectives in terms of a beneficiary consisting of one homogeneous group. He favours breaking nonprofit organizations with multiple objectives into separate autonomous parts. Alternatively he argues for reformation either to privatized organizations, or to project organizations which will be disbanded when their specific tasks have been achieved.

Other writers on strategic management take the view that the special problems encountered when the strategy process is applied to public sector and other nonprofit organizations requires that the strategy process and not the organization is changed (Nutt and Backoff, 1992). One example will be used to illustrate the public–private difference. In the private sector, the shareholders are the key stakeholder group and set the key priority as maximizing profit. Nutt and Backoff (1992) argue that the authority systems in which public sector organizations operate 'suggest that many individuals and groups can have stakes in the organizations' strategy' (Nutt and Backoff, 1992, p. 175). On this basis it may be more viable for private sector organizations to follow a strategy process in which objectives and targets are set and gap analysis is performed. In the public sector, perhaps it is both more possible and more necessary to evolve strategies on the basis of ideals rather than goals. Indeed, Nutt and Backoff recommend a strategy process for public sector organizations in which ideals rather than profit goals are used to identify organizational aims.

Private organizations, such as business firms, can assume a goal of profit. Most strategic management approaches developed for firms use some form of profit measurement to select among courses of action (Henderson, 1979; Porter, 1985). There is no equivalent for profit that applies to organizations with significant publicness. In such organizations, goals tend to be both vague and in dispute ... Ideals suggest aims that can be articulated in concrete terms to capture goallike targets and offer ways to seek compromise among competing views that dictate what the organization is (or is not) about. Our strategic management approach is designed to aid the managers of public and third sector organizations as they steer their organizations towards ambiguous ends in the context of political authority and the claims of multiple stakeholders.

Nutt and Backoff, 1992, pp. 176–7

Consequently, we might expect to find a number of respects in which the strategy process is, or should be, different between the two sectors. Not least, there may be a need to set organizational aims and identify strategic issues in very different ways.

Organizational aspects of the design of the strategy process

Organizational processes in large organizations may be set up to establish and revise goals, to monitor and analyse the environment, to instigate and plan action programmes, to monitor and measure the performance of operating units, and so on. The allocation of responsibilities for these processes forms an important design issue. In big organizations especially there are important questions about how the strategy process is designed so as to include and exclude different members of the management organization at corporate and operating unit levels. This is often seen as a choice between centralized and decentralized strategy formulation processes.

Decentralized systems may well cause strategy thinking to emphasize the maintenance of existing operational activities, whereas centralized strategy formulation by managers at the corporate level may lead to more innovations in strategy (see Figure 3.7 on McLellan and Kelly, 1989).

Figure 3.7 *Formulation processes in European companies – McLellan and Kelly (1989)*

They looked at a selection of European companies and found that they often used a standardized policy formulation process based on an annual cycle and a standard format for presenting the proposals for approval.

They also identified four different patterns of policy formulation process, defined in terms of the respective roles of operating unit managers and corporate managers.

What they described as the *Alpha* pattern of policy formulation was where operating unit managers made policy decisions which were then referred to the corporate level for approval and then combined into a corporate policy. Some of the companies fitting this pattern had informal processes through which unit level managers continuously checked out their ideas with higher level managers. Consequently, approval of unit policies at corporate level was virtually automatic in these companies. The formulation process, which was usually carried out on an annual basis, was followed by a period in which the operating unit managers implemented the policies.

In the *Beta* pattern, corporate management devised a business policy for the whole organization and the operating managers implemented it.

The *Gamma* pattern was where corporate and operating unit managers were both involved in policy formulation. Business unit managers were then required to implement the changes of policy they had previously agreed. Any lengthening of the formulation process by negotiations between the corporate and unit managers was offset by the speedier implementation process.

In the *Delta* pattern corporate managers approved but did not regularly influence unit managers' periodical policy formulation. The output of corporate policies was spasmodic and could be disruptive of the units' policies. The unit managers had to implement them even though they may not have been involved in formulating them. In other words, the corporate and unit levels were relatively isolated from each other.

McLellan and Kelly also looked at the role of corporate planners. This seemed to depend on the kind of formulation process in existence. The corporate planners' role in the organizations with decentralized policy formulation (i.e. the Alpha pattern) was relatively peripheral; they were facilitators rather than experts. In companies where the corporate managers played a more dominant role (i.e. the Beta and

Delta patterns), corporate planners behaved more as experts advising corporate-level managers on trends and future company policy.

They found some evidence that unit level managers in decentralized policy formulation processes (i.e. the Alpha pattern) were more likely to adopt what they called a maintenance orientation. This means that they were concerned to maintain existing activities and performance rather than engage in innovation. They suggest that innovation is more likely to emerge where policy formulation is centred on the corporate level.

Of course, the basic organizational form of a company – functional, divisional or matrix – is also an influence on exactly how strategy processes may be embedded within management organizations. The choice or emergence of a basic organizational form may well be contingent on factors such as the number of products or services marketed by the individual firm, the variability of the markets the firm supplies and the competitive pressures for responsiveness and innovation. On the other hand, a company's preferences for how it structures the strategy process and controls operating units may cause it to make decisions about products and markets which means it ends up choosing these to suit particular organizational forms.

There has been some speculation that even more people need to be included in strategy processes than simply senior and unit level managers. Perry, Stott and Smallwood (1993), for example, have urged companies to implement strategic improvising that widens considerably the number of potential contributors to strategy. They suggest that companies restrict the top level strategies (corporate and business strategies), leaving more space for the development of operational strategies. They envisage: 'A few key individuals may be necessary to clarify strategic direction at the corporate and business levels, but lower-level teams of individuals can assume critical strategic responsibilities' (1993, pp. 5–6).

On paper this looks like an extension of empowerment to ordinary employees of the organization. For it to work successfully there has to be some mechanism for consensus to be reached and conflicts resolved. This might, in fact, consume a considerable amount of senior management resources. Further, it is problematic to what extent such an involvement from employees is possible. It does, though, increase the information available to the organization in making strategy and could lead to improved operational effectiveness.

Key points

1 Formulating the strategy process as analysis, choice and implementation, which is the formulation which many people first encounter, is rooted in the technocratic assumptions of the modernist paradigm discussed in Chapter 2. Against this view, we have argued that identifying the critical strategic issues is the heart of the strategy process. This accords with recent calls for issues to guide the search for strategy. A move to strategic issue management need not imply the adoption of a short-term and reactive approach, providing industry foresight and strategic intent are strongly established as a result of the planning process.

2 Strategic issues have, by definition, to be dealt with urgently if the organization is to survive and prosper. It may be possible to deal with the issues as part of a regular cycle of strategic planning, but there may be cases when they have to be dealt with in nonroutine ways.

3 Strategic issues have become so fundamental to the strategic management process that formal strategic planning processes that do not enable them to be dealt with as they emerge have to be short-circuited, supplemented or abandoned.

4 The implications of a contingency theory of strategic management processes need to be considered. For example, take the problems that are experienced when attempts are made to apply private sector strategy processes to public sector organizations. Some experts have taken the view that the special problems encountered when the strategy process is applied to public sector and other nonprofit organizations require that the strategy process is changed (Nutt and Backoff, 1992). A contingency view of the strategy process would search for differences in the process not just for the sector variable but also for many others such as organizational size, market conditions, technology, etc.

5 The organizational aspects of the design of strategy processes, particularly as it affects who is involved in strategy formulation, may be important for the character of the strategies implemented (in terms of the balance between maintenance and innovation) and the performance of the organization.

References

Ansoff, I. (1968) *Corporate Strategy* (Penguin).

Ansoff, I. and McDonnell, E. (1990) *Implanting Strategic Management* (Prentice Hall).

Argenti, J (1989) *Practical Corporate Planning* (Routledge).

Beckhard, R. and Harris, R.T. (1987) *Organizational Transitions* (Addison-Wesley).

Bryson, J.M. (1988) *Strategic Planning for Public and Nonprofit Organizations* (Jossey-Bass).

Dyson, R.G. (1990) *Strategic Planning: Models and Analytical Techniques* (Wiley).

Kay, J. (1993) *Foundations of Corporate Success* (Oxford University Press).

McLellan, R. and Kelly, G. (1989) 'Business Policy Formulation: Understanding the Process' in Asch, D. and Bowman, C. (editors) *Readings in Strategic Management* (Macmillan).

Mockler, R.J. (1995) 'Strategic Management: The Beginning of a New Era' in Hussey, D.E. (editor) *Rethinking Strategic Management* (Wiley).

Nutt, P.C. and Backoff, R.W. (1992) *Strategic Management of Public and Third Sector Organizations* (Jossey-Bass).

Ohmae, K. (1982) *The Mind of the Strategist* (McGraw-Hill).

Perry, L.T., Stott, R.G. and Smallwood, W.N. (1993) *Real-Time Strategy* (John Wiley and Sons).

Rappaport, A. (1991) 'Selecting Strategies That Create Shareholder Value' in Montgomery, C.A. and Porter, M. (editors) *Strategy: Seeking and Securing Competitive Advantage* (Harvard Business School).

Smith, N.I. (1994) *Down-to-earth Strategic Planning* (Prentice Hall).

Stacey, R.D. (1991) *The Chaos Frontier* (Butterworth-Heinemann).

4

Techniques and models for analysis

Introduction

This chapter looks at the various analytical techniques and models that are popular. As we suggested in Chapter 3, a model of the strategy process can be the basis for viewing the relevance of the various techniques and models. It is important to know not only when techniques and models could be relevant in a strategy process, but also how they are used and, whenever possible, what are considered to be their limitations. Further, it is important to stress how any model or technique conditions and frames how we 'see' and consequently act upon the world.

Uses and limitations

Lenz and Lyles (1991) have pointed out that some of the many assumptions embedded in strategic plans originate from assumptions implicit in the specific analytical techniques used. For example, the BCG matrix (see below for more details) requires strategic business units to be classified according to their market share; it has been assumed that this is important because of what are called learning curve effects, whereby increased profitability is associated with a larger market share. This leads to the assumption that a strategic business unit with a high market share but only a slowly growing market is well placed to provide cash which can be invested in strategic business units that are growing.

So, analytical techniques contain assumptions, which in part explains why they can be powerful tools for analysis, but the assumptions are also the essence of their limitations. This is because the assumptions structure how reality is seen and interpreted, but also prevent certain opportunities or threats being seen. Lenz and Lyles seem to be referring to these limitations in the following remarks:

> The particular analytical model used becomes a 'filter' that frames managerial thinking. In this mode the model's parameters and structure define strategic problems in such a way that the model can deal with them ... In a sense, unqualified acceptance of a model for strategy analysis can seriously impair the capacity of an organization to spot problems sufficiently well in advance to formulate and implement a response.
>
> Lenz and Lyles, 1991, p. 62

It may be useful to distinguish between the *internal* limitations of an analytical technique or model, which arise because of the assumptions and *external* limitations, which refer to the fact that a technique or a model does not apply to all situations. Lenz and Lyles also provide a possible illustration of the external limitations of an analytical technique. They point out that the assumption that high profits are a function of market share are not corroborated by examples of small firms with small market share that are extremely profitable. This implies that the BCG matrix may have external limitations in terms of its applicability to all organizations; that is, perhaps the BCG matrix does not apply to small firms?

The student of strategic management needs to consider and assess the limitations of the more popular analytical techniques and models used in strategic analysis. Some of the most-discussed techniques and models are:

1 forecasting models
2 PEST analysis
3 benchmarking
4 resource analysis
5 competence analysis
6 scenario analysis
7 SWOT analysis
8 gap analysis
9 cognitive mapping

10 portfolio planning matrix
11 quantitative investment appraisal
12 stakeholder analysis.

Techniques

Forecasting models

It can be helpful to managers preparing to identify the key strategic issues of their organization to review trends or movements in a whole host of factors, including:

- the buying behaviour of customers, or the demand for services by clients
- the products or services marketed or supplied
- operational/business processes
- the resources of the organization
- marketing, financial, IT, HRM, etc. systems
- the environmental contexts.

Time series analysis, econometric analysis and Delphic polling may be used to study such trends and movements.

Time series data can also be used to forecast the future. Time series analysis may reveal patterns (e.g. rising demand, seasonal patterns) in, say, the buying behaviour of customers, which may be extrapolated into the future.

Econometric analysis may suggest the factors which cause variations in the behaviour of concern to a company. Econometrics is a part of economics that uses sophisticated statistical techniques such as regression analysis to model why things happen. If you can model why things happen, you can then move on to predict what would happen if something changes. An econometric model might link the value of the pound against the dollar using data about the two countries' balance of payments, interest rates, unemployment levels and so on. A model that did this well could be used to predict what the exchange rate would be if one of these items changed. A firm trading in the US could use such a model to modify its strategy when things changed.

Softer ways of forecasting are available. *Delphic polling,* where experts are asked when they think something is most likely to occur, is a popular way of 'feeling' the future. You might be interested in establishing roughly when 90 per cent of homes will have a high definition television. Asking a group of experts for their best guess on this would help you in planning your strategy for the development of such televisions.

Time series and econometric models and Delphic polling can be seen as part of a modernist mindset. They are, first, full of modernist confidence in their capability of seeing and knowing the future reasonably well. Second, they are techniques which rely on experts – managers do not normally do them.

They rely heavily on the past. They use the past to predict the future. Consequently, such modernist techniques are aligned with management habits of thinking which are also prone to rely on extrapolation of past experience. As Mintzberg has said, 'Managers may have to live strategy in the future, but they must understand it through the past' (Mintzberg, 1991, p. 114).

But is the modernist confidence in knowing the future really justified? Assumptions based on past experience may prove unreliable. There can be no guarantees, ultimately, that the past trends will continue into the future, nor that the structure of cause–effect relationships underlying those trends will continue to be reproduced. This was demonstrated by the oil crisis of 1973, which shook the confidence of many in the reliability of long-term forecasts; the dislocations caused by the oil crisis meant that past forecasts proved to be far too optimistic. It has, indeed, been found that faulty forecasts can often be attributed to erroneous underlying assumptions rather than poor methodology (Schnaars, 1990). In other words, the variables which are important in explaining past experiences may not be identical to those which will prove to be relevant in the future. And even if all the key variables that will influence the future are known, forecasting is bound to have limited success when many of these variables are too unpredictable on the basis of current knowledge (Linneman and Kennell, 1990).

PEST analysis

This directs the analyst to scan the organization's political, economic, social and technological contexts for events and trends which may be important. In practice, managers may brainstorm a list of events or trends, or they may use prepared lists as prompts. The following listing of the factors which could be considered in each of the four areas is based on Smith (1994).

Political – European law, central Government initiatives, public expenditure controls, employment law, health and safety legislation, machinery of government

Economic – economic growth, employment, costs (labour, materials/building), standards of living, competition, international trade

Social – population/demographic trends, changes in lifestyle, expectations of customers, expectations of employees, lobbies (e.g. environmental lobby, minorities lobby), family structures, attitudes to society, authority

Technological – communications at work, communications with customers, research expenditure and progress, new products.

It is not always easy to measure trends in these different areas, but their importance can be profound even so. Taking the case of 'attitudes to authority', which seem to have continued to change in the 1980s, this can have a big impact on how organizations are managed.

When a PEST analysis is done systematically, the analyst will seek data to corroborate the existence of the trends and events and will then rate them for their importance so that the analysis is concentrated on the most important of the trends and events. The criteria for judging the importance of trends and events are rarely discussed, but could include the likely impact on the organization's attainment of its corporate objectives.

Benchmarking

Benchmarking is the collection of data by management on their own organization's performance and that of other organizations and its use to make comparisons in terms of performance. The data may cover a wide range of topics – including financial performance, business processes, productivity and management style. The data may be shared by interfirm agreement, it may result from visits and discussions and it may be obtained from published sources.

There are two obvious limitations with benchmarking. First, firms will naturally want data on their best competitors and yet 'there may be an understandable reluctance to share data, for fear of enabling a competitor to catch up' (Smith, 1994, p. 75). Even if some data can be obtained, there may not be enough data to enable a firm to understand how the best firms achieve such good results. This point is made by Smith (1994) as follows.

> Benchmarking should be a learning process; establishing that another organisation has managed to reduce its stockholding to half our own figure identifies an issue, tells us we could do better. What we really need to know, however, is how to do it. Benchmarking in this sense goes beyond collecting numbers and involves sharing information about processes.
>
> Smith, 1994, p. 76

Second, benchmarking assumes that firms are trying to catch up with the best and can create a copy-cat mind set in which firms are not creating their own differentiated products and processes. In other words, it may lead to the erosion of competitors' competitive advantage, but it is not clear that it will lead to innovations which will build a competitive advantage. Of course, firms may be aware of this but be satisfied with not being left behind.

Resource analysis

In recent years there has been an increasingly influential vein within strategic management writing which takes a resource-based view of the firm (Hamel and Prahalad, 1994, p. 157). As part of this view, the organization is looked at as a portfolio of resources and the ability to use these resources is seen as critical to competitive performance. This approach is a counterpoint to Porter's emphasis on the analysis of the industry's structure (see Chapter 5). Against this background, resource analysis looks a more interesting aspect of strategic analysis than it has done hitherto.

In essence, a resource analysis looks at what resources an organization has, or what resources will be required by a new strategy. It involves, to start off, listing resources. This is done in terms of types of resources, such as:

- physical (e.g. machines)
- human (e.g. skills, knowledge)
- financial (e.g. money)
- intangibles (e.g. goodwill).

Resource analysis can be used at different stages in the strategic analysis process. They can be used as part of an internal appraisal and will then be useful as an input to a SWOT analysis. They can also be used in assessing the feasibility of proposed actions and planning the implementation of strategic action, when it is important to calculate the resources needed to realize a strategy, and their sourcing and acquisition.

When the resource analysis is used as part of an internal appraisal, the approach tends to be comprehensive and concerned with the quantity and quality of resources. When the analysis is used for the later stages of the strategy process, the analyst lists the resources required for the new strategy, assesses their criticality to the success of the new strategy and identifies who might supply them (Nutt and Backoff, 1992).

Competence analysis

This is really a set of techniques which are linked specifically to the theory of competence-based competition strategy (Hamel and Prahalad, 1994). It concerns itself with a particular type of resource – a core competence – which is seen as formed from skills. Most organizations are assumed to have just a few core competencies at most.

We will note three such techniques which have been outlined by Klein and Hiscocks (1994): skill mapping, skill cluster analysis and critical skill analysis.

Skill mapping involves identifying and assessing an organization's individual skills. The skills are researched through an examination of the formal organization structure, comparisons of the organization's products with those of competitors, interviews inside the organization and discussions with customers. For example, an organization chart will name departments and sections and the names can indicate the existence of skills; the organization's products may have superior characteristics which may indicate the skills that exist; and interviews and discussions can uncover skills that are recognized internally or externally in the market place.

These skills are then evaluated on a capability scale (e.g. for each individual skill the organization is rated as having no capability, some capability, strong capability or world-class capability); and they are then assessed for their strategic importance. Assessing the skills in terms of capability is based on evidence collected about the skills and assumes that a capability requires that people with skills are backed by the necessary capital equipment and supported by an appropriate organizational structure and culture. The assessment of strategic importance is based on two tests:

- Is the individual skill rated as strong or world-class capability?
- Is the skill of high importance to the organization's products and/or to the market?

Skill mapping produces a list of the organization's strategic skills. The skills may be technical (e.g. moulding, polymer chemistry) or managerial (e.g. finance, marketing).

Skill cluster analysis can be used to identify core competencies by looking at the occurrence of skills in a firm's existing products. It involves looking at which current skills are being combined in the making of particular products. If, for example, two skills are usually both required to make many of the firm's products, then it may indicate that the firm has a competence composed of these two skills. Conversely, if the firm uses these two skills for many of its products but they are rarely both needed in making individual products, then the firm does not have a competence which comprises these two skills.

The analysis may be used to produce a matrix in which all the strategic skills are listed horizontally and vertically and each cell shows the percentage of a firm's products in which the relevant pair of skills are both found. In the example in Table 4.1, skill 2 and skill 4 are found together in 80 per cent of a firm's products.

Table 4.1 *Skill cluster analysis*

	Skill 1	Skill 2	Skill 3	Skill 4
Skill 1	–	10	10	50
Skill 2	10	–	40	80
Skill 3	10	40	–	10
Skill 4	50	80	10	–

A large matrix with many more skills listed may be produced for real organizations and may reveal clusters consisting of two or more skills which often appear to be combined in products. The presumption is still, however, that combinations of skills which exist within a high proportion of a firm's products indicates the components of a competence.

Critical skill analysis may be useful for planning long-term skill investments. It is assumed that there is a minimum time to acquire a skill and that there is a trade-off between time and cost in the process of acquiring the skill. If the cost of acquiring a set of skills required for a product is plotted on a graph using time in years as the x-axis and this is compared with a graph showing the financial benefit to the company of manufacturing the product (also graphed using time as the x-axis), the company can work out an optimal timescale for building the skills required. These calculations require forecasts of financial benefits, which may be derived from forecasts of price and market share, which may in turn rest on forecasts of the possibility of benefits of being earlier than competitors to market the product. Costs and benefits would be forecasted using discounted figures.

Scenario analysis

Scenarios are qualitative descriptions of possible future environments of a firm, presented in a narrative format. Scenario analysis, involving the development of a set of possible future environments, may be regarded as an alternative to quantitative models for forecasting. Disillusionment with quantitative models has been seen as helping to make scenario analysis popular and the spread of its use in business during the 1970s has been linked to the oil crisis in the 1970s (Schnaars, 1990). So, scenario analysis seems to be a preferred form of forecasting when the business environment is marked by shocks and discontinuities, and forecasting based on extrapolation is unreliable.

Scenario building can also be used by not-for-profit organizations as a way of formulating desired future states, that is, for setting organizational aims (Nutt and Backoff, 1992, pp. 172–3). When used in this way, managers can envision best- and worst-case scenarios framed in terms of the characteristics of their organizations rather than their external environmental factors.

Linneman and Kennell (1990) suggest that when scenarios are used for forecasting they enable managers to appreciate the various possible future environments which may develop and thus the long-term implications of strategic decisions made in the present; they are not designed to provide a basis for detailed planning into the future. For example, managers may construct several possible scenarios and then consider the likely effectiveness of a strategic measure for each scenario. Those measures which look as though they could be effective in all scenarios are rated as more flexible than those which would only suit one of the scenarios, although it may not be appropriate to select a strategy based just on its flexibility.

The following 'inductive' approach for building scenarios used in forecasting is mainly derived from advice given by Linneman and Kennell (1990).

1 Select a planning horizon for the scenarios (e.g. most firms use five years).
2 Identify a set of assumptions for the scenarios – these are factors which can be forecasted accurately with some confidence.
3 Identify a list of critical variables that have had important effects on the organization (including effects on its products and markets) in the past or may be important in the future – some of these may be unpredictable (e.g. rate of economic growth, public expenditure plans).
4 Review the list of variables and eliminate those that (a) are thought to have a low potential impact *and* a low probability of occurrence; (b) may not happen within the planning horizon; and (c) are events which would be a total disaster.
5 Distinguish the variables which are dependent on other variables in the list (these dependent variables are used to enrich the scenarios, but are not used to form them in the first instance).
6 Aggregate variables on the list into broader variables, aiming to end up with two to five key variables.
7 Assign two or three realistic values to each of the key variables (e.g. an inflation rate variable might be assigned two values of 0–5 per cent and 6–10 per cent and a government grant variable may be assigned values of 'small' and 'large').
8 List all possible combinations of the key variables (e.g. three key variables each with two values would generate eight scenarios and three variables each with three values would generate twenty-seven scenarios).

9 Reject scenarios which are implausible (i.e. the combinations of values for the variables should be feasible) and those scenarios which
vary very little from other scenarios, with a view to ending up with a final list of three scenarios, including the scenario which is the most probable case and a worst-case scenario.

10 Write each of the scenarios in one or two paragraphs by encompassing the variables, assumptions and the dependent variables within an appreciation of the organization's environment and how it had developed, written as if it is at the end of the selected planning horizon.

Schnaars suggests that scenario analysis 'seems best suited for those situations where a few crucial factors can be identified, but not easily predicted' (Schnaars, 1990, p. 157).

SWOT analysis

A SWOT analysis is another technique based on listing. Managers begin by simply listing all the current strengths and weaknesses of the organization and all the future opportunities and threats they perceive in the environment. This may be the result of a brainstorming process; it may be the fruits of prior analysis (e.g. resource analysis, PEST analysis); it may be the results of a survey of managers.

Weihrich (1990) suggested that threats and opportunities can be grouped into the following six categories:

- economic
- social and political
- products and technology
- demographic
- markets and competition
- other factors.

The kinds of factor which managers might include in the s trengths and weaknesses of an organization can be found in work by Stevenson (1989), who classified the opinions of fifty managers on their companies' strengths and weaknesses into five major groups:

- organization (e.g. organizational form and structure, top management interest and skill, control system, planning system)
- personnel (e.g. employee attitudes, technical skills, experience)
- marketing (e.g. breadth of the product line, sales force, knowledge of the customer's needs, reputation, customer service)
- technical (e.g. production facilities, product development, research)
- finance (e.g. financial size, price–earnings ratio, growth pattern).

If it is to be done rigorously, the items listed in a SWOT analysis need to be evaluated in various ways. For example:

- Can the existence of a strength be substantiated using evidence from, say, comparisons (historically with itself or with other organizations) or is it based on opinion?
- Has an organization got any distinctive strengths, weaknesses, opportunities and threats, as shown by careful comparison with its main competitors or rivals? (If a private firm's main competitor has the same strength to the same degree, can it still be regarded as a strength?)
- Can any of the weaknesses be grouped together because they are really the same thing?
- Are any strengths causally linked to any others?
- How important are the various strengths, weaknesses, opportunities and threats – which are the most important and deserve most attention?

Such evaluation can lead to significant revision of the lists.

The placing of the SWOT analysis in the strategy process can be important in how it works in practice. For example, if the SWOT is done straight after an objective-setting exercise the results might be different from if it is done straight after benchmarking or a five forces analysis; the sequencing of the techniques can influence the implicit frame of reference used in the SWOT analysis – so, are the weaknesses weak in the light of the organization's objectives, or weak relative to rival firms?

One limitation of SWOT analysis may be seen as its subjectivity (see Figure 4.1). Managers vary in how they define strengths and weaknesses according to their position in the organizational hierarchy. This was the finding of a study of US managers by Stevenson (1989):

Top managers put a great deal of emphasis on financial issues and very little on technical ones; middle and lower managers were concerned for technical issues but almost completely ignored finance. Showing some complacency perhaps, top managers perceived more strengths than lower managers.

Whittington, 1993, p. 73

Figure 4.1 *Evaluating strengths and weaknesses – Stevenson (1989)*

Stevenson (1989) found that there was no consensus amongst managers (within the companies he studied) on the strengths and weaknesses of their companies. The managers' perceptions were strongly influenced by two individual variables: their level in the organization and the type of responsibility they held. The criteria used for judging strengths and weaknesses also varied; historical criteria (e.g. historical experience of the company) were mostly used to identify strengths and rarely used to identify weaknesses, whilst normative criteria (e.g. consultant's opinions, management's understanding of management literature) were mostly used to identify weaknesses.

The sample consisted of fifty managers, from six manufacturing companies, who were asked about the strengths and weaknesses of their organizations. The managers in each company responded with evaluations of a wide range of attributes, most of which were considered to be both strengths and weaknesses.

Managers at the top level of their company were more concerned than other managers about the financial attributes of the organization and employee attitudes, but were less concerned about marketing, product development and other technical matters.

He also found that higher level managers were more optimistic than lower level managers in terms of the balance of strengths and weaknesses.

Stevenson concluded: 'It appears that the manager's organizational level influences both his choice of which attributes to examine and his perception of them as either strengths or weaknesses' (Stevenson, 1989, p. 172).

Finally, it may be that the problem of subjectivity in the use of SWOT analysis is useful in alerting us to the pragmatic use of the technique. If management perceptions of strengths and weaknesses, and opportunities and threats, are not true in some absolute sense, can they be approximately true relative to a situation? There have been approaches to internal appraisal of organizations which are situation-based. In some of Ansoff's earlier work (1968) he argues for seeing strengths and weaknesses as existing in relation to the capability pattern of the most successful competitors in the industry and thus in relation to an organization's present product-market posture. If a firm decided to enter a new industry there would be a new set of most successful competitors and this would imply changes to the pattern of strengths and weaknesses identified for the firm. (We are identifying the situation as essentially the industry in question.)

We favour using the key strategic issues, which we assume are specific to each organization and their situation, as the basis for defining the strengths and weaknesses, opportunities and threats. Thus an attribute may be worth recognizing as a strength because it can be used to tackle a key strategic issue; or an event or trend may be worth recognizing as an opportunity because it can be exploited to tackle a key strategic issue.

There appears to be a certain illogicality in identifying strengths, weaknesses, opportunities and threats prior to identifying key strategic issues and then using them to solve the strategic issues. But it is more that the attributes of the internal or external situation are *confirmed* as strengths, weaknesses, opportunities and threats by being used to resolve the key strategic issues. (The proof of the pudding is in the eating.) It is perhaps significant that Stevenson (1989) reported that the 'most common single complaint of managers who did not feel that the definition of strengths and weaknesses was meaningful was that they had to be defined in the context of a problem' (Stevenson, 1989, p. 174). The managers, it seemed, were not happy about *a priori* definitions of strengths and weaknesses unrelated to a specific situation.

Gap analysis

Argenti's (1989) approach to gap analysis is based on the distinction between targets and forecasts. The essence of gap analysis is to determine the gap between a target and the forecast. Strategies are then selected to close the gap and thus achieve the targets.

> You set a target. You make a forecast ... The target is up to you, it is in your control. The forecast is out of your control, it represents

something that you think is going to happen in the world around you … But if the forecast does not equal the target (i.e. if you suspect that things are not going to turn out as you would like), you can take action to bring the forecast closer to your target. This is what a plan is for, to change something that has not happened, to make the outcome suit you better.

Argenti, 1989, p. 157

For a private sector company, annual targets and forecasts of profits and return on capital employed can be graphed for five years. The company can identify the factors in the past which have affected its performance and, combining this knowledge with knowledge of the future, it can make both pessimistic and optimistic forecasts of both profits and return on capital employed. Argenti insists that forecasting is worthwhile, but recognizes that forecasts are often wrong. Since it is not possible to forecast accurately, it is important to have two forecasts. The targets may also be set at two levels, a minimum one and a satisfactory one.

The graphs communicate the nature and urgency of strategic action. If there are major gaps and the forecasts suggest the company will not even achieve its minimum targets, then the analyst is warned of the need for strategies to achieve them. If there is no risk of failing to meet the minimum targets, the company can concentrate on profit-improving actions. In terms of urgency, the graphs may show a gap suddenly widening in, say, year 4 and thus indicate that strategies have to be selected which have a timely impact.

Cognitive mapping

At its simplest, cognitive mapping is about getting top managers to discover within their own ideas their embedded theories for solving strategic issues. If it works, cognitive mapping, by definition, produces analyses and solutions to strategic issues that are owned by the managers themselves.

Eden (1990) has provided a rationale for why this is an important technique, which may be summarized as follows. Real organizations undergo strategic change as a result of decisions and actions by powerful managers. These managers act on the basis of the sense they have made of their organization and its problems. Their thinking evolves subtly and incrementally. If a technique is going to help with strategic analysis and implementation it must be compatible with these realities and must be seen as useful and interesting by the powerful managers. Cognitive mapping is compatible with these realities and is acceptable and interesting to managers who like to work with their ideas and solve problems. It has the benefit that by 'surfacing' strategic thinking – strategic theory, goals and strategic options – it enables management teams to evaluate properly the value and coherence of ideas which would have guided strategic change implicitly.

A programme using cognitive mapping can consist of interviews conducted with managers on strategic issues by a facilitator, analysis to build models of the knowledge and arguments, and then workshops involving the managers who were interviewed to develop a consensus and agree on an action plan. During the interviews managers are asked broad and open-ended questions about the strategic issues. This works, according to Eden, in the following way.

> As people talk about their views on a particular problem they are drawing upon general theories they have about the organization, the market place, and the strengths and weaknesses of different courses of action. This occurs naturally and can be understood and modelled by the facilitator, without recourse to SWOT analysis questions. These theories are often expressed in highly specific terms but nevertheless imply the translation of experience into assertions about the way in which the future may unfold.
>
> Eden, 1990, p. 111

As we have noted, cognitive mapping assumes that strategic change is normally guided by the implicit or embedded theories of managers and that these can be brought to the surface and developed by discussion into agreed action plans. The mapping process may be seen as enhancing strategy making as a human and interactive process. Cognitive maps produced early in the process are turned into single group maps which are discussed and modified.

The use of cognitive mapping can be contrasted with techniques such as trend analysis, PEST analysis, SWOT analysis, etc., which highlight the importance of the environment in defining the options for action and can appear to be totally objective in their findings even though, obviously, the findings are to some extent influenced by the implicit theories of the analysts which guide their selection, understanding and rating of trends and events. It could be argued that cognitive mapping has the exact opposite problem: it does not require managers to undertake a comprehensive and systematic study of the external environment of the organization, which could influence their embedded as well as their explicit strategic theories.

Portfolio planning matrix

The most well-known portfolio planning matrix is the Boston Consulting Group (BCG) matrix, which was developed in the late 1960s and rapidly became very popular in major US companies. The matrix is used, by companies which have a number of business units, as a tool for corporate strategic thinking. The individual businesses which make up the company are classified within a portfolio planning matrix, which is defined on the basis of (a) attractiveness of the market (which could be measured by growth, or total size) and (b) the strength of the business (which could be measured by market share). Alternatively, the company's products or product lines can be classified on the same basis. It is assumed that different positions in the matrix indicate the need for different strategic measures by the company. The portfolio planning matrix was designed with private sector conglomerates in mind, but with a little ingenuity it can be adapted to public sector organizations, using factors such as political or public support and the effectiveness of services.

Portfolio planning is used by multibusiness companies to optimize their overall performance. This can be illustrated using the BCG matrix. The matrix is based on classifying strategic business units (SBUs), or products, according to their relative market share (low or high) and the market growth rate (low or high). This produces four SBU situations or product categories, illustrated in Table 4.2:

- Star – high market share in a growing market
- Question mark – low share in growing market
- Cash cow – a high share in a mature market
- Dog – low share in static or declining market.

Table 4.2 *BCG matrix categories*

Market growth rate	Relative market share	
	High	*Low*
High	Star	Question mark
Low	Cash cow	Dog

McNamee (1992) provides useful guidance on the process of constructing a BCG matrix. First, it is necessary to measure the relative market share of the business unit or the product, that is, the market share relative to that held by rivals. The relative market share is calculated by taking, say, a business unit's percentage share of a market and dividing the figure by the percentage share of its largest rival. Consequently, a business unit with a relative market share greater than 1.0 is the market leader and one with a relative market share less than 1.0 is not the market leader. If the matrix is to be plotted precisely, then the relative market share is placed on the horizontal axis of the matrix and ranges from 10 to 0.1, with 1.0 being the mid-point, so that the market leader appears on the left-hand side of the matrix and the followers appear on the right-hand side.

Second, the market growth rate of each of the company's business units, or products, is measured along the vertical axis. This is measured as a percentage. This can be calculated by working out the average annual growth rate over several years.

Third, the value of the annual sales of each of the company's business units, or products, is shown by plotting them on the matrix as a circle and not as a point (see Figure 4.2). For each unit, or product, a circle is plotted at the appropriate point in terms of relative market share and market growth rate, with an area which is calculated to be proportional to its annual sales. (The radius of the circle is found by taking the annual sales, multiplying by 7, dividing by 22 and finally calculating the square root of the resultant figure.)

When the data required to construct portfolios is not available it is sometimes possible to use other data. For example, McNamee (1992) shows how product market portfolios can be derived from figures on the number of barrels of beer shipped by the major companies in the US brewing industry in 1974 and 1978. These figures are used to calculate the growth rate of the market and the relative market shares of the different companies. He also uses the shipment figures as surrogates for their annual sales.

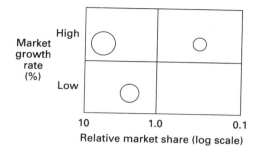

Figure 4.2 *BCG matrix construction*

So much for constructing BCG matrices. How are they then used? It is assumed that Stars require an aggressive investment strategy using cash generated by Cash Cows. Dogs are candidates for divestment. Question Marks are problematic – should a company invest in them hoping to turn them into Stars? This could pay off, but if it fails a lot of money may have been sunk hopelessly.

The usual interpretation of the BCG matrix seems plausible. A business exists to make a profit and, ideally, to increase its profitability; to do this, it must at the outset have money to invest and then it must make good profits that are reinvested to expand the scale of investment and the possibilities of profitable activity. If the existing market is saturated then the new investment must be made in new products. This is consistent with the underlying logic of the BCG matrix. A company would logically like to have a 'cash cow' and a 'star'. The cash cow is a mature business unit, or product, with a large market share in a slowly growing market. It is assumed that the high market share indicates a high profit margin (due to experience curve effects which produce relatively low costs). Since the market is growing slowly for the cash cow, it is assumed to generate cash in excess of the amount needed for reinvestment. In contrast, the star is a business unit, or product, with a high market share enjoying high growth. It is assumed that growth requires added assets and therefore the star may not generate all its own cash; later when growth slows it will become a cash generator – i.e. it will become a cash cow. The question mark business unit, or product, might become a star, provided a lot of cash is provided, but could end up being a dog, which is regarded as a waste of time.

The general limitations of portfolio planning are that it neglects the nonquantified success factors, pays too little attention to the individual businesses themselves and does not grasp the company as a coherent assembly of businesses (Ohmae, 1982). More recent approaches to corporate strategy place considerable emphasis on sharing activities and transferring skills between business units which make up the company (see Chapter 7).

McNamee (1992) notes a number of criticisms and doubts about the BCG matrix, including criticisms of the reliance on just two factors to determine strategic position; criticisms of the assumption that small relative market shares are always a problem; criticisms of the assumption that high growth markets are best; and doubts about the link between relative market share and profitability. On that last point, about the link between market share and profitability, it is useful to look at Baden-Fuller and Stopford's (1992) arguments. They quote a study by Buzzell and Gale (1987): 'only 4 per cent of the differences in profitability of one business unit versus another could be explained by differences in market share' (Baden-Fuller and Stopford, 1992, p. 25). They conclude that, 'Many successful businesses do have a large market share but the causality is usually from success to share, not the other way' (1992, p. 24).

Others have also been concerned about the BCG matrix's imagery and oversimplification (Seeger, 1991). A core business of the company may be neglected because it is seen as just a cash cow (Whittington, 1993, p. 72).

Quantitative investment appraisal

The discounted cash flow technique involves working out the economic value of an investment by discounting the expected cash flow by the cost of capital. It is often recommended as a technique for evaluating the profitability of capital investment at a project level. But it can also be extended and used at the corporate strategy level. 'By estimating the future cash flows associated with each strategy, a company can assess the economic value to shareholders of alternative strategies at the business unit and corporate levels' (Rappaport, 1991, pp. 382–3).

We will illustrate the use of the discounted cash flow technique at the project level. The assumption behind the technique is that people prefer money now rather than the same nominal amount at some future point in time – even assuming zero inflation. Therefore, the expenditures and returns of a project associated with future years need to be discounted at an appropriate rate to find out its net present value (NPV; see Figure 4.3).

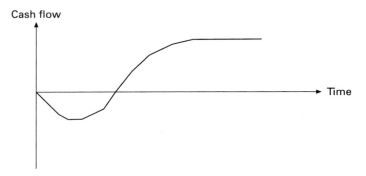

In the early period there are likely to be high costs and no benefits as the firm spends money on activities such as market research, product development, market testing, designing tooling and developing marketing and distribution capabilities

Figure 4.3 *A typical cash flow profile for a strategic move*

To be able to calculate future expenditure and benefit streams from a strategic project designed to increase profitability and calculate them at their net present value, the analyst needs to decide on how much will be spent on, say, buying any equipment required, the spending associated with each year, the increased sales associated with each year and an appropriate discount rate. The discount rate may be chosen to reflect likely interest rates and inflation (see Figure 4.4 for an example of a discounted cash flow calculation for a farm business investment project).

Figure 4.4 *An example of a silage harvester investment proposal*

Silage harvesting entails mowing the grass crop at its optimum quality stage, leaving the crop to dry on the ground for about twenty-four hours. It is then picked up, chopped and blown into trailers by the silage harvester. The crop is then drawn into the storage area and sealed to ensure an anaerobic fermentation.

At present the operation is carried out by a contractor. The farm business is considering a silage harvester and carrying out the operation itself. Adequate back-up machinery is already in place.

Table 4.3 *Net present value calculation*

	Year 0	Year 1	Year 2	Year 3	Year 4	
Machine purchase	−11 000	0	0	0	3500	
Running costs	0	−2000	−2000	−2600	−2800	
Seasonal labour	0	−1100	−1200	−1300	−1400	
Contractor fees saved	0	6600	6600	6900	6900	
	−11 000	3500	3400	3000	6200	
@15% cost of capital						
Discount factor	1.000	0.870	0.756	0.658	0.572	
	−11 000	3045	2570	1974	3546	136
						NPV
@16% cost of capital						
	1.000	0.862	0.743	0.641	0.552	
	−11 000	3017	2526	1923	3422	−111
						NPV

The costs over five years are given in Table 4.3. NPV at 15 per cent cost of capital is positive and negative at 16 per cent.

The internal rate of return = 15 + (136 ÷ 247) = 15.6 per cent.

On the basis of these figures the farm business will decide whether the mowing operation will continue to be carried out by the contractor.

Stacey (1991) has criticized the use of such techniques for appraising long-term investments in conditions where change is open ended (i.e. where discontinuity is a feature). Commenting on modern methods of investment appraisal using discounted cashflow procedures, where cash flow for an investment in, say, the next six months is projected for twenty-five years, he has said: 'This whole procedure is pure fantasy when the dynamics are chaotic' (Stacey, 1991, pp. 186–7).

He refers to the product development cycle for the pharmaceuticals industry (more than ten years to develop a new drug) and the aerospace industry (more than fifteen years to produce a new aircraft). Projections of costs, revenues and consequent profits may be estimated, but 'no one can forecast the snags that may be encountered in the development, the costs that will be incurred in year 10 or the market demand that will prevail in year 15, simply because there are too many unknowns' (Stacey, 1991, p. 187).

He believes that managers in successful companies manipulate the figures to fit their judgement. 'It may also be that experience-based intuition is a more reliable approach to the overall shape of a dynamic business system than any analytical methods presently available to us' (Stacey, 1991, p. 186). Long-term planning and quantitative investment appraisal are alleged to be dangerous when they are actually used for decision making and waste time and distract managers from the real issues (p.189).

If Stacey is correct, quantitative investment appraisal techniques are useful in more predictable and stable situations but useless in situations marked by unpredictability.

Stakeholder analysis

Stakeholder analysis can be used early in the strategy process in order to influence judgements made about the strategic issues and it can be used to plan the implementation of strategic action.

The analysis begins, essentially, as a listing technique. All those individuals or groups who can affect the organization, or are affected by it, are listed. These stakeholders may, for example, have ownership, managerial, political or professional interests in the strategies pursued by the organization. It is useful at this stage to spend time specifying the ways in which the stakeholders affect, or are affected by, the organization, thereby corroborating their status as stakeholders. Their relative importance or power in relation to the organization should also be rated.

If the stakeholder analysis is being undertaken prior to the analysis of strategic issues, the next step is to analyse the expectations of the stakeholders. These expectations may be divided into their current and future expectations. Smith (1994) offers the following advice about doing the analysis:

What do the stakeholders expect from us? What criteria do they use when judging our performance? It is at this stage that information collected from the stakeholders needs to be available. Some of this may be collected regularly as a matter of routine, for example, from users' surveys or regular feedback meetings ... The risk in a stakeholder analysis is that the management team simply record their present perceptions whereas any planning cycle must be used as an opportunity to stand back and change perceptions if necessary. Therefore, if we wish to record the criteria used by stakeholders to judge our performance and to record their views of our performance, we need to ask them.

Smith, 1994, p. 47

If the stakeholder analysis is being used to plan the implementation of a strategy, it can be useful to plot the key stakeholders on a simple matrix as in Table 4.4. This involves:

1 Considering which stakeholders will be affected by the new strategy that has been selected.
2 Ranking stakeholders in terms of their importance (low through to high) and likely response to the strategy (opposition through to support).
3 The stakeholder assessments are then plotted on a grid, enabling the managers to plan in detail different tactics for building stakeholder commitment to the new strategy.

Nutt and Backoff, 1992, pp. 196–7

Table 4.4 *Stakeholder assessment (and examples of possible tactics)*

Importance	Likely response	
	Opposition	*Support*
Low	problematic (e.g.take precautions)	low priority (e.g. educating)
High	antagonistic (e.g. bargaining)	advocate (e.g. co-opting)

Argenti (1989) is very critical of stakeholder theory. He has specifically rejected it because he sees it as unrealistic and because he considers that it is unclear who is a legitimate stakeholder and on what grounds their demands can be approved or rejected. In these respects, he seems to be concerned about the dangers of stakeholder theory confusing the setting of corporate objectives by clouding the issue of who is the intended beneficiary of the organization and what is the intended benefit. These arguments, if they are accepted, may suggest that stakeholder analysis has limitations as a technique used in preparation for an analysis of the strategic issues, but is more useful in connection with planning strategic implementation. The protagonists of stakeholder theory do not accept that corporate objectives should only reflect the priorities of a single group of beneficiaries (e.g. shareholders).

Using the techniques in a strategic planning process

It will have been evident from our discussions of the relevance of different techniques and models that they can often perform more than one function in an analysis and planning process. For instance, scenario analysis can be used to make qualitative forecasts and to set corporate aims. In Figure 4.5 we suggest some of the ways in which the techniques are relevant in a process of analysis and planning. As different techniques have within them different assumptions, we would suggest, whenever feasible, the use of more than one technique. This would highlight the built-in assumptions of each technique and the way it uniquely frames your view. For instance a combination of techniques, such as scenario planning and PEST, could be used for examining an organization's environment.

Table 4.5 *Processes and relevant techniques*

Step	Purpose	Relevant techniques
Step 1	Trend analysis	Forecasting techniques
Step 2	Environmental and resource analysis	Forecasting techniques Scenario analysis PEST analysis Benchmarking Resource analysis Competence analysis

Step 3	Target setting	Stakeholder analysis
		Scenario analysis
		Cognitive mapping
Step 4	SWOT analysis	SWOT analysis
Step 5	Identification of strategic issue(s)	Gap analysis
		SWOT analysis
		Cognitive mapping
Step 6	Formulation of strategic actions	Portfolio planning matrix
		Cognitive mapping
Step 7	Evaluation of actions	Quantitative investment appraisal
Step 8	Planning implementation	Stakeholder analysis
		Resource analysis

Key points

1 Analytical techniques contain assumptions, which in part explain why they can be powerful tools for analysis, but the assumptions are also the essence of their limitations.

2 Assumptions structure how reality is seen and interpreted, preventing certain opportunities or threats being seen. Thus, as Lenz and Lyles (1991) say, analytical models 'filter' managerial thinking, defining strategic problems in particular ways and structuring the capacity of an organization to react to problems. This suggests the need for using more than one analytic model at any one time.

3 Many of the techniques can be relevant to different stages of the strategy process, reflecting the fact that the strategy process is not reducible to a set of techniques.

References

Ansoff, I. (1968) *Corporate Strategy* (Penguin).

Argenti, J. (1989) *Practical Corporate Planning* (Routledge).

Baden-Fuller, C. and Stopford, J.M. (1992) *Rejuvenating the Mature Business* (Routledge).

Buzzell, R. D. and Gale, B. T. (1987) *The PIMS Principles* (Free Press).

Eden, C. (1990) 'Cognitive Maps as a Visionary Tool: Strategy Embedded in Issue Management' in Dyson, R.G. (editor) *Strategic Planning: Models and Analytical Techniques* (Wiley).

Hamel, G. and Prahalad, C.K. (1994) *Competing for the Future* (Harvard Business School Press).

Klein, J.A. and Hiscocks, P.G. (1994) 'Competence-based Competition: A Practical Toolkit' in Hamel, G. and Heene, A. (editors) *Competence-based Competition* (Wiley).

Lenz, R.T. and Lyles, M.A. (1991) 'Paralysis by Analysis: Is Your Planning System Too Rational?' in Asch, D. and Bowman, C. (editors) *Readings in Strategic Management* (Macmillan).

Linneman, R.E. and Kennell, J.D. (1990) 'Shirt-sleeve Approach to Long-range Plans' in Dyson, R.G. (editor) *Strategic Planning: Models and Analytical Techniques* (Wiley).

McNamee, P.B. (1992) *Strategic Management: A PC-based Approach* (Butterworth-Heinemann).

Mintzberg, H. (1991) 'Crafting Strategy' in Mintzberg, H. and Quinn J.B. (editors) *The Strategy Process: Concepts, Contexts and Cases* (Prentice Hall).

Nutt, P.C. and Backoff, R.W. (1992) *Strategic Management of Public and Third Sector Organizations* (Jossey-Bass).

Ohmae, K. (1982) *The Mind of the Strategist* (McGraw-Hill).

Rappaport, A. (1991) 'Selecting Strategies That Create Shareholder Value' in Montgomery, C.A. and Porter, M. (editors) *Strategy: Seeking and Securing Competitive Advantage* (Harvard Business School Press).

Schnaars, S.P. (1990) 'How to Develop and Use Scenarios' in Dyson, R.G. (editor) *Strategic Planning: Models and Analytical Techniques* (Wiley).

Seeger, J.A. (1991) 'Reversing the Images of BCG's Growth/Share Matrix' in Mintzberg, H. and Quinn, J.B. (editors) *The Strategy Process: Concepts, Contexts and Cases* (Prentice-Hall).

Smith, R.J. (1994) *Strategic Management and Planning in the Public Sector* (Longman).

Stacey, R.D. (1991) *The Chaos Frontier* (Butterworth-Heinemann).

Stevenson, H.H. (1989) 'Defining Corporate Strengths and Weaknesses' in Asch, D. and Bowman, C. (editors) *Readings in Strategic Management* (Macmillan).

Weihrich, H. (1990) 'The TOWS Matrix: A Tool for Situational Analysis' in Dyson R.G. *Strategic Planning: Models and Analytical Techniques* (Wiley).
Whittington, R. (1993) *What is Strategy – and Does it Matter?* (Routledge).

5

The strategic environment

Introduction

Environmental assessment is important in a number of different approaches to planning strategy. For instance, some writers have approached strategy formulation from the point of view of the need to match the organization and its strategy to the environment. Then there have been those who argued that environmental assessment is important so that strategy can be used to position the firm *within* its environment. Obviously the former approach tends to imply that there is a unitary environment which can be matched by the firm, although this simple picture can be made more complex by assuming that the environment is evolving and that industries may be lagging or leading the overall pace of evolution. The second approach suggests that there are more favourable and less favourable, locations contained within the environment and that the firm should position itself at the location that is most accommodating to its interests.

In the last decade there has been a rise in interest in the structuring of the business environment by the interfirm relationships known as strategic networks and strategic alliances. Whereas the industry structure analysis popularized by Porter emphasized the competitive relations between firms, their suppliers, their customers and their competitors, a number of writers have been probing the co-operative relationships which sometimes exist between firms. This work has highlighted the fact that the business environment is to some degree composed of complexes of businesses, which may be co-operating to such a degree that they virtually form a single organization, even though they are formally independent of each other. This has a profound implication for the conceptualization of the relationship between the environment and the firm's strategy. Where there is co-operation with certain other firms through strategic alliances or strategic networks, the firm can pursue a strategy in which it co-operatively adapts with its partner organizations. Since the alliances and networks are in fact important elements of the business environment, we can say that this co-operative adaptation amounts to a joint evolution of the firm and its environment.

Surprisingly little attention has been paid to understanding the different views of the environment–strategy relationship. We look at some of these different views – what they are and how they are used to appraise organizational environments. The implications of using different perspectives needs to be brought out clearly, otherwise strategic analysis is in danger of drawing conclusions which reflect the conceptual framework of the perspective and mistaking these for the situation itself. The three views we will look at are:

- postindustrialism
- competitive environments
- strategic alliances and networks.

Postindustrialism

The term 'postindustrialism' has long been used by many different writers to signify many different things. The 1980s fascination with postmodernism brought another rash of interest in the term, especially by those who claimed that the emergence of postindustrialism resulted from the decline of a Fordist-based industrialism. There was much in this analysis for businesses to pay attention to. For example, it was suggested that there was a fundamental shift from the importance of producers and towards the importance of consumers. Under Fordism the producer had dictated to the consumer: the mass-produced standardized products were easily marketed because of the low prices which were achieved through massification of the workplace and the consequent economies of scale. Now, in the 1980s, it was argued, consumers mattered. Much of the postmodernist analysis focused on the social experience of consumption. Postmodernists emphasized the very special nature of the shopping mall as a site of spectacle and drew parallels between the atmosphere and appearance of the mall and carnivals. Other cultural developments associated with this postindustrialism included the increasing emphasis on the importance of simulation, the accent on the immediate present, the shift from class-determined tastes to life-styles, and the growing diversity of these life-styles.

These remarks are extremely pertinent to the businesses that are directly impacted by these social and cultural developments. The products they made, or the services they provided, and how they marketed them had to change dramatically. A manager at Direct Response Group (DRG), an American direct marketing insurance company, illustrates this development clearly:

> In 1988, DRG president Norm Phelps and other senior executives decided that for our company, the days of mass marketing were over ... DRG would have to offer customer service, not just products and it would have to offer products designed to serve particular, identifiable classes of customers.
>
> Hammer and Champy, 1993, p. 183

Postindustrialist ideas have been entertained within academic business policy in terms of the assumptions of rapid technological change (which is assumed to be self-sustaining within postindustrialism) and of competitive threats posed by technological obsolescence and shortening product life cycles. These assumptions of postindustrialism are, now, quite commonplace. For example, Hammer and Champy (1993) conclude their popular book on re-engineering with the following assessment: 'The world of the industrial revolution is giving way to an era of a global economy, powerful information technologies and relentless change' (1993, p. 216).

An exceptionally thorough attempt to incorporate systematic strategic diagnosis of the business environment into strategic management is to be found in Ansoff and McDonnell (1990). They discuss the convergence of countries towards what they term the 'postindustrial predicament'. They assume that the environment is evolving and that industries are at different stages in evolving. Consequently, they argue that each firm must diagnose the challenges of its environment and the response required. They describe environments using four variables:

- the complexity of the environment
- the novelty of the environmental challenges
- the rapidity of change
- the visibility of the future.

Using these variables they describe a set of environmental conditions which they suggest vary in terms of their turbulence. For example, the most turbulent situation is where the environment changes faster than the firm can respond, the events which occur are novel and the future cannot be predicted. The next most turbulent environment is labelled by them as 'discontinuous'; firms in this environment are challenged by events which are familiar but discontinuous and the future is only partially predictable. The least turbulent setting – the 'repetitive' environment – presents firms with familiar events, recurring challenges and relatively slow-paced changes (i.e. the firm can respond faster than the environment changes). The last one is said to be found rarely in free market economies and Ansoff and McDonnell claim that most managers expect to face an environment at level 4 on their turbulence scale (i.e. discontinuous).

They suggest that firms need to assess the level of turbulence and then plan an appropriate level of strategic aggressiveness. By this they mean that the firm must introduce new products or services, enter new markets and launch new marketing strategies in an appropriate way and at an appropriate pace. Thus, a firm facing a future in a discontinuous environment that cannot easily be predicted will be in difficulty if it makes incremental changes; its changes must also be made on a discontinuous basis, using the results of environmental scanning, making frequent reassessments of the competitive factors and constantly seeking opportunities for growth and profitability. They describe this level of response as fitting an 'entrepreneurial' pattern of aggressiveness. Firms in a surprising environment (level 5 on the turbulence scale) have to respond with a 'creative' pattern of behaviour, which means being 'a leader in developing products/services incorporating the cutting edge of innovation and technology' (Ansoff and McDonnell, 1990, p. 34). In contrast, firms in an expanding environment (level 2 on the turbulence scale) can respond in a 'reactive' way, which means that they have ample time to respond incrementally to any threats posed by their competitors.

In addition, they suggest that there is a need to diagnose the required responsiveness of the firm's capability. So, in effect, it is necessary to line up the aggressiveness of the strategy and the responsiveness of capability with the turbulence of the environment (see Figure 5.1).

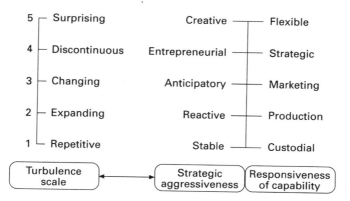

Figure 5.1 *Classifying environments, strategic aggressiveness and responsiveness of capability. Source: Based on Ansoff and McDonnell (1990)*

This is all quite plausible. For example, the experience of Hallmark Cards, Inc. of the United States seems to bear out the overall view that strategic aggressiveness needs to be increased when the turbulence of the environment increases. The following assessment by one of Hallmark's managers brings out a sense of the growing turbulence of the environment, increasing difficulties in making predictions about the future and the need for faster responses:

Our markets and channels of distribution had been reasonably homogeneous for a long period of time. But in the 1980s, consumers started fragmenting into many, many groups ... Our eleven thousand-plus specialty retailers ... had to move more product, faster. Major retailers ... were also demanding tailored product and marketing programs ... we needed new and more lines of cards and related products to accommodate more market segments, as well as marketing and promotional programs tailored to our different channels. In addition, when market segments are less homogeneous, you have to respond to those segments faster, which means you have less time to figure out which products are winners and which are losers. But when your product offering broadens that much, your historical basis for forecasting sales is suddenly in jeopardy.

Hammer and Champy, 1993, p. 160–1

And, like Ansoff and McDonnell, this manager emphasized the need for an appropriate responsiveness in terms of capability: 'We are building the organizational capability that will enable Hallmark employees to react swiftly and successfully to continuous, unpredictable change' (1993, p. 168).

But is it more than plausible? Ansoff and McDonnell report that there is evidence to confirm that a mismatch between environmental turbulence and strategic response does depress the performance of firms. They conclude: 'The results show that strategic diagnosis is a scientifically validated instrument for use in planning the future strategic response of organizations' (Ansoff and McDonnell, 1990, p. 38).

As a first step, the work of Ansoff and McDonnell is very useful, because it begins the task of suggesting that different firms need to adopt different strategies depending on their environment. This is a contingency perspective. It is easy to underestimate the need for such simple first steps. As Ansoff and McDonnell themselves shrewdly remark: 'The major aim of an effort to understand a previously unstudied part of reality is to reduce the complexity of the real world to a model which is comprehensible and manipulable by man' (1990, p. 467).

Whilst the remarks of real managers in major organizations, noted above, show that there is a rough approximation between some of their immediate experiences of business and the Ansoff and McDonnell model, there are nevertheless legitimate questions to be asked about the validity of the model and about whether it has hit the right level of complexity. In the next section we look at the work of Porter which indicates to us that more complex models involve firms more than merely matching the requirements of an environment. His work puts the emphasis on environmental structures and the need for organizations to position themselves within the environment.

The competitive environment

Michael Porter, the guru of competitive advantage, has written influentially about the competitive environment at both the industry level and the global level. His ideas are not altogether consistent between the two levels – as shown by the way he posits that intense rivalry with competitors harms profitability at the industry level, whereas local rivalry is seen as a key factor in being globally competitive as a result of innovation. At both levels, however, Porter is keen to suggest that firms must choose carefully how they position themselves within the business environment.

In a 1979 article Porter (1991a) picked out five critical forces determining the profitability of an industry:

1 Bargaining power of suppliers — *bulk, same supplier.*
2 Bargaining power of buyers *drop prices .*
3 Threat of substitute products or services — */FINANCE/.*
4 Threat of new entrants — *Development Abroad!*
5 Rivalry among existing companies. — *Competitors* — *Product Difference.*

He conceptualizes an industry's structure in terms of the interplay of these five forces. In fact, in his 1979 article, this interplay was seen primarily as competition. And the firm's strategy was assumed to be primarily a matter of coping with competition, a competition which he characterized as encompassing relations with customers, suppliers, potential entrants and substitute products – not just competition from rival firms in the industry.

Porter argued that company profitability depends in an important way on industry structure. The scale of this importance can be inferred from the variation in industry averages of company performance, as measured by, say, return on equity. For example, taking the United States in recent years, industries typically achieved average returns on equity of 12–16 per cent, but there were industries with averages over 25 per cent and industries with averages well below 10 per cent.

Porter was, by definition, also arguing that profitability depended on the interplay of competitive forces, since these constituted the structure of the industry. An industry structure with very strong competitive forces in total (current competitors are jockeying for position, entry to the industry is easy, substitute products or services pose real threats, etc.) had the worst prospects for long-run profitability. And, conversely, high average rates of return in an industry would be the result of high entry barriers, suppliers and buyers with little bargaining power, the absence or unimportance of substitute products or services and stable rivalry between competitors. 'The weaker the forces [are] collectively ... the greater the opportunity for superior performance' (Porter, 1991a, p. 11).

Within this framework, the strategist is seeking a 'position in the industry where his or her company can best defend itself against these forces or can influence them in its favour' (1991a, p. 12).

This model (see Figure 5.2) may be used in strategic analysis. The analyst can use it to organize his or her knowledge about rivals, suppliers, customers and so on, so as to bring out the critical strengths and weaknesses of the company in its industry. In this way, the five forces analysis can be used as an input to a SWOT analysis (see Chapter 4). It may also be used to assess industry trends which have been previously identified in a PEST analysis; the model then enables the analyst to interpret the trends as significant opportunities or threats.

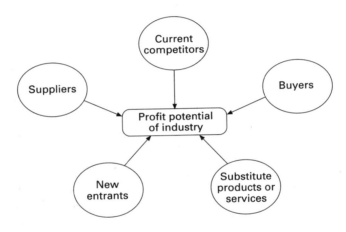

Figure 5.2 *Industry structure decomposed to five forces. Source: Based on Porter (1991a)*

If the five forces model is to be used as part of an environmental appraisal, then the specific nature of each industry structure needs consideration. Porter's work provides more detailed indications of the characteristics which may be involved in determining the strength of an industry's competitive forces.

In terms of threats of entry, he drew attention to: economies of scale, product differentiation, capital requirements, cost disadvantages independent of size, access to distribution channels and government policy. Porter suggested that powerful suppliers in an industry:

- are relatively large compared to the buyers
- have a unique or differentiated product
- have built up high switching costs
- enjoy an absence of substitute products
- can make credible threats of forward integration
- perceive the customers in that particular industry as relatively important.

He suggested that buyers with the following characteristics were thought to be powerful:

- buyers purchasing in large volumes
- buyers purchasing standardized products
- buyers who purchase products which are a high proportion of their own costs
- buyers with poor profitability
- buyers for whom the purchased product is not important to the quality of their own products or services
- buyers for whom the purchased products do not save them money
- buyers who can make credible threats of backward integration.

He suggests that the availability of substitutes was more of a threat where developments might increase their price–performance trade-off with the industry's own product, or where the substitutes were made by industries which were very profitable.

Porter suggested industries with intense rivalry between competitors were characterized by:

- numerous equally sized and equally powerful competitors
- slow growth of the industry
- no differentiation
- no switching costs
- high fixed costs
- perishable products
- capacity that has to be expanded in large increments
- high exit barriers
- overcapacity
- rivals who differ strongly (strategies, origins, personalities and ideas about how to compete).

This analytical model of the forces governing competition in an industry has been very popular since it was first published in 1979. Yet it provides now a clear example of the internal limitations of an analytical model. Porter saw strategy as building defences against, or influencing, competitive forces which were imbued in all relationships – with suppliers, customers, rivals, etc. All these relationships were adversarial ones. All the different groups were posited as threatening profitability. This can be seen in his arguments about the effects of suppliers and buyers (two of the five forces).

> Powerful suppliers can thereby squeeze profitability out of an industry unable to recover cost increases in its own prices … Customers likewise can force down prices, demand higher quality or more service and play competitors off against each other – all at the expense of industry profits.
>
> Porter, 1991a, p. 16

His views of generic strategies are integrated into this analysis and thus are also based on an assumption of competitive forces and bargaining power as the determinant of strategic thinking. He argued that selecting suppliers and buyers was a key strategic decision and that companies should choose them on the basis of selecting those who possessed the least power to influence the company adversely. The point about generic strategy is made in relation to the company facing powerful buyers: 'As a rule, a company can sell to powerful buyers and still come away with above-average profitability only if it is a low-cost producer in its industry or if its product enjoys some unusual, if not unique, features' (1991a, p. 18). In other words, low cost or differentiation strategies are needed in the face of strong buyers.

This advice on strategy may be contrasted with the growing literature of strategic networks and the advice of management gurus to seek win–win relations with suppliers and customers. The focus has shifted to partnerships and co-operation, in place of bargaining and competitive forces. Porter's five forces model made it difficult to envisage becoming profitable by being innovative *with* the help of suppliers and customers.

This advice can also be compared with Porter's more recent statements about the importance of innovation as the basis for competitiveness in his work published in 1990 on the competitive advantage of nations (Porter, 1991b). This is so despite the fact that this more recent thinking could be seen as a development of earlier ideas – with innovation seen as a course of action intent on differentiating a firm's products or services. However, in the competitive advantage of nations model, Porter viewed intense domestic rivalry and sophisticated and demanding domestic buyers as beneficial for innovation, which at the very least cuts across the five forces analysis thinking. It may be possible at some level to argue the consistency of Porter's ideas; the important point here is that the strategic analyst using the five forces model is not likely to consider opportunities for using alliances and partnerships with suppliers and buyers.

The view that the industry matters, which is Porter's view, has also been challenged. If industries do have structures in terms of the competitive forces which determine their ultimate profit potential then it would be sensible for firms to choose their industry carefully. If they want high profitability then they enhance their prospects by selecting 'good' industries. Baden-Fuller and Stopford (1992) suggest that recent evidence did not support the view that the choice of industry matters. They say, 'At best only 10 per cent of the difference in profitability between one business and another can be related to their choice of industry' (Baden-Fuller and Stopford, 1992, p. 16). And, they argue, even if there is a statistical relationship between industry and profitability, it could be down to the industry having a high proportion of successful businesses, rather than the industry causing the firms to be successful.

However, Montgomery and Porter (1991, p. xiv) say that recent studies had 'repeatedly shown that average industry profitability is, by far, the most significant predictor of firm performance'. They cite a study by Wernerfelt and Montgomery (1988) showing that 19.48 per cent of the variation in firm performance was due to an industry structure effect. In their judgement, 'it is now uncontestable that industry analysis should play a vital role in strategy formulation' (1991, pp. xiv–v).

Porter has been influential in defining the context of competitive advantage at the global level, through another classic work – *The Competitive Advantage of Nations* (1991b) – published in 1990. He reviewed the leading global competitors and discovered that even successful economies had less than successful industries and were not uniformly leading the way. Furthermore, although countries had industries and firms that were very successful in global terms, they were, paradoxically, concentrated in specific regions. The location in a country and within a particular part of a country was, it seemed, important for global success. So, globally successful firms, marketing in many countries and producing in many countries, were exploiting locational advantages of a particular place within a country.

Furthermore, Porter has argued that innovation is now the key to successful international competition. His position on this can be contrasted with that of Levitt (1991), who saw globalization as resulting from modernity: standardized products being made by companies reaping enormous economies of scale, and increasingly drawing more and more customers away from culturally specific tastes because of low cost and good quality products. Porter did not emphasize low costs. He argued that innovation had supplanted competitive advantage based on the factors of production (natural resources, low labour costs) or on low costs (achieved through investment to achieve economies of scale and a large home market).

Because of his coupling of the global drive with exploitation of locational advantages in order to achieve competitiveness through innovation, he views nations now as platforms for global strategies. And if a country does not provide a good platform for a multinational, the firm should move its headquarters to a country with the locational advantages it requires.

So, what are the locational determinants of global competitiveness? There are four:

- firm strategy, structure and rivalry
- demand conditions
- related and supporting industries
- factor conditions (see Figure 5.3).

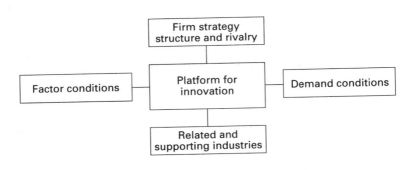

Figure 5.3 *Locational determinants of global competitiveness. Source: Based on Porter (1991b)*

He has been quite clear about these determinants operating to create competitiveness in global terms. This can be illustrated briefly. First, he claims that vigorous rivalry amongst firms in close proximity spurs innovation. Second, he suggests that having local customers who are very demanding helps. Third, a concentration of very good local suppliers is important. Fourth, a good supply of factors of production, especially knowledge resources and human resources, is a key advantage.

This set of locational advantages is said to produce clusters of competitive industries, such as the Italian footwear cluster which Porter cites. A cluster is a set of competitive industries which are interlinked by means of buyer–seller relations and common buyer relations. In the case of the Italian footwear cluster, the interconnected industries included shoe producers, leather manufacturers and design services, as well as makers of leather handbags and gloves, makers of leather clothes and makers of leather-working machinery.

He seems to envisage a circular relationship between innovation and competition. Successful competition requires innovation – and competitive forces spur innovation. Consequently, firms should place themselves in conditions which create the right sorts of competitive pressures and they should not seek to evade them. For example, firms should:

- locate headquarters and other key operations so as to take advantage of concentrations of sophisticated customers who are demanding
- they should not seek to reduce domestic rivalry by merging with other domestic competitors
- they should only use alliances with foreign companies selectively and temporarily, or in respect of noncore activities.

He also places a great emphasis on the need to invest in skills and knowledge and on the benefits of close working relationships with suppliers and buyers through which information flows and technical interchange can occur. So this leads to advice that firms should:

- locate where there are universities, laboratories, etc., which produce skilled people and knowledge
- locate where there are important suppliers.

So, even though Porter suggests that multinational firms should help to upgrade their home environment by, for example, playing an active role in forming clusters and helping their suppliers and buyers to improve their competitive advantage, nevertheless we still have a notion of the organization 'fitting into' its environment, even if it is not a simple matching of the environment's requirements. The difference is that achieving a fit is partly about selecting where to be in the environment, not simply taking on the strategies and capabilities required by it. But his work also provides a bridge to the third approach to the environment, which we consider next, because he does envisage that firms can adjust their environment to suit themselves. In this third case, a fit is achieved by changing the environment to match the firm's requirements.

Strategic alliances and networks

We are concerned here to look at strategic alliances and networks as an environmental feature. The strategic opportunities of these co-operative relationships are explored briefly in Chapter 7.

Strategic alliances and strategic networks are two forms of co-operative relationships between businesses. A *strategic alliance* is an agreement between two companies to co-operate. The agreement can centre on 'joint research efforts, technology sharing, joint use of production facilities, marketing one another's products, or joining forces to manufacture components or assemble finished products' (Thompson and Strickland, 1995, p. 165). The alliance can be based on a formal pact or just an informal agreement – but it stops short of a merger or full partnership (1995, p. 165). Japanese companies such as Toshiba appear to have derived great benefit from them, but in more recent times they have been of interest to non-Japanese firms wishing to develop a global strategy: ' ... leading companies from different parts of the world have formed strategic alliances to strengthen their mutual ability to serve whole continental areas and move toward more global participation' (1995, pp. 165–6).

According to Dunning (1993) crossborder strategic alliances have increased markedly in recent years. It seems that they have been concentrated in high technology industries and have generally involved large corporations. Dunning suggests that technological innovation lies at the heart of these crossborder alliances. Interfirm links provide access to technology and markets and also allow risks to be pooled. Dunning paints the following picture of the emerging structure of crossborder alliances.

> The world's leading MNEs are operating through an intricate global web of formal or informal coalitions, most of which are in the advanced industrial countries. These developments induce the formation of oligopolistic galaxies with the major world producers at the hub of the galaxies.
>
> Dunning, 1993, p. 191

Japanese firms have also been prominent in strategic networks, which are where a whole set of firms co-operate to produce and market a product or service and one firm – the 'hub' firm – co-ordinates and controls the network. For example, Jarillo (1993) credits Toyota, the car manufacturer, with having 'invented' some of the key features of strategic networks. Toyota had more than 150 primary subcontractors and they, in turn, relied on more than 5000 subcontractors; and then there were up to 40 000 more companies that were subcontractors to these second-tier subcontractors, or subcontractors used on a noncontinuous basis. Thus, Toyota was at the centre of a massive network of suppliers.

An essential feature of the *strategic network* is that the contractual relationships are operated co-operatively, whereas traditional outsourcing in Britain and elsewhere has been based on larger companies having an arm's length relationship with suppliers. This co-operation is thought to require trust and fairness, and the exploitation of suppliers by the large company forcing the suppliers to bear all the risks (e.g. fixed price contracts when there are big fluctuations of cost) would seem to imperil such co-operation. Jarillo (1993) reports that a study by Kawasaki and McMillan of a large sample of subcontracting relationships in Japan found that the large company often absorbed some of the risk of fluctuating demand and that contracts were often close to the cost-plus variety. He commented that risk sharing by the larger company was important for the success of the co-operative relationship in the long term: 'The supposed exploitation is certainly nowhere to be found' (Jarillo, 1993, p. 147).

It is easy to see how strategic alliances and strategic networks may feature as a consideration in the development of strategic action. But how can a business environment in which they are important elements be conceptualized and mapped as an aspect of a situational assessment by an organization? To date much of the work on these co-operative relationships has been descriptive and aimed at typifying them as forms of strategic behaviour. A systematic formulation of a multiplicity of environmental situations in terms of these co-operative relations would be a first step in developing a framework which could be used for situational assessment.

Burgers, Hill and Kim (1993) have provided an example of an attempt to map the environment of the global car industry in terms of horizontal strategic alliances, which are defined as alliances between competitors. They were interested in the period 1978–87, a period during which all the world's major car manufacturers entered into alliances with each other. According to Burgers and his colleagues, a web of cross-shareholdings, joint ventures and joint manufacturing emerged over this time span, possibly as a response to increasing uncertainty.

They collected evidence on the co-operative linkages between the twenty-three largest global car firms and they went on to map three subnetworks of alliances amongst them. Two consisted of American–Japanese subnetworks and the third was primarily a European one. Subnetworks were identified on the basis that a majority of the firms in a subnetwork have a majority of their partnership links with competitors also in the same subnetwork. One subnetwork had GM and Toyota at its heart, a second one had Ford at its heart and Volkswagen was important in the European one. There were some linkages across subnetwork boundaries, but the two American–Japanese subnetworks were connected only through a link between GM and Mazda. BMW lay outside of these three subnetworks although it had an alliance link to Ford. (See Table 5.1.)

This mapping of the strategic alliances in the global car industry suggests firms can be in one of three positions in relation to alliance networks: in alliances within the boundaries of a subnetwork, in alliances both within and across subnetwork boundaries or (like BMW) relatively isolated outside of subnetworks.

The actual positioning of firms in the subnetworks of the global car industry seemed to be far from arbitrary. First, the large car firms tended to have alliances with small firms and small firms tended to have alliances with large firms. Second, large and small firms formed co-operative partnerships within the boundaries of the subnetworks but intermediate-sized firms had links with competitors in other subnetworks. This might suggest that the large and small firms in a single subnetwork are the core of a virtual organization which competes with the other virtual organizations centred on other subnetworks. The intermediate-sized firms may be only loosely bound into these virtual structures and seek alliances which do not compromise their independence (i.e. alliances across boundaries) or 'put all their eggs in one basket'.

Table 5.1 *Strategic alliances between competitors in the global car industry –*
Burgers et al. (1993)

GM-Toyota subnetwork	Ford subnetwork	Volkswagen subnetwork
General Motors	Ford	Volkswagen
Toyota	Hyundai	Nissan
Daewoo	Mitsubishi	Daimler-Benz
Suzuki	Chrysler	Saab-Scania
Isuzu	Honda	Peugeot-Citroen
Fuji-Subaru	Mazda	Renault
Daihatsu		Rover Group
		Volvo
		Fiat
		Skoda

The strategic management literature sometimes seems to imply that co-operative relationships of all kinds are becoming the norm. At the very least it is implied that strategic alliances and strategic networks are spreading throughout industry and are becoming important at the global level. 'Given the pervasiveness of alliance formation in nearly every important industry today, our present understanding of the firm as an independent agent may lose much of its current meaning' (Burgers *et al.*, 1993, p. 431). To the extent that this is true, co-operative relationships become a very important feature of the business environment and need to be understood in terms of the patterns they form and the consequences of firms taking up different positions in relation to the networks which exist.

What happens when a firm does not want to fit its environment ?

Hamel and Prahalad (1994) develop the idea of stretch for those instances when a firm's ambition is seemingly greater than its resources. There are cases when a firm does not have the resources to achieve the market position it wishes. Instead of finding a strategy that allows them to survive in the market but not as an industry leader, the organization uses its creativity and ambition to lever what resources it does have, in new and imaginative ways, to take on its competitors in such a way that it eventually 'rewrites' the industry rule book. Hamel and Prahalad give the example of Canon taking on and beating Xerox. They suggest that firms that are to become 'winners' are ones with extraordinarily high ambitions coupled with a high degree of capacity to leverage resources.

This is quite a radical point. Instead of accepting their place in the environment firms should, if they want to become 'winners', stretch to do even better, to have ambitions above their present ones and to find new ways of achieving them. Hamel and Prahalad propose resource-based strategies for seizing control of industries and creating the markets of tomorrow. This is discussed further in Chapter 7.

Key points

1 One of the most influential ways of conceptualizing the business environment has been based on the view that it is changing rapidly, becoming more complex, more surprising and less predictable. To some extent this has resulted from customers becoming more diverse and less happy with standardized products or services. It is requiring faster and faster responses from firms in terms of introducing new products, entering new markets and developing new distribution channels. This leads to a concern to match, which usually means upgrade, the organization's strategic response and its capability to the competitive conditions. Environmental diagnosis can be based on a classification of environments according to the amount of change (technological or otherwise) they exhibit. One such approach relies on a typology of environmental conditions which range from a 'repetitive' through to a 'surprising' environment (Ansoff and McDonnell, 1990).

2 Perhaps the most popular of all frameworks for analysing the business environment is Porter's framework for looking at industry structure. This decomposes industry structures to five forces which determine the long-term profit

potential of the industry. This approach encourages the analyst not only to consider which industries offer the best prospects, but also suggests that the strategist needs to think about how the company should be positioned within the industry. This is a matter of selecting a position in the light of the competitive forces that make up the basic structure of the industry.

3 Porter's work on competitive advantage in a global context continues the theme of the need to position a firm wisely in the competitive environment. Thus he suggests that firms can seek out markets with sophisticated buyers because of the stimulating effect of customer demands on innovation. And, as a second example, Porter urges multinational companies to choose a national location for their home base to support competitive advantage. It may be suggested that Porter's work indicates that there is an important difference between the concept of the firm fitting into its environment and that of the firm simply matching the environmental requirements.

4 Strategic alliances and networks are seen as spreading fast and proving themselves to be a superior form of organizational format. The strategic alliance is seen as offering a quick and easy route to global strategic action and there is evidence that they have been increasing in number since the 1970s. It is possible that they are a response to increased uncertainties and intensified global competition. However, whilst they offer some interesting additional options for strategic action, it is not yet clear how a systematic approach to environmental diagnosis could incorporate a concern with these co-operative relationships.

5 As an antidote to much of the thinking about the relationship of organizations to their environments, Hamel and Prahalad argue the case for strategy as 'stretch' and the ability of industry leaders to rewrite the rules of their industry.

References

Ansoff, I. and McDonnell, E. (1990) *Implanting Strategic Management* (Prentice Hall).

Baden-Fuller, C. and Stopford, C. (1992) *Rejuvenating the Mature Business* (Routledge).

Burgers, W.P., Hill, C.W.L. and Kim, W.C. (1993) 'A Theory of Global Strategic Alliances: The Case of the Global Auto Industry', *Strategic Management Journal*, Vol. 14, pp. 419–32.

Dunning, J.H. (1993) *The Globalization of Business* (Routledge).

Hamel, G. and Prahalad, C.K. (1994) *Competing for the Future* (Harvard Business Press).

Hammer, M. and Champy, J. (1993) *Reengineering the Corporation* (Nicholas Brealey).

Jarillo, J.C. (1993) *Strategic Networks* (Butterworth-Heinemann).

Levitt, T (1991) 'The Globalization of Markets' in Montgomery, C.A. and Porter, M.E. (editors) *Strategy: Seeking and Securing Competitive Advantage* (Harvard Business School Press).

Montgomery, C.A. and Porter, M. (1991) 'Introduction' in Montgomery, C.A. and Porter M.E. (editors) *Strategy: Seeking and Securing Competitive Advantage* (Harvard Business School Press).

Porter, M.E. (1991a) 'How Competitive Forces Shape Strategy' in Montgomery, C.A. and Porter, M.E. (editors) *Strategy: Seeking and Securing Competitive Advantage* (Harvard Business School Press).

Porter, M.E. (1991b) 'The Competitive Advantage of Nations' in Montgomery, C.A. and Porter, M.E. (editors) *Strategy: Seeking and Securing Competitive Advantage* (Harvard Business School Press).

Thompson, A.A. and Strickland, A.J. (1995) *Strategic Management* (Irwin).

6

Evaluating company performance and activities

Introduction

Some attention is paid to evaluating strategies in books on strategic management, but very often there is, strangely, relatively little attention paid to the evaluation of company performance. So, whilst the question of the feasibility of a strategy is treated systematically, questions of how well the business is currently doing, or how well it has done following the implementation of a strategy, are glossed over. The main emphasis is put on evaluating company performance by calculating accounting ratios from financial statements (the profit and loss account and the balance sheet).

Nonfinancial managers often feel that the complexities of measuring and interpreting company performance using financial data are beyond them. The production of financial data involves the use of specialist language and procedures, as a matter of technical necessity. This is not unique to accountancy, but it does lead to a degree of alienation from financial statements for nonfinancial managers. There is, however, the further barrier to using financial statements for strategic purposes due to the impact of creative accounting in recent years (Smith, 1992). On this point, there is also a view that accounting standards just need to be sorted out and then the financial statements will be more reliable guides to company performance.

But even if financial reporting could be shorn of its technicalities and even if accounting standards were ideal, there is an important point about how managers relate to quantitative data. We are going to subject this to a detailed analysis and look at how the process of evaluating companies can be located at three levels: profit figures, cash figures and value-adding activities.

Observing and measuring in general

When we look at any organization there are countless things we could observe with a view to measuring. The famous philosopher Karl Popper used to set his students a task of observing. After a little while they would come back to ask, 'Observe what?' There was so much they could be observing and they needed to know exactly what Popper wanted them to look at. He pointed out that observation has to be guided. We also have to have something in mind when we observe company performance, else we will end up like his students, unsure of what to observe.

Not only does observation have to be focused, but also who does the focusing makes a difference. This is our first warning. Observation is always directed by someone. What they want you to observe is what *they* want you to observe.

Some things we observe are pretty easy to measure with a fair degree of accuracy. For example the production output numbers of a certain type of car we made last year, or the number of size fifteen white shirts we sold last month or the temperature at noon. Other things we want to observe are more difficult to measure with certainty. For instance, the organization's core competencies or stakeholders' support for a proposed strategic action.

Often another observation is measured that stands in for the one you are really interested in. It is a proxy. For example, the attractiveness of a market may be proxied by the total size of the market or the market's growth rate (as we saw when we looked at portfolio planning in Chapter 4).

Our second word of warning is that a lot of measurements are made in organizations because they are the easy, or easier, ones to make. They may, or may not, be of any use. And, related to this, some observations are measured as they are assumed to be good approximations to what we would really like to know. They may or may not be.

Organizations collect lots of measurements because they have to by law. Increasingly organizations are required not only to collect financial information for audit purposes, but other information that is required by Central and Local Government as well as other agencies. Other things they might wish to measure are not measured, as their resources are already deployed for the statutory ones. There is a tendency for the measurements the firm has to collect to become drivers in the organization. They concentrate on how well they are doing on these, as they have to have them, as opposed to other things.

Our next warning, then, is about collecting too much information that is not much use to the firm. Unfortunately they might have to because of statutory requirements, or whatever, but they need to be careful that this does not start to drive them away from collecting other information that would be of more use to them.

Our final word of warning concerns the modern nature of measurement. As will be recalled from the first two chapters, modernism is based on the application of scientific rationality to the world. Modernists would see any measurement, at least in principle, to be either true or false. There would be agreed procedures that could be utilized to enable us to distinguish between a true measurement and a false one. On the whole, modernists assume that people would (or should) agree, after these procedures had been applied, whether there had been a true or false measurement. This view is challenged by the postmodernists. For them, 'true' has no meaning. It is meaningless. There is simply no way of sifting the 'true' from the 'false'. There are some measurements that are privileged over others, that have the label 'true' attached to them. There are others that are labelled 'false'. The labelling is done by powerful individuals or groups, who have the power to pronounce what is 'true' and what isn't. After the accounts have been audited successfully the auditors state that the accounts present a true and fair picture of the business. Only some people are allowed by law to make such statements.

Pragmatically speaking, despite these words of warning, we accept that traditional accounting systems are valuable in strategic management as they provide the bedrock of financial information necessary for controlling the businesses, planning for the future and undertaking 'what if' analysis.

Financial statements

Two of the key sources of financial information are the balance sheet and the profit and loss account. From these two financial statements standard accounting ratios can be calculated that can be used in running the business. For instance, the rate of return on capital employed, the net profit margin and so on (see Figure 6.1).

Figure 6.1 *Accounting ratios analysis*

The use of accounting ratios to monitor organizational performance may be tailored to suit the specific organization concerned; for example, the analyst may concentrate on ratios which are particularly important in understanding its key strategic issues. The ratios may be calculated from the profit and loss account and the balance sheet and cover, say, each of the last five years. This means that the ratios for different years can be compared. They can also be compared with industry averages or those of particular competitors in the same industry. The ratios may be used to look at company performance or used to identify problems or weaknesses. Some of the financial ratios which are used for studying an organization's operating profitability and financial base (Ellis and Williams, 1993) are summarized in Table 6.1. This whole area of financial ratios is a complex one and requires further study before nonfinancial managers can confidently apply the commonly used ratios strategically.

Table 6.1 *Summary of accounting ratios*

Ratio	Calculation
Return on capital employed	(operating profit ÷ average capital employed) x 100
Net profit margin	(operating profit ÷ turnover) x 100
Asset turnover	turnover ÷ average capital employed
Earnings per share	profit attributable to shareholders ÷ number of ordinary shares issued
Gearing ratio	(total borrowings ÷ capital employed) x 100
Debt–equity ratio	(total borrowings ÷ shareholders funds) x 100

Current ratio	current assets ÷ current liabilities
Acid test	(current assets – stocks) ÷ liabilities

The return on capital employed, the profit margin and earnings per share are all measures of profitability, or measures of performance. The first of these ratios – *return on capital employed* (ROCE) – can also be calculated by multiplying the net profit margin by asset turnover. This suggests that the long-term prosperity of a business depends not only on how much profit it makes in proportion to its sales, but how rapidly capital can be made to turn over. Peters and Waterman (1982, p. 138) seem to be getting at this point when they claim that 'most young men in big organizations behave as if profit were not a function of time'. They attribute Jerry Lambert's success with Listerine to the fact that he reviewed his advertising and profits every month and not just once a year and speeded up the marketing process.

The *net profit margin* is another useful tool for management and shows the ratio of net profit to turnover (sales). Extraordinary items (e.g. profit made by the disposal of a subsidiary) should be excluded from the calculation of the profit margin to give a fairer picture of the ongoing or normal operating performance.

Earnings per share (EPS) is a widely used ratio, but may be reported so as to conceal poor performance by a business.

The *debt–equity ratio* tells us about the capital structure of a business. There is an optimum level of gearing. A low ratio means that the firm has reserve borrowing power. A high ratio may indicate that management is making the most of its capital to borrow money for investment, but, if too much long-term debt is used to finance a business (referred to as being overgeared), the firm will struggle to generate enough profit to meet the interest payments on its borrowings. Some financial professionals believe that equity should be greater than the amount of long-term debt (Wheelen and Hunger, 1995, p. 404).

The *current ratio* can be seen as indicating the short-run survival prospects of a business: has it got the current assets to meet its short-term liabilities? The acid test provides a more exacting measure of short-term health by excluding stocks (which might be difficult to sell).

The biggest limitation of financial ratios discussed in recent years concerns the integrity of the figures produced. It appears that there are a large number of creative accounting techniques which can be used by companies to exaggerate the growth in earnings per share and to reduce the appearance of overgearing (Smith, 1992, p. 193).

The expression 'the bottom line' comes from the bottom of the accounts where we see whether or not a profit has been made. In a very real sense, for most organizations, the accounting bottom line is 'the bottom line'. Businesses are in business to make money. They have to know how well they are doing, or else they could go bust. Using accounting information allows them to control and monitor the organization. It gives them the information they need, in part, to explore different strategies.

Careful reading of the accounts and use of the standard accounting ratios gives us insights into how well firms are doing different things. It can show us, to a degree, where profits are being made and where losses are occurring. For large multinational companies the accounts provide a picture of how well they are doing in operations in different strategic business areas. Performance in one country can be contrasted with that of another and, if necessary, corrective action taken. Accounts can be used to benchmark performance against competitors or the best elsewhere. Accounting information can be looked at over a period of years to see if any trends emerge. This allows us to monitor and correct today's performance in light of past performance.

Understanding what the financial statements show is not an easy task. Large companies employ financial directors and accountants to prepare and interpret what they mean. This may seem a pretty obvious point but in an age when organizations are increasingly turning to teams and where delayering of the bureaucratic pyramid is commonplace, organizations still employ experts to do the accounts.

Appreciating what the balance sheet and the profit and loss account, along with the standard ratios, tell us about the business does require a very high level of technical expertise. But, leaving aside the technical aspects of the accounts, who is reading the figures also matters. Different 'stakeholders' will read into the accounts different things. For example, the firm's shareholders will want to see a 'realistic' dividend to make sure they have earned a return on their investment. The firm's bankers will want to make sure that if things go wrong their money is protected. The firm's employees might view the directors' remunerations differently from the directors. Views about undertaking investment will not just depend on what the figures say but on who you ask.

A firm's stakeholders might include its shareholders, its employees, its managers, its directors, its suppliers, its bankers, its local community, the national and even the international community. Subgroups within the stakeholders might also be present. In its local community there could well be conflicts between those in the local community who favour jobs and those who are worried about the potential for pollution if more jobs are created locally. While conflicts between stakeholders will encompass more than just the accounts, the accounts and the information contained in them will form an important part of the 'facts' being argued over.

One way of partially reconciling different values stakeholders have is by using a 'balanced scorecard'. This approach takes the organization's strategy and then gets managers to identify a few key indicators of performance in their area targeted towards the strategy. Managers are asked to think about this from different perspectives. (See Table 6.2.)

Table 6.2 *Balanced scorecard*

Perspective	Possible indicators
Financial	Cash flow, dividends to shareholders
Customer	Customer satisfaction, quality of product
Internal	Health and safety training, participation
Innovation and learning	Number of new products launched

Apple Computer is one company that is using this approach at present with its managers, who think in terms of the shareholders, the customers and employees. This is only a partial reconciliation as only some stakeholders are included and things still have to be measured for it to work. If it cannot be measured then it cannot be included in the scorecard. At least it realizes that not everyone will see the world the same way.

Of course disputes over the 'facts' start even before the 'facts' are printed in the accounts. To put it simply, it is not only what the numbers tell us that we argue over, but also the way the figures are reached before they get into the accounts.

Profits and cash

For firms in financial difficulties the temptation is to use 'creative' accounting to put the firm in the best possible light (see Figure 6.2). This temptation proves at times to be irresistible.

Figure 6.2 *Accounting for growth (Smith, 1992)*

Smith (1992) raises the issue of just how much of the apparent business growth in the UK during the 1980s was genuine. His work implies that a lot of the growth could have been false and that some apparently profitable companies achieve this appearance by the use of accounting techniques. His conclusions are based on an examination of the financial statements of the largest UK companies, which he probed for the use of specific accounting techniques.

He was centrally concerned in his analysis with assessing a company's 'true profitability' and its real gearing. So, for example, he looked at the way in which disposals of fixed assets confused matters. He reports:

> It is quite common for companies to take the profits on the disposal of fixed assets through the profit and loss account...the investor should be aware of the size of these items and the extent to which they are one-off or recurrent in order to assess a company's true profitability.
>
> Smith, 1992, p.37

The point of this and some of the other techniques examined may be to inflate profits above the level of cash generated through ongoing trading performance.

These techniques may involve changing the balance sheet position in order to preserve a favourable appearance in the profit and loss account. This is illustrated by Smith with reference to a decision by Midland in 1984 to redefine an associate company as a trade investment. In consequence, Midland did not have to show a £20 m loss in its profit and loss account.

Some of the techniques, such as the use of off-balance sheet items, can reduce the apparent gearing of a company.

He reports the results of updating an earlier report in 1991 which surveyed over 200 large UK companies to see if they used certain accounting techniques. In that earlier 1991 report companies were surveyed on the use of eleven techniques. He warns that it is not possible to simply equate the fact of using a technique with the conclusion that the company was indulging in creative accounting. However, companies using a relatively high number of these accounting techniques had a marked tendency to exhibit an indifferent or disastrous relative share performance in 1991. Three companies – Maxwell, British Aerospace and Burton – all topped the list with seven of the eleven accounting techniques surveyed and each performed badly in 1991. Most sensationally, Maxwell Communications Corporation's shares fell in 1991 from a peak of 241p to 77.5p and were then suspended.

Clearly, organizations want to portray themselves favourably and as business activities change, grey areas in accounting practice develop and need clarifying. Changes in legislation mean some practices that were legal are no longer so and others that were illegal are now legal. Recently, accounting practices aimed at putting the company in a good light to influence, for example, its share price or profit and loss account have come under scrutiny. Here the line between sharp but legal practice and sharp and illegal practice is hard to define. With the increasing complexity of modern business, accounting practices are being looked at by the courts to see whether a crime has been committed.

The realization that profitability and indebtedness can be engineered by creative accounting may lead to a search for more robust measures of company performance and company worth. It may be suggested that cash flow is a better basis for evaluating company performance. The assumption is that cash flows are the real basis of trading activity and that the rest is just a smokescreen. Of course, firms that continue to have a net cash outflow will go bust sooner or later, even if profitability and gearing is camouflaged through creative accounting techniques.

The shareholder value contribution from a company's strategic plan can be calculated by estimating future cash flows associated with the current strategy. Rappaport (1991) has recommended making calculations for data over the previous period (which may be five years, ten years, etc.) and projecting it forward maybe five or more years. So, capital investment per dollar of sales increase is calculated in this way. He also recommends the use of risk-adjusted costs of capital, which involves making a number of judgements in applying different costs of capital to different business units within the company. In other words, the calculation of the shareholder value contribution from a company's strategy depends on all the vagaries of predicting the future.

This can be used in determining the worth of a business using cash flows. The value of a company – its shareholder value – is defined by Rappaport as comprising two main elements:

> The present equity or shareholder value of any business unit, or the entire company, is the sum of the estimated shareholder value contribution from its strategic plan and the current cash flow level discounted at the risk-adjusted cost of capital less the market value of outstanding debt.
>
> Rappaport, 1991, p. 396

But attempts to compare businesses in terms of their current cash flow levels are also problematic. Two firms with similar net cash flows can be performing quite differently. For instance, they may have a similar scale of net cash inflow (and increasing profitability), but one firm may have achieved this by cutting costs against a static sales revenue situation, while the other may have done it by increasing sales revenue and controlling costs. Does this matter if they both achieve the same result – a positive cash flow (and profitability)? Hamel and Prahalad (1994, p. 9) suggest, and we agree with them, that it is more desirable for a firm to make productivity gains by 'growing its revenue atop a slower growing or constant capital and employment base' than it is for a firm to achieve these gains by cutting the capital and employment base whilst maintaining the level of its revenue. A gradually deteriorating performance can be shored up by repeated bouts of cost cutting.

Our conclusion is that a valid appreciation of company performance has to take in the real activities of the company as well as its financial status. These activities are the bearers of value which underpins the financial performance of the company. It is to these activities we turn next when we look at Porter's concept of the value chain.

Evaluating activity – value chains

> Oh Mr Porter I don't know what to do; I started off for Birmingham and here I am at Crewe!

The line above is from a popular musical hall song. In it the singer is complaining to a railway porter that he is lost, confused by the complexity of the railway system. The railway system at the time this song was popular, was growing in size and many people had little or no experience of navigating the network. For the song to work, being lost must have been quite a common experience. Asking the porter what to do was a common-sense thing to do. In theory the porter would help you to reach Birmingham even if you were at Crewe!

M.E. Porter in his work on competitive advantage gives managers similar help in deciding what to do. One of the tools he uses is called the value chain. Just as the porter in the song might have advised the lost traveller to take the next train from platform three, Porter advises managers to use value chains to gain competitive advantage. In the modern business environment we often feel like the traveller lost, needing help and advice to find the right thing to do. Unlike the traveller who can be easily put back on the right train, seldom in business is it that simple.

How does value chain analysis help us find our way in this complex and ever-changing world? To answer this we need to find out what Porter means by value chains. Let us go right back to the beginning and ask what is the purpose of a firm? Porter in answering this stresses the purpose of the firm in terms of providing goods and services for its customers. In providing these goods and services firms engage in activities. In doing things – activities – products or services are produced that customers are prepared to pay for. Next he asks us to examine these activities from two perspectives: one, to see what they add for the customer and, two, to see if we perform them at lower cost than our competitors.

Take the first perspective. Customers are prepared to pay a price for our product or service. This represents in Porter's eyes the value attached to it. When we look at the activities that make up our produce or service can we work out the value attributed to this activity by the customer? If the value attached to the activity is greater than the cost incurred in doing the activity we have made a profit.

The second perspective takes the activities and asks whether we are doing them cheaper than our competitors. If we do an activity cheaper than our competitors we have an advantage.

Gaining competitive advantage in the market means finding activities that our customers are prepared to pay more for than the cost of doing them. It also means doing these activities cheaper than our competitors. It could also mean offering our own unique bundle of activities that differentiate us from our competitors to gain a premium price over our competitors' products.

Value is what customers are prepared to pay for our product or service. If we can get them to pay more for it, that is value it more highly, then as long as we hold our costs constant we are making more profit. If we can reduce how much it costs us to make the product or service and consumers are prepared to pay the same price for it, that is, they give it the same value as before, we will make more profit. If we put together the activities involved in making the product or service in a different way we might be able to reduce our costs and again make profit. Or by recombining our activities we might be able to get our customers to value the product or service more and then we make more profit.

This may appear pretty obvious stuff but compared to the way we usually view what we do it forces us to look at how profits arise in our organization as opposed to looking at, say, cost alone. It links activities to profit. It is another way of evaluating the organization.

Linkages between activities

The next step in value chain analysis is to look at linkages between activities on the value chain and how these linkages contribute to value. In doing this we have to not only look at activities within our firm but activities outside of it. Porter emphasizes the totality of the value chain, stretching from our suppliers, through us, perhaps to other organizations, to the final consumer. Here the normal boundaries of our organization are broken down. Porter wants us to look at what we produce through the eyes of the final consumer. The final consumer is not interested so much in what we have contributed to the product or service as in the final, total product.

Some double-glazing firms have a poor reputation for correcting faults in their work. Often the company that sells you the double-glazing does not manufacture it or install it. When something goes wrong the company you have the contract with claims that it's not their fault, it's the installers' fault or the manufacturer's fault. As a customer we are not that interested in attributing blame but we want it put right. The company we dealt with should sort it out for us. Similarly when we go on a package tour and the accommodation turns out to be substandard, we do not want the package company to deny responsibility for this. These are not only legal problems, but are to do with the way Porter wants us to see how our activities in the production of goods or services link with other firms' activities. Instead of blaming the installers or the foreign hotel for the problem we need to work with them to guarantee a high standard for our products or services.

Porter divides activities internal to the firm into primary and support. Figure 6.3 shows the divisions Porter used. The primary activities are divided into five areas: inbound logistics, operations, outbound logistics, marketing and sales and, lastly, service. The support activities are divided into four: procurement, technology development, human resource management and firm infrastructure.

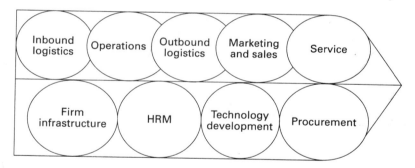

Figure 6.3 *The value chain elements*

These activities are inter-related. For instance, procurement is concerned with getting the resources required, while inbound logistics is to do with receiving, storing and taking the resources to the operation activity. The first does not physically handle the resource but obtains it, while the second actually physically receives it and eventually passes it on. Immediately, the linkage between these two is apparent. These two activities need to act together to ensure costs are minimized and value added to the inputs. Every subdivision needs to act in concert with the others to either reduce costs or to enhance value. Looking at the list of activities again it should be clear how, once you commit yourself to a value chain analysis, functional areas are reduced in importance and linkages between them increase. This is because any change in one activity will affect others. It is conceivable that by attempting to lower costs or enhance value in one activity we will increase the cost or lower the value in others and in the product or service overall.

For instance, in deciding to reduce storage costs by having raw material shipped direct to production, production might be adversely affected because of nondelivery of vital stock or simply because of congestion in the production area. Just-in-time methods mean getting guarantees from suppliers to get the material to you when you need it. Your suppliers might not be able to do that.

Giving a no-quibble one-year replacement or money-back warranty might mean customers are prepared to pay more for your product or service than competitors but if quality is low this could lead to problems later on. For example you often see twenty-year guarantees for damp proofing. This often leads to problems later on if the product is low quality as more and more resources have to be diverted to replacement and maintenance as products age and fail. If you make offers that enhance the value of your product or service over competitors you need to make sure you can live up to them – or else you will be in trouble. Hoover offered free airline trips a few years ago to customers who purchased Hoover products. After a while it became clear that, although Hoover had managed to enhance the value customers placed on their products, it could not cope with the demand for free airline tickets. The damage this did to its reputation was immense.

The value chain concept should allow analysts to evaluate the company and its activities and to plan specific changes for achieving competitive advantage. It does this by focusing us on the customer's perception of value and by suggesting some pointed questions we can ask of the company and its subunits. Let us have a look at some of the questions we can ask.

Do we know what attributes, either physical or mental, customers value in our products or services? Where customers attribute value might not align with where you think value is being created. How do we work out if a change in one of the firm's activities will enhance overall the value the customer places on our product or service? Sometimes we can get a good idea from market research. Imagine we have for the last few years only offered our hi-fi range in black and we are now thinking about offering it in a variety of colours. We calculate that the total extra cost involved in doing this would add 10 per cent to the market price. If our market research found that customers were prepared to pay an extra 20 per cent for this it would be worth doing. On the other hand, if they were only prepared to pay an extra 5 per cent it would not. The need to think clearly about what customers value or need can be illustrated with an extreme example. Going back to the Hoover case, while the free trip promotion was on, many customers did not buy Hoover products because of their reliability or superior technology but simply because it was a very cheap way of buying an airline ticket. In other words, the customers needed airline tickets. Consequently, Hoover were, for a while, not in the business of making washing machines or vacuum cleaners but were in the business of selling cheap airline tickets. Even in less extreme cases, the value customers place on an activity can differ from that the company perceives. One simple question that could be asked of any individual, subunit, etc., is 'How does what you do create value for the customer?' If it does not, does it need to be done? Another would be 'Can we find ways of reducing costs across activities without reducing the value perceived by the customer?'

Above we have sketched out the activities which exist in part or in total in any organization and how, after reflection, it is clear they need to act together to produce value for the customer. This is an important point when we evaluate the full implications of a change. Taking the case of the hi-fi range which is to be offered in a variety of colours, there are problems waiting for us if we do not see the firm and its activities in total. When we calculated that the any-colour option would only add about 10 per cent to the final price did we check to make sure no hidden extra costs were incurred. If just production were involved in the costings, extra costs associated with storing different paints might have been missed, as might extra costs in ordering the different paints. Training of staff in the application of more colours might have been overlooked. Suppliers of existing inputs might charge more for the colour option. Problems to do with the finish of the hi-fi might emerge with new colours leading to customer complaints. New marketing and sales literature would need to be produced and product information and training given to retailers and so on.

Value chain analysis forces us to think across boundaries. Value is not only created by activities in isolation but by activities working together. So instead of seeing the firm as divided internally by function, we should attempt to see it as value creating activities working together. One traditional way firms organize themselves is by giving each subunit a fair degree of independence. This independence might manifest itself by making the subunits compete against each other. Secrecy and low trust between subunits might mean that value is reduced rather than enhanced. Projects spanning subunits would be frustrated because of enmity between them. This might result in an internal culture appearing of 'us against them'. So there is a need to counter rivalry between activities inside the organization which might lead to a lowering of value to the customer. A good question to ask would be 'Can we form teams that span activities on the value chain to create even more value by combing activities in novel and imaginative ways?'

Value chain analysis should help to focus organizational subunits on how they are contributing to the value of the product or the service and how they can work with other subunits to enhance value and create competitive advantage.

The value chain analysis and cost drivers

The value chain can be useful, as we have noted, in the checking and if possible reducing, of costs as compared to our competitors. If we can provide the same value to our customers at a lower cost than our competitors we will make more profit. Porter gives a list of ten influences on costs, which he calls 'cost drivers'.

- Economies and diseconomies of scale
- Learning or experience effects
- Capacity utilization
- Linkages within the value system
- Shared resources with other strategic business units
- Vertical integration
- Timing of market entry
- Discretionary (decision-driven) costs
- Location
- Institutional (legal and regulatory) costs.

A pragmatic approach to defining the value chain

Porter has warned that accounting classifications and value activity classifications are rarely the same. This is because accounting classifications separate and group costs in ways which disregard distinct activities within the business. Traditional accounting systems tend to look at the firm quite differently from the way a manager needs to analyse it in order to develop competitive advantages out of the activities. The accounting systems are concerned with measuring/recording costs and income, not with the proactive development of activities and technologies to create maximum value as perceived by the customer. Partridge and Perren (1994a, 1994b) in two articles in *Management Accounting* contrast various accounting systems with what would be required under value chain analysis, as shown in Table 6.3.

Table 6.3 *Value chain cost analysis*

	Traditional costing systems	*Value chain cost analysis*
Focus	Manufacturing operations	Customers
		Value perceptions
Cost objects	Products	Value creating activities
	Functions	Product attributes
	Expense heads	
Organizational focus	Cost and responsibility centres	Strategic business units
		Value creating units
Linkages	Largely ignored	Recognized
	Cost allocated and transfer prices used to reflect interdependencies	Maximized
Cost drivers	Simple volume measures	Strategic decisions
Accuracy	High apparent precision	Low precision indicative answers

The traditional accounting model can be seen as being part of a modernist view of the world. Its function within the modernist view is to stand apart from the wealth creating activity of the firm and provide financial information on the company's performance and individual decisions. The financial information is the basis of judgements of performance and of decisions in terms of the flows and balances of money, debt and credit. It is perceived as keeping tabs on the health and state of the business and provides a basis for management to plan and control. At the individual level, the accountant's operation is modernist in style. He or she starts with his or her categories and fits into them data from the individual firm in such a way that a mass of detail can be marshalled and generalizations about, say, the health of the business produced. These generalizations may be seen as having some absolute truth about the health of the business – it is, for example, profitable or bankrupt. The measure of the business is thereby taken, with apparently high precision, and forms a link in the chain of planning and control.

Analysis using the value chain, by contrast, is less concerned with judging things than with improving a firm's competitive advantage. The style of conducting the analysis is more pragmatic. First, the firm carries out an identification of its activities. These will be specific to itself – those which are important for competing in its industry. Second, it must decide on the appropriate degree of disaggregation of its activities, bearing in mind that the number of such activities is quite large within many businesses. This, according to Porter, depends on the economics of the activities and the purpose of the analysis. More disaggregation is needed as and when the analysis reveals evidence on matters with an important bearing on competitive advantage. Third, the firm must allocate specific activities to specific categories and this will require judgement. Porter uses the example of order processing (a specific activity) – does it belong to the category 'outbound logistics' or, alternatively, to the category 'marketing'? Porter suggests activities should be allocated to the category which best represents their contribution to competitive advantage.

Arguably, process maps used within business process re-engineering can be seen as a kind of company analysis of its activities. According to Hammer and Champy (1993, p. 118), business processes in a company 'correspond to natural business activities'. They suggest that the principal processes can be made more visible by giving them names. Examples of names are:

- procurement to shipment process
- product development: concept to prototype
- sales: prospect to order.

Apparently companies rarely have ten or more principal processes. The process map shows the principal processes and how they are related. The principal processes can be 'exploded' into their sub-processes. The process map is specific to the company and, it seems, may be produced in several weeks.

As can be seen, the value chain analysis contains elements of judgement, but it is not overly concerned with judging the firm. It is committed to making judgements which can be used to enhance the firm's development and performance. This is one sense of its pragmatism – it is analysis for learning where and how to make the firm better. It is pragmatic also in the sense of refusing to be captured by subjectivism in analysing the firm. It acknowledges that there are potentially many different ways of seeing the firm (depending on how far you disaggregate and then allocate activities to categories) but argues that some are more useful in assisting attempts to increase competitive advantage.

Key points

1 The two basic building blocks of financial information are the balance sheet and the profit and loss account. From these two financial statements, standard financial ratios can be calculated that can be used in running the business. For instance, the rate of return on capital employed, the net profit margin and so on.
2 What can be put into the accounts and what should not be is a matter of some controversy. For firms in financial difficulties the temptation is to use 'creative' accounting to put the firm in the best possible light. This temptation proves at times to be irresistible.
3 Traditional accounting models designed for high precision answers are less useful than value chain analysis which develops an analysis specific to the firm and its industry and which helps with increasing competitive advantage. The view of a firm as expressed by traditional accounting may be at variance with what emerges from a value chain

analysis. More importantly the value chain analysis offers firms a device for experimenting with new corporate identities, as they reconceptualize what they are good at. For example, a firm might have thought it was good at manufacturing, when in reality it was good at trading, as demonstrated by a value chain analysis.

References

Ellis, J. and Williams, D. (1993) *Corporate Strategy and Financial Analysis* (Pitman Publishing).

Hamel, G. and Prahalad, C.K. (1994) *Competing for the Future* (Harvard Business School Press).

Hammer, M. and Champy, J. (1993) *Reengineering the Corporation* (Nicholas Brealey).

Jarillo, J.C. (1993) *Strategic Networks: Creating the Borderless Organization* (Butterworth-Heinemann)

Partridge, M. and Perren, L. (1994a) 'Assessing and Enhancing Strategic Capability: A Value-driven Approach', *Management Accounting*, July/August, pp. 28–9.

Partridge, M. and Perren, L. (1994b) 'Cost Analysis of the Value Chain: Another Role for Strategic Management Accounting', *Management Accounting*, June, pp. 22–6.

Peters, T. and Waterman, R. (1982) *In Search of Excellence* (Harper Collins).

Rappaport, A. (1991) 'Selecting Strategies That Create Shareholder Value' in Montgomery, C.A. and Porter, M.E. (editors) *Strategy: Seeking and Securing Competitive Advantage* (Harvard Business School Press).

Smith, T. (1992) *Accounting for Growth* (Century Business).

Wheelen, T.L. and Hunger, J.D. (1995) *Strategic Management and Business Policy* (Addison-Wesley).

7

Corporate and competitive strategies

Introduction

This chapter is concerned with strategic management in competitive sectors of the economy and the seemingly simple question: How can businesses compete successfully?

We will be examining acquisition and diversification strategies and how diversified companies devise corporate strategies; then we will look at popular theories of how individual businesses can use competitive strategies in order to improve their competitive position (see Figure 7.1 for definitions of terms).

Figure 7.1 *Some key terms*

A firm's *competitive position* is its ranking in an industry in terms of profitability and/or market share.

A *corporate strategy* is a company-wide strategy for a multibusiness company; it deals with what businesses the company should be in and how the relationship between the headquarters and the businesses should be structured.

A firm's *competitive strategy* is reflected in its decisions about products, markets, distribution channels, etc. that are made in order to improve its competitive position; it can be defined as concerning the creation of competitive advantage at the level of individual businesses.

A firm's *competitive posture* is the resultant of its competitive strategy, its capability and its strategic investment.

There are two key points to bear in mind as we consider different views and theories on this matter. First, changing circumstances have accompanied and may have partly caused, changes in ideas about how best to compete. In the 1960s, a period of expansion and confidence, businesses used acquisitions and mergers to build better competitive positions. In the early 1980s, after the onset of economic difficulties around the world, some experts were advising against such strategies and popular ideas turned towards the use of other strategies, such as the low cost and differentiation strategies proposed by Michael Porter and innovation recommended by Tom Peters and others. In the early 1990s, as businesses hoped for global recovery, interest has grown in ideas about strategic investments in competence (see the discussion of the work of Hamel and Prahalad below) and strategic alliances as ways of improving competitive postures.

The second key point is that the actual profitability of a business is a function of strategic activity and operating activity. The selection of a good strategy creates the potential for profitable activity which can be realized if the operating activities are efficiently and effectively organized. Consequently, poor profitability by a firm often leads to action to improve its operating efficiency and effectiveness; it may only respond with strategic measures if the operating measures do not create sufficient improvement in profitability. Ansoff and McDonnell (1990) refer to such businesses as 'reactive firms'. The important point here is that some popular techniques such as total quality management and business process re-engineering may be taken to be strategic in nature, although in fact they could be just operating measures.

Acquisitions, diversification and corporate strategies

Diversification and acquisitions were popular strategic measures in the United States during the 1960s. Diversification through new corporate ventures required a willingness to continuing investing in the new business even though profitability might not be achieved for five or more years (see Figure 7.2). Many of the moves to diversify into new industries were effected by acquisitions. There is evidence to suggest that many of these moves could have been ill-advised. Porter (1991a) studied the acquisitions of thirty-three large US firms that had diversified over the period 1955–86 and, using the subsequent divestment rate as a measure of the success of acquisitions, reported in 1987 that over half had been divested by 1980. The indications were even worse for unrelated acquisitions (acquisitions in unrelated new fields): 74 per cent of the acquisitions made by 1980 were then divested. Assuming that companies divested acquisitions that had been a mistake, this was a dismal record.

Figure 7.2 *The costs of diversifying by launching new businesses –*
Biggadike (1989)

Biggadike (1989) found that most diversifications based on new business ventures were still not profitable by the end of the fourth year.

His sample included sixty-eight ventures launched in the late 1960s and early 1970s by thirty-five of the top 200 US companies. He defined a corporate venture as a business (a division, product line or profit centre) marketing a product or service which was new for the company and which required the acquisition of new people, knowledge or equipment. The corporate ventures in his sample had entered existing markets (they were not attempting to create new markets) and had survived. Two-thirds of the sample had been operating for at least four years.

He found that major losses were made by the corporate ventures in their first four years. The median business made big losses in the first two years and suffered from a huge negative cash flow (see Table 7.1). The median business in years 3 and 4 was still suffering from losses and a negative cash flow. Amongst those that had been operating for four years, only 38 per cent had been making a profit by the end of the fourth year.

Table 7.1 *Financial performance in the first four years*

	Median value	
	Year 1/2	*Year 3/4*
Return on investment	–40%	–14%
Ratio of cash flow to investment	–80%	–29%
Sample size	(n = 68)	(n = 47)

Using data from the PIMS project, he concluded that new ventures might need, on average, some eight years before they became profitable.
He suggested that large-scale entry could reduce the time needed before businesses became profitable – on the basis that larger market shares are linked to better profit performance. However, he suggested that executives might see small-scale entry as being prudent. He quoted one executive as saying, "Far better to enter small, learn as you go and expand with experience' (Biggadike, 1989, p. 189).

Porter was not the first to strike a pessimistic note about diversification, nor was he the first to produce evidence on the success rate of conglomerates acquiring businesses. Peters and Waterman (1982) summarized their assessment of the results of acquisitions as follows:

It is a simple fact that most acquisitions go awry. Not only are the synergies to which so many executives pay lip service seldom realized; more often than not the result is catastrophic. Frequently the executives of the acquired companies leave. In their stead remains only a shell and some devalued capital equipment. More important, acquisitions, even little ones, suck up an inordinate amount of top management's time, time taken away from the main-line business.

Peters and Waterman, 1982, p. 293

Drawing on comparisons of their own sample of 'excellent companies' with other companies and making reference to research findings by Rumelt in the 1970s, they advocated some diversification based on 'sticking close to the knitting'. They gave the example of 3M, a company which had diversified around a single skill – coating and bonding technology. Peters and Waterman said that diversifying around a single skill was better than related diversification, which was similarly more likely to be successful than unrelated diversification. Excellent companies tended to acquire very small businesses, ones that were easily incorporated within the business and small enough so that there was limited financial damage if they had to be divested or written-off. They acquired and diversified in an experimental fashion, taking manageable steps and ready to pull out if it did not work. Such acquisitions were sometimes motivated by a desire to acquire a 'window on a new skill'. But, whilst they backed this modest approach to acquisition, Peters and Waterman stressed that the main method of growth was internal development and not acquisition.

Porter (1991a) indicates that some successful diversifiers may acquire a company in an attractive industry 'as a beachhead' and then use its skills to build on the position. This would involve transferring skills to the new business. In some respects, these suggestions put us in mind of Peters and Waterman's views on acquisitions, in terms of growth being fostered by both acquisition and internal development and in terms of the importance of skills as a consideration in successful acquisition. Porter, like Peters and Waterman, cites the example of 3M.

Planning acquisitions

Acquisitions that are planned are more likely to be successful than those which are not planned (see Figure 7.3). But what criteria should be applied when planning to make an acquisition? Porter (1991a) suggests three:

- How attractive is the industry?
- What is the cost of entry?
- Will the business be better off?

Figure 7.3 *Ansoff et al. (1970) – Planning and acquisitions in US manufacturing firms, 1947–66*

They studied ninety-three large US manufacturing firms using a questionnaire and secondary analysis of financial data. (They mailed questionnaires to 412 firms, achieving a response rate of 22.6 per cent.)

They used the questionnaire to study how, if at all, firms planned acquisitions and if they systematically executed the plans made. They found that firms which planned their acquisitions also planned their execution and so they divided the sample into planners (n = 22) and nonplanners (n = 41). They compared the financial performance of these firms before and after they had acquired other firms.

The planners appeared to perform much better than the nonplanners when the ratios of postacquisition to preacquisition performance were compared. Some of the highlights of these differences are shown in Table 7.2.

Table 7.2 *Planners and acquisition*

Performance variable	Planners	Nonplanners
Sales growth	2.64	−6.08
Earnings growth rate	17.51	0.05
Earnings/share growth rate	16.70	−1.24

Note: median values of changes (%) in ratios in pre- and postacquisition measures.
Source: Ansoff and McDonnell, 1990, pp. 248–51.

Industries vary in their structural characteristics (entry barriers, bargaining power of suppliers and buyers, availability of substitute products or services, and the state of rivalry amongst competitors) and thus, claims Porter, they vary in their average rate of return. Picking industries with low average rates of return probably means acquiring businesses with poor long-term prospects of profitability. Then there is the issue of the cost of entry to attractive industries: firms may have to pay a premium to acquire a business with good future prospects in the industry and this premium has to be considered in calculating the return on the investment. Finally, a firm acquiring a business needs to consider whether it can increase its own or the business's competitive advantage.

Portfolio management

The result of successfully pursuing an acquisition strategy is the creation of a company with multiple businesses. It then needs a strategy to run the company successfully – a corporate strategy.

Portfolio management (see Chapter 4) can be seen as one way of planning corporate strategy based on circulating capital in the multibusiness company. In fact, in the late 1970s, large diversified companies in the US were often using portfolio planning as an analytic tool at the corporate level (Haspeslagh, 1992, p. 149). The essence of this approach is transferring resources from businesses which are cash generators to those which need cash, coupled with acquisitions and divestments to create the optimum portfolio of businesses inside the company.

Corporate strategies can rest on the transfer of skills between businesses. Porter (1991a) suggests that transfer-of-skills strategies can be built on the use of acquisitions and internal development.

> a company diversified into well-chosen businesses can transfer skills eventually in many directions. If corporate management conceives of its role in this way and creates appropriate organizational mechanisms to facilitate cross-unit interchange, the opportunities to share expertise will be meaningful.
>
> Porter, 1991a, p. 246

Sharing common activities (e.g. distribution channels) may be the object of a corporate strategy, where, says Porter (1991a), it:

- achieves economies of scale
- boosts utilization or
- moves the company down the learning curve (which is thought to lower costs).

There are costs attached to transferring skills or sharing activities and the company headquarters may have to work at creating the organizational support needed to encourage co-operation between its business units. Porter lists some of the requirements and measures which might be needed to get business units to share activities:

- a sense of corporate identity
- an appropriate mission statement
- an incentive system
- cross-business-unit task forces.

In fact, contemporary opinion is turning against the use of portfolio management as a basis for corporate strategy, in favour of treating the constituent businesses in a more integrated way and with the company managing them so as to build synergies between them (Ohmae, 1982; Porter, 1991a). Consequently, it has been asked why portfolio management was so popular in the past. There have been suggestions that portfolio management was attractive to managers because it talked the 'financial language' of business and characterized the company 'as a bundle of liquid assets rather than a concrete collection of factories and people' (Whittington, 1993, p. 77). There is increasingly a presumption, or at least a warning, that companies run on the basis of portfolio management may get complacent and left behind, in terms of competitive position, by companies following a strategy of product innovation (Lenz and Lyles, 1991). Indeed, it has been claimed that the limitations of the portfolio approach were eventually seen by US businesses in the 1980s: 'Slowly, beginning in the early 1980s, they began to refocus their energies on creating better capabilities within manufacturing operations, creating better engineering organizations, rationalizing suppliers, improving response time and "service empathy," and generally tightening operating standards' (Johansson, McHugh, Pendlebury and Wheeler, 1993, pp. 10–11).

The control of multibusiness companies

Given that multibusiness companies do operate different corporate strategies, and assuming that structures should be correlated with strategies, there is also an issue about how the relationship between corporate headquarters and the business units is best organized. The nature of the relationship between company headquarters and individual business units can be examined in terms of questions such as:

- Who decides strategy?
- Who sets the budget for individual business units?
- What measurements are used by company headquarters to evaluate the performance of business units – do they use indicators to measure the effectiveness of strategic measures or are they concerned with financial ratios that track short-term performance?

The logical answer is that the style of managing should reflect the situational requirements of the company. One contingent factor is the degree of diversification (see Figure 7.4 on the work of Goold and Campbell, 1991). But it may be that companies can exercise some degree of choice about these contingent factors; for example, a company may wish to operate a particular style of management and thus acquire or divest itself of businesses to accommodate that style.

Figure 7.4 *Goold and Campbell (1991) on corporate strategy*

In 1987 Goold and Campbell (1991) identified three successful styles of managing corporate strategies on the basis of a study of sixteen diversified British companies.

Strategic planning – This is a centralized style where the company headquarters decide strategy, making it possible for the strategies of its individual units to be integrated and co-ordinated. It is a style which can encourage bold planning and ambitious strategies at business unit level and it is able to take the pressure of business units to achieve short-term financial results.

Financial control – This is a decentralized style of managing; unit managers decide strategy and the headquarters are interested primarily in short-term budgetary control. Business units are evaluated in terms of their return on capital and annual growth rates. The performance of business units is closely monitored and variances against plan investigated.

Strategic control – This style attempts to balance control and decentralization. The business units are responsible for their strategies, but headquarters have the right to approve them. A separate budgeting process produces financial targets and, again, the units' budgets are subject to headquarters' approval. Individual business units are monitored in terms of their strategy and financial ratios.

Successful strategic planning companies tended to have a low degree of diversification and were criticized for cumbersome planning processes and the limited autonomy of the unit managers. The financial control style, say Goold and Campbell, is effective in highly diversified companies, but is not conducive to long-term strategies and long-term investments. The strategic control companies can cope with more diversified portfolios of business units, but can suffer from problems of unclear accountability and ambiguity.

Each style of corporate management seemed to have its own area of success when financial data for the period 1981 to 1985 were examined (see Table 7.3). Thus, strategic planning companies did well on a measure of internal growth, financial control companies performed well in respect of growth through acquisition and strategic control companies achieved the best improvements in terms of profitability ratios.

Goold and Campbell conclude that all styles have drawbacks as well as strengths. They suggest that successful companies accept trade-offs in terms of contradictory tensions implicit in the role of corporate management (e.g. strong leadership and co-ordination of units versus autonomy and motivation of business unit managers) and 'draw on the combination that best fits the businesses in their portfolio' (Goold and Campbell, 1991, p. 345).

Table 7.3 *The successes of corporate management styles*

	Strategic planning	Financial control	Strategic control
Average annual growth of fixed assets due to growth through existing businesses (%)	10	3.5	5
Average annual growth of fixed assets due to growth through acquisitions (%)	7	27	−1.5
Average percentage change in return on capital ratio (%)	−4	−6	20

Note: data relates to the period 1981–5.

Generic strategies

Porter's ideas on success based on sustainable competitive advantage are much quoted. He has argued that firms require a unique position in order to have a competitive advantage. This unique position can be based on one of the following:

- cost leadership strategy (low cost)
- differentiation strategy (non-price value).

Only via one or other of these can a firm achieve competitive advantage.

The basic idea is that a good profit margin can be achieved either by selling at or below the industry-average price whilst achieving comparatively low costs; or by selling a differentiated product at above the industry-average price to an extent that more than compensates for higher costs.

Porter sees a *cost leadership strategy* as being the result of cost advantages achieved by management paying attention to cost drivers. These lower costs have to be achieved whilst producing the same value for the buyers, that is, cost leaders are not producing inferior goods or services, merely lower cost ones.

The *differentiation strategy* is where the firm sets out to meet the common needs of buyers in a unique way. This involves not only a differentiated product but also differentiated activities. Whilst this means additional costs, the premium price paid by the buyers produces above average profit margins.

Undoubtedly Porter sees cost leadership and differentiation as the basic strategy options. However, a focus strategy is also identified by him. This is where a segment of buyers are targeted with a product or service that is tailored to their needs which are relatively unusual. The firm targets a narrow scope of buyers and is thus able to lower costs (because existing products or services exceed their needs) or add nonprice value (which other customers would not be prepared to pay for). Consequently, there is a strategy labelled as a 'cost-based focus' and one labelled a 'differentiation-based focus'.

Peters and Waterman (1982) in their book *In Search of Excellence*, examined fifty top performing companies and concluded: 'we find high-performing companies in different industries to be mainly oriented to the value, rather than the cost, side of the profitability equation' (p.186).

Innovation

There has been considerable interest in the possibility of using innovation to create competitive advantage. This is not altogether surprising. Innovation has been an integral part of business activity for at least the last 200 years. It has consistently involved reinvesting profits in new products and services, stimulating and awakening customer needs for them, and developing new processes and competences to deliver the new products and services.

In companies in the United States, the UK and elsewhere in Europe, there is concern about the difficulty of keeping up with a quickening pace of innovation. Jarillo (1993) says, 'it is more and more frequent that even successful companies cannot sit back for a while and catch their breath' (Jarillo, 1993, p. 7). In the UK there is public concern about the effects of a poor record of innovation on national competitiveness (DTI/CBI, 1993, p. 5).

This concern over the quickening pace of innovation coincides with shifts in global trading relations and the emergence of the successful Japanese and the Pacific Rim economies. During the 1970s

Japanese companies developed a new technology gap towards firms in the rest of the world (Mjoset, 1992, p. 74). European companies found themselves with technology which was 'behind the times'. But the issue is wider than just technology – it concerns the whole range of innovation activities and stretches from mundane incremental changes through to major breakthroughs (Porter, 1991b). (See Figure 7.5 for a variety of measures which can be used to measure a firm's performance on innovation.) In the West there is some concern that innovation and the associated human resource development, is still occurring more rapidly in Japan and the Pacific Rim countries. 'And if Western managers were once anxious about the low cost and high quality of Japanese imports, they are now overwhelmed by the pace at which Japanese rivals are inventing new markets, creating new products and enhancing them' (Prahalad and Hamel, 1991, p. 280).

Figure 7.5 *The innovation report by the UK's DTI/CBI (1993) – Possible performance measures for innovation*

Product innovation

- number of new product ideas, product enhancement ideas evaluated last year
- percentage sales/profits from products introduced in the last three (five) years
- percentage sales/profits from products with significant enhancements in the last three (five) years
- product planning horizon – years, number of product generations
- market share – global, EC, UK.

Product development

- time to market (average concept to launch time; time for each phase-concept, design, initial production launch; average overrun, percentage of products overrunning planned finish date; average time between product enhancements, redesigns)
- product performance (product cost, technical performance, quality, return on sales, market share)
- design performance (manufacturing cost, manufacturability, testability).

Process innovation

- process parameters, cost, quality, work-in-progress (WIP) levels, lead time, etc. (performance versus competitors, percentage improvement over one, three years)
- installation lead times (start to trouble-free working, percentage of new processes/process, innovations considered successful)
- number of new processes, significant process enhancement in year
- continuous improvement (number of improvement suggestions per employee; percentage implemented; average annual improvement in process parameters – quality, cost, lead time, WIP, reliability, downtime, capability)
- progress to lean production, WIP, lead times, quality.

Are these innovation worries important? Do technology gaps really matter? Porter (1991b), one of the most influential writers on competition, has insisted that innovation is the cornerstone of business success. Innovation, he says, always involves investment in skill and knowledge and must be continuous. He warns companies that they must keep on improving and innovating or they will eventually be overtaken by their competitors.

Leaders and followers

Whilst Porter throws the weight of his reputation behind the agenda for innovation, others have considered the options of being a leader (i.e. innovator) or a follower (i.e. an imitator). The general opinion seems to be moving Porter's way, but the discussions of the options reveal some of the issues which strategic management may need to consider.

European firms in the 1950s and 1960s benefited from the diffusion of technologies and work organization methods which were developed by US companies (Mjoset, 1992, p. 72). Miles and Snow (1978) coined the term 'Prospectors' to describe firms which find and exploit new product and market opportunities; and they stressed, as Porter did later, the implications for the investment in skills and knowledge. The followers are labelled 'Analyzers' by Miles and Snow. They say that the Analyzers imitate the actions of successful Prospectors and thereby save on research and development.

But imitation may be a short-term bet. Soichiro Honda, one of the two founders of Honda, had a personal motto which was 'be original'. It is said that his regard for originality went back to the 1930s when there was a big technology gap between the US and Europe on the one hand and Japan on the other. He believed Japan could catch up by developing its technology and was opposed to merely copying. Then Honda began making motorcycles.

> At first Honda's motorcycles came nowhere near their rivals, but Honda could not bear the thought of simply imitating foreign models: no matter what, he was determined to come up with a better, original machine of his own. It took a long time and a great deal of effort but the company eventually caught up with its rivals, and later overtook them. The companies that had prospered by imitating did well at first, but lost out later on ... Honda understood the temptations of taking the easy way but mere copying gives the technician no pride of creation.
>
> Mito, 1990, p. 2

In the last twenty-five years the pitfalls of imitation have become more evident in Europe – or so it has been claimed by Mjoset (1992). Being a follower is now risky:

> Since the 1970s, such a strategy has become more risky. Production technology is no longer standardised and stable. International competition is fiercer, growth of demand is sluggish and the dangers of tariff protection are ever present. Thus, companies cannot wait too long to apply new technologies. These developments shorten the life cycle of products considerably. When the life cycle was longer, a follower could be sure to offer a similar cheaper product somewhat later, but with shorter life cycles, the technology gap may develop cumulatively: when the imitated product is available, the leader has already developed a new one.
>
> Mjoset, 1992, pp. 73–4

The leader–follower dilemma has been explored in relation to major breakthroughs, but the evidence to date suggests winners and losers are to be found amongst both leaders and followers. (This is shown in Figure 7.6.)

Figure 7.6 *Leaders and followers in major breakthroughs*

Craig and Grant (1993) classified a number of major breakthroughs and found that companies could be successful in playing leader or follower roles in innovation, but there were examples of unsuccessful leaders and followers too (see Table 7.4).

Table 7.4 *Innovators and imitators*

	Innovator	Follower–imitator
Win	Pilkington (float glass)	IBM (personal computer)
	G.D. Searle (Nutra Sweet)	Matsushita (VHS video recorders)
	Dupont (Teflon)	Seiko (quartz watch)
Lose	R.C. Cola (diet cola)	Kodak (instant photography)
	EMI (scanner)	Northrop (F20)
	Bowmar (pocket calculator)	DEC (personal computer)
	Xerox (office computer)	
	De Havilland (Comet)	

Source: Craig and Grant (1993), Figure 5.3, p. 88.

So, what leads to success in being a leader or follower? Craig and Grant (1993) emphasize two other key factors apart from R&D capabilities. First there are resources needed to exploit the innovation. 'These complementary resources include finance, manufacturing facilities and capabilities, marketing resources, and the ability to offer customer service' (Craig and Grant, 1993, p. 88). Second, there are resources needed 'to overcome the hesitation customers feel regarding an unfamiliar, unproven product' and they identify the importance of 'investment in distribution and service support in an effort to soothe customers' (1993, p. 88). The implication is clear: a firm which is good at R&D may not have these other resources and although it is first to the market, it may not be as successful as followers who have such resources.

John Kay (1993) suggests that there have been many cases of firms which innovated but could not develop a sustainable competitive advantage. He points out that the 'British company EMI was one of the most effectively innovative companies there has ever been' (Kay, 1993, p. 101) and yet, despite pioneering activity in television, computers, the music business and scanner technology, only in the music business was it able to sustain a position.

One reason why it is difficult to create competitive advantage from innovation is that 'the rewards of innovation are difficult to appropriate' (1993, p. 101) Innovation alone, Kay argues, is not the answer: firms need to be able to protect and exploit their innovations. He discusses the protection of innovation by patents and copyright laws and by commercial secrecy, but concludes that they provide very little protection. 'The most effective way of turning innovation to competitive advantage is generally to deploy it in conjunction with another distinctive capability' (1993, p. 106). He suggests that innovation and reputation and innovation and architecture are two particularly effective combinations. A good reputation is important for firms – if a firm has a good reputation, customers will try innovations because they trust them. Sony has a reputation for successful innovation; customers are more likely to buy Sony's new products because they trust that successful record of innovation. Architecture – which is an organizational feature of a firm and is defined by Kay as a system of relationships within the firm and between the firm and its suppliers and customers – can be important either to facilitate a stream of innovations by a company or to enable it to adopt existing available technology quickly and effectively. For example, Kay claims that Hewlett-Packard has had an architecture which enabled it to develop innovative products. And he suggests that successful high technology companies that acquire the ability to undertake technological adaptation have extensive networks of relational contracts (i.e. relationships based on trust and co-operation) which enable speedy responses and information sharing (1993, p. 110).

Organizational and other factors in innovation

Kay's suggestion that architecture was important in explaining successful innovation is consistent with a wider body of opinion positing a link between the importance of organizational characteristics and a capacity for innovation. Profiles of appropriate organizational forms have been identified. See Figure 7.7 for more evidence on organizational forms suited to innovation.

Figure 7.7 *Innovation factors*

In 1992 the Technology Group of the CBI and the Innovation Unit of the DTI interviewed chief executives or senior managers of seventy-six firms. They claim that a number of them were innovative or had aspects of the innovative process. They further claim to pinpoint key ingredients of successful innovation practice (partly based on a literature review).
  Perceived ingredients relating to successful innovation are as follows.

1 Company culture: strong commitment to innovation, vision, leadership, market driven, customer focus, global perspective, openness and flat hierarchies
2 Internal processes: teaming, communication levels and frequency, project champions, adaptability/flexibility, continuous improvement, total quality management, performance measurement, training and technology
3 External influences: other industry-joint or collaborative partnerships, academia (research, training consultancy), investors, government (regulations, standards, support schemes) and community.

The DTI/CBI (1993) conclusions are in line with a lot of contemporary thinking in the 1990s.

However, there can be a tendency to see innovation as just requiring the right type of organizational form, or just requiring the right style of top management (charismatic, visionary and empowering employees and front-line managers to be innovative). The one-sided accentuation of the importance of organizational structure or management style is probably overoptimistic. Circumstances, resources, core competencies, organizational metaskills in learning and innovation (Klein and Hiscocks, 1994) and much more are also bound to be important factors in successful innovation.

Perhaps the most detailed corporate agenda for innovation can be found in Porter's (1991b) analysis of national competitive advantage. He lists the following strategic measures to stimulate the pace of innovation.

1 Create pressures for innovation (e.g. sell to sophisticated and demanding buyers, exceed regulatory standards, source from advanced suppliers and treat employees as permanent).
2 Seek out the most capable competitors as motivators (best man-

agers always run a little scared).
3 Establish early-warning systems (e.g. serve buyers with the most anticipatory needs, maintain relationships with research centres).
4 Improve the national 'diamond' (e.g. help home-nation buyers, suppliers and channels to upgrade and extend their own competitive environments; encourage local suppliers to compete globally; put headquarters where there are concentrations of buyers, suppliers or universities or laboratories).
5 Welcome domestic rivalry (do not complain about excessive competition).
6 Globalize to tap selective advantages in other nations (e.g. identify sophisticated buyers in other countries; take advantage of foreign research).
7 Use alliances only selectively (use as a short-term transitional device; use on a temporary basis only or in respect of noncore activities).
8 Locate the home base to support competitive advantage (crucial since competitive advantage is created at home; move to a country which stimulates innovation).

Competence-based strategy

Competence-based strategy is primarily concerned with the conduct of corporate strategy rather than competitive strategy. It represents a further consolidation of the rejection of the portfolio management thinking criticized by Ohmae (1982). Instead of thinking of the company as a portfolio of independent businesses and as a set of financial assets, this view of strategy focuses on core competencies (the 'real' resources?) of firms and how these can be built speedily and relatively cheaply and then leveraged in multibusiness companies. Big claims have been made for this rethinking of business competition. For example, Prahalad and Hamel (1991) have said that top managers will be judged in the 1990s on 'their ability to identify, cultivate and exploit the core competencies that make growth possible' (Prahalad and Hamel, 1991, p. 277).

These core competencies have been defined as 'the collective learning in the organization, especially how to co-ordinate diverse production skills and integrate multiple streams of technologies' (1991, p. 281). Examples of core competencies, as suggested by Prahalad and Hamel, include:

- Canon's core competencies in optics, imaging and microprocessor controls
- Citicorp's core competence in operating systems
- Honda's core competence in engines
- 3M's core competencies in substrates, coatings and adhesives
- NEC's core competence in digital technology
- Sony's core competence in miniaturization.

Core competencies are embodied in core products, which are components in end products. The core products are incorporated into a range of end products made by a company's business units (see Figure 7.8). A competence-based strategy deliberately and intentionally pursues competitiveness by building the competencies out of which new businesses will be grown, by building them quickly and relatively cheaply, and by creating products which are new. 'The real sources of advantage are to be found in management's ability to consolidate corporate wide technologies and production skills into competencies that empower individual businesses to adapt quickly to changing opportunities' (Prahalad and Hamel, 1991, p. 281).

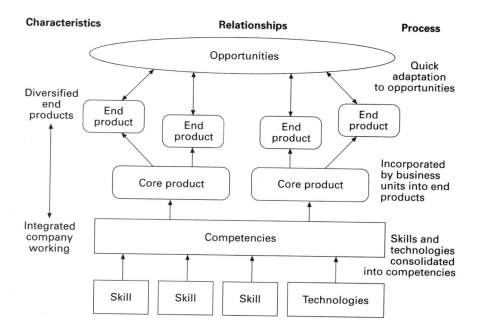

Figure 7.8 *Competence-based strategy*

Prahalad and Hamel have suggested that most companies will have at most five or six core competencies and propose three tests for the identification of core competencies in a company:

1 Could it enable the company to enter a wide variety of markets?
2 Is it an important contributor to the perceived customer benefits of the end product?
3 Is it difficult for competitors to imitate?

Competencies are constituted from the skills of individuals; people can be seen as competence carriers. Competencies may be built over quite long periods of time – ten years and more – and built through continuous efforts to improve them and enhance them. They may be built by companies entering licensing deals and alliances. In the case of alliances, companies learn from their alliance partner the particular skills they need in respect of their chosen core competencies. This learning has to be an organized effort to be effective: 'learning within an alliance takes a positive commitment of resources – travel, a pool of dedicated people, test-bed facilities, time to internalize and test what has been learned' (Prahalad and Hamel, 1991, p. 287). Perhaps surprisingly, there is not thought to be a simple correlation between the scale of research and development spending and the success of a company in building core competencies.

Competence-based strategy has an important implication for measuring corporate performance. Measuring businesses by their market share (which is a key measure in portfolio management) is not really appropriate when competitiveness is based on proliferating products out of core competencies and multiplying the number of applications for its core products.

There is also an implication for the structure of companies: core competencies are corporate resources. Therefore, competence-based strategy requires top management to behave quite differently from top management in the decentralized conglomerate structures based on portfolio management or financial control as described by Goold and Campbell. The company may end up being quite diversified in terms of its end products, but has to be run in a more integrated way to build and exploit core competencies. 'Core competence is communication, involvement and a deep commitment to working across organizational boundaries' (Prahalad and Hamel, 1991, p. 283). The company needs technical and production linkages across business units. It needs company-wide objectives for competence building, and product and market diversification have to be subordinated to competence building and competence exploiting. The company needs top management to allocate and reallocate core competencies to businesses, just as portfolio management required them to allocate capital.

Hamel and Prahalad (1994) actually see the building of core competences as only one component of the total approach to successful competition. For a company to become an industry leader it has to compete in three distinct ways:

- for intellectual leadership (gaining industry foresight)
- in the management of 'migration paths' (building core competences and creating strategic alliances and coalitions with other companies)
- for market share (market positioning strategy, etc.).

This approach, as we have noted in Chapter 1, implies a very long-term process, measured in decades, although the third and final stage may be a short and intense fight for industry leadership. Hamel and Prahalad's approach, by stressing industry foresight and competence building, leads to a view that companies can restructure industries – rewrite the industry rules as they put it. It is markedly different from what we might call Michael Porter's market-based view of competitive strategy. His approach advocates the use of structural analysis to understand the competitive forces and the selection of strategic positioning within the market place through the choice of a low cost or differentiation strategy. This seems to offer a much more conservative view of strategic management. Viewed in this way, the ideas of Michael Porter on one hand and those of Hamel and Prahalad on the other seem to offer radically different views of competitive strategy.

Strategic networks and alliances

Strategic networks and strategic alliances have become a major topic of interest in the last decade, both in the academic journals and in the business pages of newspapers. They represent two forms of co-operative relationships between businesses (see Figure 7.9).

Figure 7.9 *Definitions*

Strategic network: 'In a strategic network one company takes the role of "central controller" and organizes the flow of goods and information among many other independent companies, making sure that the final client gets exactly what he or she is supposed to get, in an efficient way' (Jarillo, 1993, p. 6).

Strategic alliance: These are partnership agreements (formal or informal) between two firms who may agree to co-operate in a variety of ways – including joint ventures, joint product development, transfer of skills, etc. Horizontal alliances are where the partnership is between competitors.

Why have these developments towards co-operation between businesses happened? Presumably they enable firms to compete more successfully. But how?

Strategic networks allow formally independent firms to achieve some of the benefits of larger scale organization whilst retaining a high degree of entrepreneurial motivation. Planning and co-ordination are achieved through co-operation, without the high costs of bureaucratic hierarchy or the high costs of arms'-length subcontracting (see Figure 7.10). Benetton in Italy, the US fast-food chain McDonald's and Toyota in Japan have all been analysed as having characteristics of the network organization.

Figure 7.10 *Co-operation between Ford and ABB*

Frey and Schlosser (1993) examined the co-operative relationship established by Ford and ABB.

Ford wanted to build a new paint plant costing about $300 m that would use the latest paint technology to enhance the value placed on its finishes by customers. In doing this it had committed itself to a 25 per cent to 30 per cent reduction in the usual costs of such projects. Could Ford work with a supplier of such facilities to get it built, operational, at a lower price than before and incorporating the latest paint technology? ABB, a large European company specializing in, amongst other things, power generation, power transformers and distribution, had some capacity and expertise in providing large-scale paint facilities but realized that it was not doing as well as it could with car manufacturers. It was interested in working with a major car maker to show others it had the ability to do this.

In January 1990 Ford asked ABB to tender for the paint facility. Ford only gave ABB one week to put in a bid. Because of this ABB played safe and responded with a price of $300 m, about what was normal for such a plant but too high for Ford with their objective of a reduction of 25–30 per cent.

What happened next was different. Instead of falling out, arguing endlessly about price and delivery, Ford and ABB entered into a deferred fixed price contract. This had three features. First, ABB would deliver the paint plant at least 10 per cent off its quoted price of $300 m. ABB judged that it could achieve cost reductions in excess of 10 per cent by working with Ford. It agreed with Ford a way of dividing up any cost savings resulting from working together on the project. Second, a three month co-operative stage was agreed. Here the two companies would bring together their own expertise in designing the facility. Third, if after this the price ABB quoted was not giving Ford the savings it required both sides could terminate the agreement.

After the three-month joint collaboration ABB quoted a price of about 25 per cent below its initial bid which Ford accepted. How was this possible?

1 Ford established early on with ABB how to divide up any cost reductions resulting from working together.
2 Both sides brought to the project skills that helped the other, leading to significant cost reductions.
3 Ford was better able to communicate with ABB the trade-offs amongst various specifications and pass on some of its knowledge about operating large paint plants.
4 Both parties were made more aware of possible delays and had time to discuss possible solutions to these delays.
5 ABB used the time to contact its own subcontractors to firm up on estimates (and obtain lower subcontracting prices).
6 ABB and Ford used this time to establish trust between each other.

The project resulted in lower costs to Ford and a reduction in risk for ABB, as well as showing other car makers that ABB could design, build and equip such plants. The project had resulted in a win–win situation with both parties getting what they wanted.

Strategic alliances also have benefits for competition. They allow firms to acquire skills, gain entry to new markets, develop new products or services, etc. more cheaply than they would otherwise. For example, NEC, a Japanese firm specializing in semiconductors, telecommunications products and computers had over 100 strategic alliances in 1987 (Prahalad and Hamel, 1991, p. 279). It used these alliances to learn the skills possessed by its partners in the collaborative relationships.

There is some evidence in respect of horizontal alliances between competitors in the world car industry that poor company performance causes firms to seek alliance agreements, which may suggest that such agreements were used to provide access to necessary competencies when a firm was suffering a decline in terms of market share (see Figure 7.11).

Figure 7.11   *Poor company performance and strategic alliances with competitors in the global car industry – Burgers et al. (1993)*

Burgers, Hill and Kim (1993) were interested in the possibility that environmental uncertainty causes the formation of alliances between competitors. In particular, they were curious about the effects of unpredictable changes in consumer demand and uncertainty stemming from competitive moves by rival firms. They were not able to measure either of these types of uncertainty directly and had to make do with measures of company performance and company size. They reasoned that poorly performing companies were less able to deal with unpredictable changes in consumer demand and would therefore be more likely to enter into alliance agreements to access key strategic capabilities possessed by partners. They also reasoned that medium-sized firms' competitive actions would be more noticeable than those of small firms and that they were more vulnerable to sustained competitive battles than large firms because they lacked the resources required. Consequently, they expected medium-sized firms to seek more alliance partners in order to reduce competitive uncertainty.

Their sample comprised the twenty-three largest global car firms in the free world in 1987. They obtained data on the competitive alliances from the United Nations Industrial Development Organization and from a number of other sources. They also had data on worldwide car production published by the Motor Vehicle Manufacturers Association. They found 214 horizontal alliance agreements established by 1988 and fifty-eight pairwise linkages between the twenty-three firms. They assessed firm performance using change in market share (across the period 1978–87), rather than profit data. 'In the global setting market share data for different firms are more nearly equivalent than are firms' reports of profit performance since the latter: (1) are subject to national differences in accounting methods, (2) are of uncertain comparability due to persistent differences in firms' cost of capital, and (3) will vary greatly with currency fluctuations' (Burgers *et al.*, 1993, p. 426).

They found that firms with higher levels of performance had entered into fewer alliance agreements. When they looked more closely at the data they found that previous performance correlated with subsequent entry into agreements, suggesting that poor performance causes firms to enter into agreements.

They also found that intermediate-sized firms had linked to more competitors through strategic alliances than had small and large firms.

The neglect of the study of co-operation between firms until recently is an interesting theoretical issue. It has been suggested that this occurred because of the influence of the theories of competitive advantage, which promoted an atomistic conception of the firm, emphasized the behaviour of competitors as rivals and regarded suppliers and customers as motivated to capture a firm's profit (Jarillo, 1993).

Jarillo (1993) claims that strategic networks are 'winning over in more and more industries' (Jarillo, 1993, p. 11). Hard evidence is not presented to substantiate this.

Porter (1991b) warns firms about the costs of using alliances and cautions them to use them only selectively. He sees several costs in entering into alliances: 'They involve co-ordinating two separate operations, reconciling goals with an independent entity, creating a competitor, and giving up profits' (Porter, 1991b, p. 164). However, Prahalad and Hamel (1991) consider that there are real benefits to be obtained from strategic alliances, but they have to be part of an intention to build competence:

> Clearly, Japanese companies have benefited from alliances. They've used them to learn from Western partners who were not fully committed to preserving core competencies of their own ...
>
> Prahalad and Hamel, 1991, p. 287

Business process re-engineering

Hammer and Champy (1993, p. 35) define a business process as 'a collection of activities that takes one or more kinds of input and creates an output that is of value to the customer'. Business re-engineering is about making radical improvements in these processes, achieved by rethinking the design of the whole of these processes and not working within the constraints of traditional organizational structures. Hammer and Champy give the example of Ford Motor Company in the early 1980s which had acquired an equity interest in Mazda, a Japanese car company, and which redesigned its procurement process after it compared the relative costs and efficiency of its accounts payable department with that of Mazda's set-up. The results of re-engineering were summarized as follows:

> Ford's new accounts payable process looks radically different. Accounts payable clerks no longer match purchase order with invoice with receiving document, primarily because the new process eliminates the invoice entirely. The results have proved dramatic. Instead of five hundred people, Ford now has just 125 people involved in vendor payment.
>
> Hammer and Champy, 1993, pp. 41–2

It is clear from this and other examples that re-engineering is about making radical improvements in performance by doing the processes right (see Figure 7.12). It is about efficiency: 'Re-engineering ... means doing more with less' (1993, p. 48). By designing the process without regard to organizational boundaries (e.g. departments), by designing to keep the process simple and work sequenced in terms of the needs of the process, much unnecessary work can be eliminated. (See Figure 7.13.) It is assumed that cumbersome bureaucratic structures were created to suit the fragmented and now overspecialized tasks; that the internal demands of the organizational structure spawned many otherwise unnecessary tasks; and that many tasks have nothing to do with meeting the customer's needs. New organizational structures to replace the old bureaucratic structures can, Hammer and Champy argue, only be put in place after the business processes are re-engineered. Attempts to do away with the bureaucracy whilst keeping the old fragmented processes will produce chaos – bureaucracy is needed to integrate and manage the overspecialized tasks.

Figure 7.12 *Definition of business process re-engineering*

The fundamental rethinking and radical redesign of business processes to achieve dramatic improvements in critical, contemporary measures of performance, such as cost, quality, service, and speed
Hammer and Champy, 1993, p. 46

Figure 7.13 *Kodak*

Hammer and Champy (1993) describe a re-engineering project at Kodak which illustrates the scale of improvements in operational effectiveness which can be achieved. The project concerned its product development process and involved the work of product designers and manufacturing engineers. Kodak brought in the use of computer-aided design and computer-aided manufacturing (CADCAM) for the design of a single-use camera. This allowed design groups to work concurrently on camera design and enabled the manufacturing engineers to begin tooling design more quickly. The results were good: the product development process was shortened substantially and tooling and manufacturing costs for the single-use camera were reduced by 25 per cent.

Why do firms do business re-engineering? Hammer and Champy suggest that three types of company carry out re-engineering.

1 companies in trouble (e.g. costs are much higher than those of their competitors)
2 companies currently enjoying success but forecasting more difficult times ahead (e.g. new competitors)
3 aggressive companies that are doing well and want to do better.

The existence of three types of firms may be due to different circumstances, but it is useful to remember the work of Ansoff and McDonnell (1990) on corporate responses to surprising changes. This suggests that there may be internal processes which create delays in responding to changes. Observing, interpreting, discussing and verifying the changes can take time. Then there are managers and departments that will fight delaying actions because they may lose out from company responses to the changes. And then there are delays caused by managers having to come to terms emotionally and intellectually with changes.

Hammer and Champy argue that the old bureaucratic structures are ceasing to work effectively because customers, competition and change demand flexibility and quick response. This suggests that Ansoff and McDonnell's ideas of delays may be relevant to understanding the three types of company that undertake re-engineering: the three types could be companies who have delayed too long, those that are reacting to forecast changes and those which respond before specific changes have even been identified. If we follow Ansoff and McDonnell's ideas one step further, we note that what they call reactive firms initially assume that drastic operating countermeasures may deal with their difficulties and only after some time will consider the need for strategic measures. The question arises: is business re-engineering really a drastic operating measure, or is it a strategic measure?

The views of Hammer and Champy seem to suggest that re-engineering is essentially an operating measure:

> Some people think companies should cure what ails them by changing their corporate strategies. They should sell one division and buy another, change their markets, get into a different business. They should juggle assets or restructure with a leveraged buyout (LBO). But this kind of thinking distracts companies from making basic changes in the real work they actually do. It also bespeaks a profound contempt for the daily operations of business.
>
> Hammer and Champy, 1993, p. 25

Re-engineering is, in Drucker's terms, concerned with, primarily, businesses doing the *thing* right and not with the company doing the *right* thing. Of course, not all problems are due to strategic issues – there may be times when the problem is operational and requires operational measures. On those occasions, then re-engineering may provide a valuable framework for undertaking radical improvements in business processes.

We started the chapter with an overview of how different strategic responses were fashionable at different times, dependent, in part, on historical circumstances. It would be nice now to be able to predict the next 'fashion' in strategic thinking based on the new environment of the twenty-first century. In a few years time it may be that no one will be using business process re-engineering (BPR) because new responses will have emerged to cope with the new world. For example, a growing concern with environmental issues might alter the balance of power between senior managers in a firm and its stakeholders. Strategies aimed at sustainable development, evolved with a range of partners (both within and outside of the firm) could become the norm (Welford, 1995).

Key points

1 It is important to distinguish between corporate strategies needed by multibusiness companies and competitive strategies concerned with developing competitive advantages at the level of individual businesses.

2 Thinking on corporate strategies has moved away from a belief in the use of portfolio management towards strategies which integrate the business units within a company to achieve synergies. Different styles of corporate management can achieve good results, but the selection of a style is contingent on factors such as the degree of diversification and leads to different results and weaknesses.

3 Discussions of effective competitive strategies at the level of individual businesses have in recent years looked at the need to fit the strategy to industry structure (Porter's generic strategies) and at the universal importance of innovation. The work on innovation has shown that there is much more to it than simply coming up with new product ideas. There is, according to Kay, a need for competitive advantages to back up the exploitation of innovations, including reputation and architecture (i.e. internal organizational structures and external relationships with customers and suppliers). There have been some attempts to define the organizational characteristics conducive to innovation. The most original approach to defining a company agenda for innovation is to be found in the work of Porter (1991b), who sees innovation as vested in 'clusters' of firms that benefit from a favourable set of conditions, which they should seek to create, take advantage of and upgrade.

4 Strategic networks and strategic alliances represent an important growth in strategic repertoires and both imply that competitive advantages and superior performance can be built on co-operation between firms as well as competi-

tion between them. Care must be taken that a firm's own core competencies are not 'hollowed out' by its partners. Alliances require trust and vigilance for them to work to the benefit of all participants.

5 Business process re-engineering has achieved major improvements in company efficiency and has enormous implications for the organizational structures of companies. Nevertheless, it is not a strategy but a philosophy for taking operating measures. It is concerned with ensuring that business processes are designed properly, that work tasks are necessary and logically sequenced and that company organizations can match contemporary requirements for flexible and quick responses.

6 The recent growth of interest in competence-based competition represents a significant break with the competition-based approach of Michael Porter. It suggests that regaining competitiveness requires foresight, persistence and a capacity to build capabilities over long periods of time.

7 Just as in the past there have been changes in strategic management there is no reason to think that this will not be the case in the future. For example, there could be a move towards strategies based on sustainable development as environmental concerns become more important. Such a development could entail changes in strategic planning such as a shift towards longer planning horizons, more decentralized strategic decision making and a greater concern for ethical and social responsibilities.

References

Ansoff, H. I., Avner, J., Brandenberg, R., Portner, F. and Radosevich, R. (1970) 'Does Planning Pay? The Effect of Planning a Success of Acquisitions in American Firms', *Long Range Planning*, December.

Ansoff, I. and McDonnell, E. (1990) *Implanting Strategic Management* (Prentice Hall).

Biggadike, R. (1989) 'The Risky Business of Diversification' in Asch, D. and Bowman, C. (editors) *Readings in Strategic Management* (Macmillan).

Burgers, W.P., Hill, C.W.L. and Kim, W.C. (1993) 'A Theory of Global Strategic Alliances: The Case of the Global Auto Industry', *Strategic Management Journal*, Vol. 14, pp. 419–32.

Craig, J.C. and Grant, R.M. (1993) *Strategic Management* (Kogan Page).

DTI and CBI (1993) *Innovation: The Best Practice* (DTI/CBI).

Frey Jr, S.C. and Schlosser, M.M. (1993) 'ABB and Ford: Creating Value Through Co-operation', *Sloan Management Review*, Fall, pp. 65–72.

Goold, M. and Campbell, A. (1991) 'Many Best Ways to Make Strategy' in Montgomery, C.A. and Porter, M.E. (editors) *Strategy: Seeking and Securing Competitive Advantage* (Harvard Business School Press).

Hamel, G. and Prahalad, C. K. (1994) *Competing for the Future* (Harvard Business School Press).

Hammer, M. and Champy, J. (1993) *Reengineering the Corporation* (Nicholas Brealey).

Haspeslagh, P. (1989) 'Portfolio Planning: Uses and Limits' in Asch, D. and Bowman, C. (editors) *Readings in Strategic Management* (Macmillan).

Jarillo, J. C. (1993) *Strategic Networks: Creating the Borderless Organization* (Butterworth-Heinemann).

Johansson, H.J., McHugh, p. , Pendlebury, A.J. and Wheeler, W.A. (1993) *Business Process Reengineering* (Wiley).

Kay, J. (1993) *Foundations of Corporate Success* (Oxford University Press).

Klein, J.A. and Hiscocks, P.G. (1994) 'Competence-based Competition: A Practical Toolkit' in Hamel, G. and Heene, A. (editors) *Competence-based Competition* (Wiley).

Lenz, R.T. and Lyles, M.A. (1991) 'Paralysis by Analysis: Is Your Planning System Too Rational?' in Asch, D. and Bowman, C. (editors) *Readings in Strategic Management* (Macmillan).

Miles, R.E. and Snow, C.C. (1978) *Organizational Strategy, Structure and Process* (McGraw-Hill).

Mito, S. (1990) *The Honda Book of Management* (The Athlone Press).

Mjoset, L. (1992) *The Irish Economy in a Comparative Institutional Perspective* (National Economic and Social Council).

Ohmae, K. (1982) *The Mind of the Strategist* (McGraw-Hill).

Peters, T. and Waterman, R. (1982) *In Search of Excellence* (Harper Collins).

Porter, M.E. (1991a) 'From Competitive Advantage to Corporate Strategy' in Montgomery, C.A. and Porter, M.E. (editors) *Strategy: Seeking and Securing Competitive Advantage* (Harvard Business School Press).

Porter, M.E. (1991b) 'The Competitive Advantage of Nations' in Montgomery, C.A. and Porter, M.E. (editors) *Strategy: Seeking and Securing Competitive Advantage* (Harvard Business School Press).

Prahalad, C.K. and Hamel, G. (1991) 'The Core Competence of the Organisation' in Montgomery, C.A. and Porter, M.E. (editors) *Strategy: Seeking and Securing Competitive Advantage* (Harvard Business School Press).

Welford, R. (1995) *Environmental Strategy and Sustainable Development* (Routledge).

Whittington, R. (1993) *What is Strategy – and Does it Matter?* (Routledge).

8

Internationalization

Introduction

There is much talk about global strategies in the academic literature these days. It is also an issue for practitioners. A Coopers and Lybrand survey of executives in US manufacturing companies in 1991 found that most of the large companies (more than $1 billion in sales) already had production in other countries. The survey also suggested that most of the executives thought that global competition was affecting their business and that globalization of their own business was inevitable (Johansson, McHugh, Pendlebury and Wheeler, 1993, p167). There are probably different pressures towards globalization, but in some industries it appears the rise in development costs of innovation are being accompanied by a drive to achieve larger and larger global market shares.

Globalization can be defined as an advanced state of internationalization, with the latter seen as comprising three main stages:

- exporting
- international activity
- global activity.

The international stage is defined as occurring when marketing, production, R&D or local diversification activities are conducted in other countries (Ansoff and McDonnell, 1990). At the global stage there is integration of production activities, R&D activities and resources on a crossborder basis; there is a global strategy; and the firm's structure and culture is suitably evolved (Ansoff and

McDonnell, 1990).

Ansoff and McDonnell, who have identified a three-stage model of internationalization (but who label the third stage as the muliti-national stage), claim that progression through the various stages of internationalization has been observed, although they say that not all firms do, or should, follow the respective stages.

If we accept that some process of internationalization and global-ization is underway, we might expect that current theories will tend to accent particular phases of the evolution and thus overempha-size some features at the expense of neglecting others. Arguably, this is precisely what we observe.

There is what we call a modernity model, put forward by Levitt (1991), which appears applicable to an early phase of international-ization. When multinational firms (defined in the usual sense of having operations in more than one country) are producing prod-ucts or services outside of the home country, but are not undertak-ing R&D in other countries, then it may seem logical to talk about standardized products being produced for the whole world. Later, when internationalization has proceeded further and products and services are being adapted for and developed in these other coun-tries, then the theories may reflect the importance of adapting prod-ucts, and organizational cultures, to the countries involved. Finally, when firms are beginning to search for global integration between their activities in different countries and beginning to produce glob-ally informed strategies, then theories of global strategy become applicable (Yip, 1991).

We need to consider in this chapter not only the theories of glob-al strategy, but also the theories and ideas about how firms make the transitions involved in internationalization. We will also look at the growth of joint ventures and strategic alliances which appear to be a feature of the current transition to a genuinely global economy. First, however, we begin with Levitt's (1991) ideas on global strate-gies and those developed by Yip (1991).

The modernity model

Theodore Levitt (1991, p. 204) provides a model of how a company can develop and can become global. His ideas revolve around his distinction between the 'aging multinational corporation' and the 'modern global corporation'. (Note that this terminology does not correspond to that used by, say, Ansoff and McDonnell, who see multinationals as capable of developing activities which are global. Thus the special sense of multinational which is used by Levitt needs to be kept in mind.)

According to Levitt, the multinational adapts to national differences (and even differences within national markets), whilst the *modern* global corporation 'will seek sensibly to force suitably standardized products and practices on the entire globe' (Levitt, 1991, p. 204). The multinational adjusts its products and practices in each country, but the global corporation 'sells the same things in the same way everywhere' (1991, p. 187).

Levitt assumes that difference and diversity within consumers is relatively unimportant. But this is not to say that Levitt does not recognize the fact of differences amongst consumers. Indeed, this recognition of existing differences in consumer preferences explains the use of the phrase '*force* suitably standardized products and practices on the entire globe' (our italics). He argues that 'the global corporation accepts and adjusts to these differences only reluctantly, only after relentlessly testing their immutability, after trying in various ways to circumvent and reshape them' (1991, p. 203). However, whilst he recognizes these differences in consumer preferences, he sees the trend as being towards a convergence of preferences. This is because the standardized products of global corporations enable them to enjoy economies of scale. This is part of the power of globalization to reproduce and extend itself:

> When the global producer offers his lower costs internationally, his patronage expands exponentially. He not only reaches into distant markets, but also attracts customers who previously held to local preferences and now capitulate to the attractions of lower prices.
>
> 1991, p. 192

The implication of Levitt's analysis, and one that is often accepted, is that there is a trade-off between responding to local (i.e. national) preferences and achieving economies of scale. His point is that successful globalization occurs because the economies of scale have priority over local preferences.

The new products of the global corporation are not just low priced. They have to be high quality and reliable. He says:

The Japanese ... have cracked the code of Western markets. They have done it not by looking with mechanistic thoroughness at the way the markets are different but rather by searching for meaning with a deeper wisdom. They have discovered the one great thing all markets have in common – an overwhelming desire for dependable, world-standard modernity in all things, at aggressively low prices.

1991, p. 200

Companies must move in this direction: 'Companies that do not adapt to the new global realities will become victims of those that do' (1991, p. 204).

Levitt's view of global strategy has some connection with the modernist view of strategy in as much as it assumes that the main features of the environment are largely knowable and the desired change can be programmed according to a formula, leading to an impression that change is essentially a matter of innovation. It is to be noted here that the modernist confidence of Levitt's position is shown by his assertion that *all* markets demand these things.

Levitt's evidence to corroborate this modernist model is basically a list of well-known companies. He cites in the consumer field the success of McDonalds, Coca-Cola, Pepsi-Cola, rock music, Greek salad, Hollywood movies, Revlon cosmetics, Sony televisions and Levi jeans. Johansson and Yip's (1994) study of thirty-six multinational companies supports the view that globally common customer tastes and global scale economies cause or enable companies to make and market products that are standardized globally (see Figure 8.1).

Figure 8.1 *A comparison of US and Japanese multinationals – Johansson and Yip (1994)*

Johansson and Yip (1994) carried out an empirical analysis of a small sample of companies which suggested that industry drivers were an important factor in the emergence of more global strategies and that such strategies were linked to better company performance.

Their sample consisted of thirty-six multinational companies, selected because they were large and had a high proportion of international revenue. The companies were not selected randomly. Over half the businesses sampled were domestic market leaders in their industry. Johansson and Yip comment at one point that global leaders 'almost inevitably have a large share in their home base' (1994, p. 586).

Two managers in each of the US companies sampled completed a questionnaire covering industry globalization drivers, organizational structure, management processes, global strategy and performance. A researcher was present as the managers completed the questionnaire. The procedure was changed for the Japanese sample: the questionnaire was left with one person who polled others in the company and completed the questionnaire according to the consensus view. This was justified in terms of the different realities in terms of management positions and decision making. The data collected related to one line of business within each company.

Their approach was very quantitative. The respondents gave answers which yielded measures on five-point scales; they analysed this data by developing formal models and using a technique known as 'partial least squares' to see how well the data fitted the models they explored.

Their reported findings were as follows.

1 Industry drivers (the effects of homogeneous global markets and global cost economies) affected the level of global strategy found in a company (measured partly by reference to the marketing of globally standardized products and the integration of competitive moves).

2 A more global strategy was linked to a higher company performance level.

3 Organization and management processes had 'important effects on the ability of firms to implement global strategy' (1994, p. 596).

4 Japanese companies had more global strategies than US companies.

5 Japanese companies had more global management processes, which enabled them to implement more global strategies (global group meetings and global budgeting).

It is only fair to say that they were not sure about the causal role of organization structure in the actual relationship between strategy and performance. They also noted that, whilst Japanese companies were more global in strategic terms than their US counterparts, they actually had lower performance scores, as measured by global market shares and relative profitability. They suggested, finally, that there was a need for larger sample studies allowing more complex types of analysis and more confidence in the findings. They also suggested that more conceptual development, alternative testing instruments and scales, and more rigorous data collection techniques were necessary to claim scientific validity.

Globalization by integration

Yip (1991) partly follows the distinction made by Levitt between multinational and global approaches. He claims that multinational companies 'set up country subsidiaries that design, produce, and market services tailored to local needs' (Yip, 1991, p. 693). However, he formulates the global approach as an *integration of the results of internationalizing* (whereas Levitt talked about standardized marketing and products).

Thus, Yip argues for three steps in a method for developing a total worldwide strategy:

1 developing the core strategy (usually for the home country first)
2 internationalizing the core strategy (international expansion and adaptation)
3 globalizing (by integrating the strategy across countries).

Obviously, this method implies that the strategy of a business which is undertaking the internationalizing step will be different from that of a business engaged in globalizing. Yip suggests firms that are internationalizing will:

- enter national markets on the basis of their individual attractiveness
- tailor products to meet local needs
- develop marketing locally
- locate all the required activities in each country
- make competitive moves which make sense in the national context.

In contrast, globalizing firms will:

- want to build a significant share in major world markets
- offer standardized products
- use a uniform marketing approach
- build an integrated set of activities worldwide
- make competitive moves which are integrated across countries.

Yip's ideas about the leveraging of a core strategy developed in the home country into international activity seems to be borne out by the success of Honda in the US. It is clear that the Japanese car firm established a competitive advantage first (innovative, technological developments, workforce involvement in making improvements, low costs, high quality, etc.) and then went international. That is, it did not begin to internationalize until after it had developed a core strategy. Yip's ideas are also consistent with Porter's (1991) later analysis of the importance of the home country as a platform for creating competitive advantage (see Chapter 5).

However, understanding the process of leveraging a domestic strategy into an internationalizing strategy and the process of integrating that into a globalizing strategy, are obviously very important. Indeed, the latter process of integrating strategy is very topical in the light of current concerns in a number of industries (e.g. cars, telecommunications). Yip is more helpful in suggesting the circumstances which favour and impede the process of developing a global strategy, rather than in characterizing the process itself.

Numerous circumstances which affect the likelihood of globalization – which Yip labels 'drivers' – are considered. For example, globalization is encouraged by customers in different countries wanting essentially the same type of product or service (a market driver), and by the existence of potential economies of scale produced by standardization or concentration of activities (a cost driver). Globalization is impeded by government policies (governmental drivers) which create problems in terms of local content requirements, differences in technical standards between countries and different marketing regulations (e.g. rules governing advertising on television). Globalization may be speeded up by competitive pressures created by firms that globalize to gain cost advantages – other firms are motivated to follow their example in order to catch up (competitive driver).

In many ways, Yip's ideas resemble those of Levitt's. However, the importance of becoming global via responsiveness to the differences between countries is also incorporated.

Globalization as a cumulative process

The model of a cumulative movement towards a global strategy needs to be completed in terms of both the process by which the core strategy can be leveraged into international activity, and the integration process which moves a firm from a multidomestic strategy to a global one. A possible model of the first process is provided by Ansoff and McDonnell's ideas of a 'progressive commitment process'. A model for the integration process is not obvious, but business process re-engineering (BPR) does seem to offer an approach to enhancing the results of the integration process.

Progressive commitment process

Honda's move to the United States is often held up as an interesting and successful case of internationalization. This move was achieved in stages:

> Honda at first relied on an agent for distribution ... [then Honda] established an overseas unit [for distribution] reporting directly to corporate headquarters to give Honda a better presence in the market, especially in post-sale servicing ... American Honda had to operate on a cash basis, building its inventory, advertising and distribution systems.
>
> Quinn, 1991, p. 289

In 1979 Honda opened its motorcycle plant in Ohio and took the decision 'to build a 15,000 unit US auto assembly plant' (1991, p. 295).

The case of Honda seems to bear out the validity of what Ansoff and McDonnell (1990) call a 'progressive commitment process in internationalization'.

What is a progressive commitment process in internationalization? This can involve either a stepwise or an opportunistic entry. The stepwise entry is where firms commit themselves to entering a strategic business area (SBA) and do so in steps. The opportunistic entry is used when firms are unsure about committing themselves because of uncertainty over the attractiveness of an SBA, or the strategy to use within it, and so they make a low cost entry to learn about the SBA. 'The opportunistic entry should be designed and executed as a strategic learning experience' (Ansoff and McDonnell, 1990, p. 233).

In either case the assumption is that the strategic information held by the company is limited. 'An explanation for such a gradual approach is to be found in the cost of strategic information ... the cost of information for internationalization is very much higher than the cost of domestic information, and some of the vital knowledge about foreign environments can only be acquired through first-hand experience' (1990, p. 232). However, Ansoff and McDonnell say that stepwise entry is advisable even if information on the attractiveness of the SBA is available: ' ... it is still advisable to proceed in steps using strategic learning at each step, but with more confidence and boldness, not only to confirm/deny the previous decisions, but also to modify the global internationalization strategy' (1990, p. 233).

The company using progressive commitment is also able to control its risk by making limited and measured investments. In the case of the opportunistic entry, the information gained may persuade the company to move into a stepwise and permanent entry; alternatively the information may lead it to withdraw, or withdraw after short-term profit making is exhausted. The importance of respecting the risks attached to internationalizing has been brought out by some recent research by Mitchell, Shaver and Yeung (1992) on the medical diagnostic imaging equipment industry in the United States. It seems that firms with their own manufacturing facilities outside the US and firms with extensive multinational activity had better records in terms of US market share and survival, suggesting that firms with a more developed international status performed better. However, both increasing and decreasing internationalization were associated with negative effects in terms market share and actual survival, suggesting that whilst there are benefits of becoming global, getting there is risky (see Figure 8.2).

Figure 8.2 *Changing international presence in the medical diagnostic imaging equipment industry – Mitchell et al. (1992)*

Mitchell *et al.* (1992) were interested in the risks associated with firms becoming international, whilst being aware of evidence suggesting that multinational firms achieve superior performance in some industries.

Their sample comprised 111 manufacturers of human diagnostic imaging equipment systems that marketed their products in the US market between 1975 and 1989. Data was obtained on the firms' internationalization strategies for their medical sector activity from a series of trade guides. In the case of seventy-four of these firms, they also had this data on strategies at the level of the operating units which included the imaging businesses. In the other cases it was difficult to get information on business unit strategy. They also had data on US market share in different periods, and survival records in terms of participation in the American market.

Their measurement of international strategy was based on five categories:

- firms in which there was no significant international activity
- firms that imported for sale in the US
- firms that exported from the US
- firms that owned and operated facilities outside the US
- firms (classified by them as multinational) that had a combination of domestic and foreign manufacturing, as well as importing an exporting activities.

They found that firms in the last two categories – those with overseas facilities and those they called multinational – had performed better than the rest in terms of market share. The multinational firms also had better survival records.

In terms of increasing or decreasing internationalization at the level of the firm, they found:

1 decreased internationalization (e.g. ceasing to manufacture overseas) was associated with smaller market share increases and shorter survival
2 increased internationalization (e.g. starting to manufacture overseas) was associated with shorter survival and was not significantly related to market share.

At the business unit level they also found negative effects of both decreasing and increasing internationalization.

They comment: 'While being international may be associated with superior performance, as it is in the diagnostic imaging equipment industry, becoming international is a difficult and risky process' (Mitchell *et al.*, 1992, p. 429)

The similarity of this approach and the ideas of Quinn on strategic change through logical incrementalism is evident in the common assumption of a strategy of incremental steps and limited knowledge. In both cases there is a notion of testing, feedback and learning. Perhaps the chief difference between Quinn's logical incrementalism and Ansoff and McDonnell's progressive commitment is that the former emphasizes the role of precipitating events which require urgent decisions, whereas Ansoff and McDonnell see the process in normative terms and launched by the management's formulation of a global internationalization strategy. They see opportunistic entry as under the *control* of the management, not as a successful response to urgent and unexpected matters. They are, therefore, still working within a quasimodernist paradigm, although they have accepted the powerful impact of limited knowledge on the strategy process.

Global re-engineering – enhancing the integration process?

Ford Motor Company, the second largest vehicle producer in the world in the first half of the 1990s, has been international for decades and has had an integrated European operation for nearly thirty years. It is currently embarked on a programme called 'Ford 2000' which, according to its chairman will make the company 'the world's leading automotive company by the end of the century – the best in customer satisfaction, the best in quality and value of product' (Lorenz, 1995). The company is expecting massive cost cuts (£1.9 billion a year) and to reduce the product-development cycle of its vehicles from three to two years. The aims also include increasing the returns on investment by achieving massive total sales of new models. The streamlining of the company by Ford 2000 has been described as a globalization drive and the biggest restructuring in modern corporate history. It has even been linked to business process re-engineering (BPR), although how well it deserves that label is difficult to say on the basis of the report.

The advocates of applying BPR to the global business, such as Johansson and his colleagues (1993), believe that there are cost advantages if products are standardized. They also advise worldwide scheduling of plant rather than centralized production where transport costs are not significant and suggest that BPR can be used to get the best of both worlds (decentralization of some responsibilities, feature-rich but customer-specific products and rationalization applied to core processes leaving other processes to be designed locally). Let us look at these two points in more detail.

Cost savings

Global domination is assumed to be based on a process orientation rather than economies of scale, that is, providing value to the customer and paying attention to core business processes (Johansson *et al.*, 1993, p. 165). Major cost gains are thought to be made by adopting a single global way of manufacturing so that products manufactured in one plant can be shipped to another plant's customers (1993, p. 166). Worldwide scheduling of plant usage can deal with surges in demand so that use of production capacity can be made optimal and buffer stocks can be avoided (this assumes the declining importance of transport costs and the existence of standardized products) (1993, p. 183).

This is an economy of standardization rather than an economy of scale. It requires co-ordinated and integrated production systems, rather than massified ones.

Best of both worlds

Within the overall commitment to standardization, BPR offers several attempts to reconcile the centrally controlled standardization with the local market differences.

1 Local businesses within the global setup have the responsibility for identifying local market preferences and can specify new products, but the actual design of new products and process roll out is centralized to ensure standardization.
2 Products can be designed that are 'simultaneously feature rich and customer specific (1993, p. 186). This involves designing products with more features than specific customers require, so that the same products can be marketed to customers in different countries who have different requirements. The nonrequired features should not be apparent to the customers.
3 It is possible for core business processes to be re-engineered globally and support processes to be designed locally to take advantage of local practices (1993, p. 177).

This particular view of BPR shows an attempt to balance economies of standardization and local preference, and to balance responsibilities between the centre and the country managers. In this sense,

BPR offers a process for designing a firm which is consciously managing the major dilemmas of global business activity. But in the notions that products are standardized (albeit that products are feature rich and customer specific), that new products are rolled out by the global centre and that only the noncore processes are designed locally, we have BPR offering a process to achieve an operationally sophisticated global strategy model. That is, above all, it is offering to optimize the operational effectiveness of a model of globalization based on standardized products. Therefore, in our opinion, BPR applied to globalizing businesses produces an enhanced integration process.

A synthesis

The model of a cumulative movement towards a global strategy is represented diagramatically in Figure 8.3. This suggests that the home country is the platform for creating a core strategy (Yip, 1991) and competitive advantage (Porter, 1991), which is leveraged internationally. We would suggest that Porter's (1991) analysis of the home country environment as a platform for international success is relevant to an understanding of whether or not the core (or domestic) strategy can be successfully leveraged.

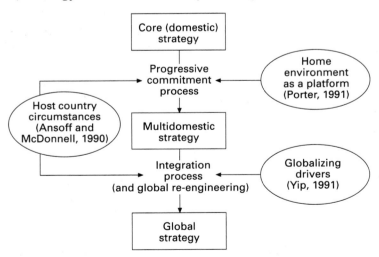

Figure 8.3   *Globalization – a synthesis*

Host country circumstances are also important for the move to multidomestic strategy. A useful listing of important host country circumstances has been provided by Ansoff and McDonnell (1990) in their discussion of situations in which firms develop strategy specific to the strategic business area. They say that such specific strategies are more likely where:

- customer demand is very specific to the country concerned
- competition within the strategic business area is intense
- customer pressures/discrimination is intense
- the market is relatively large
- government regulation is intense
- there is a lot of nontransferable or implicit information.

Implicit information is vital information which is not perceivable from outside and is acquired first hand by operating there (Ansoff and McDonnell, 1990).

Some of these factors obviously make the effort to enter the market more worthwhile or make careful attention to strategic issues more necessary (e.g. the size of the market, intense competition, intense customer pressures/discrimination), but the others relate fairly obviously to the difficulties of learning about and adapting to the strategic business area. Thus some of these host country circumstances function as barriers to internationalization.

The process of leveraging the core strategy – *how* the core strategy becomes a multidomestic one – is explained by the progressive commitment model provided by Ansoff and McDonnell (1990, p. 232).

The difficulty of moving to a global strategy depends on the prevailing host country circumstances and on Yip's (1991) drivers, which are global level circumstances. The process of creating a global strategy is an integration process which can be enhanced by undertaking global re-engineering.

Do firms have to pass through a multidomestic strategy (i.e. a strategy for the international phase) before they can successfully create a pure global strategy? Figure 8.3 does seem to suggest that this is the case, although Yip's identification of globalization drivers may indicate that under certain circumstances (i.e. when these drivers are extremely favourable to globalization) the duration of the phase of multidomestic strategy may be relatively brief, or may even be skipped over entirely. Of course, under these circumstances the model would simplify to approximate Levitt's ideas about global strategies.

Conversely, if the globalization drivers are very weak, will the firms remain in the multidomestic strategy phase for a long time? Getting fixed in a multidomestic strategy might be more likely when the home circumstances predisposing a firm to develop a strategy specific to the country are strong and Yip's global level drivers are weak.

According to Hamel and Prahalad (1994), in the past, there was little incentive to co-ordinate worldwide product roll-outs, and multinational head offices were wary of attempting global integration in the face of host country variations. 'In a world of national markets fragmented by tariffs, regulatory differences, and unique customer preferences, there were few opportunities to capture global-scale economies' (1994, p. 262). Country managers had considerable product line autonomy. 'Traditionally, local executives were free to adopt or ignore new products created in other countries or at the head office' (1994, p. 262). But, they argue, in effect, that globalization drivers are now strengthening. The factors mentioned by them include:

- increasing economic integration
- the dismantling of tariff and nontariff barriers
- the growth of international media
- customers with a more global consciousness
- competitors increasingly capable of developing global products.

Their observations are broadly consistent with the model of a movement towards a global strategy via a multidomestic strategy stage.

Organizational culture and structural design

Ansoff and McDonnell (1990) argue that internationalization has profound implications for the organization of a business. They see the major need to reorganize a business as being produced by the shift from the international to multinational status (which we suggest might be better termed a global status). This reorganization is conceptualized on the cultural level and the structural level.

Culturally firms have to go from an ethnocentric to a polycentric focus (i.e. to a genuinely multinational culture). The Honda case can be used to illustrate the shift to a polycentric focus which can accompany internationalization. Setsuo Mito (1990), who has written on Honda management, claims:

> Honda management is not precisely the same in every country. As it is put into practice in Europe, the United States or South-east Asia, it is tailored to specific needs and conditions. There is nothing surprising about this, especially for Honda, where attention is customarily paid to 'individual differences'. Honda management is a mix of many elements drawn not only from Japanese experience but also from overseas experience and this includes the response of users in the countries and local management know-how.
>
> Mito, 1990, p. 101

The move towards a global strategy also impacts on the decision-making structures of companies. In those multinationals which have in the past allowed their country managers a good deal of autonomy, and where there has been little attempt at global integration of activities, centralized co-ordination or even shared authority could represent reduced decision-making discretion. Some multinationals are involving the country managers in regional and global decisions and in transnational teams. These initiatives and global branding may be useful in overcoming the divisions which exist within the multinational setup.

According to Ansoff and McDonnell (1990), however, firms moving from an international to a multinational status have to change from the principle of unity of authority to that of shared authority. The principle of shared authority is applicable to situations where at least three key managers are involved in decision making. One manager has the responsibility for approving and controlling decisions, a second manager has responsibility for making and implementing decisions and a third manager has a responsibility to agree or disagree with the decision made by the second manager. This may sound much more complicated than in the usual hierarchical setup, but is applicable to matrix organizations (Ansoff and McDonnell, 1990, p. 223).

Asea Brown Baveri (ABB) appears to have developed a matrix organization to manage its multinational business activities (Johansson *et al.*, 1993, pp. 170–1). ABB has more than 1100 companies (in manufacturing, services and sales) covering fifty business areas worldwide. Each business area has a leader who is responsible for global optimization. At the same time there are national organizations. Consequently, each company's president reports to a business-area president and a national president. In these circumstances, it is likely that decision making is based, to some degree, on the principle of shared authority.

Quite a different view of the organizational implications of global strategies emerges from Johansson and Yip's (1994) empirical work on multinational companies. They suggest that Japanese companies can meet global strategy requirements more easily than US companies because they have had centralized direction of their business activity. In fact, they found that companies with one global head (i.e. unitary authority) and no separate international divisions (i.e. splitting the international activities off from the domestic ones) were more likely to have a more global strategy. Moreover, they point to the role of specific organizational processes (global group meetings and global budgeting) as assisting the implementation of more global strategies.

The logic of internationalization

Different accounts are provided for the waves of internationalization which have occurred. For example, after the Second World War many US firms moved into Europe because the domestic market was saturated and they were looking for more demand to continue their growth; whereas a desire to enhance profitability is reputed to have motivated the 'Japanese invasion of the profitable computer markets' (Ansoff and McDonnell, 1990, p. 218). Whilst competitive pressures and the search for opportunities to increase profits may often be important factors, in specific cases there are sometimes other reasons, such as a search for political stability.

It may be that the motive to globalize is different from the motive to internationalize. In the face of emerging global competition, perhaps as in the case of the telecommunications industry, the drive is against competitors rather than simply the conquest of markets: 'The goal of many businesses in globalizing their activities has become domination over the competition rather than merely to reach new markets' (Johansson *et al.*, 1993, p. 167). However, in our view, it is hard to separate for long the desire for conquest over competitors, or survival in the face of their competition, from the search for profit-making opportunities. Each is the medium for the other.

Joint ventures and strategic alliances

Various forms of cooperation and partnership between businesses have been getting attention in recent years. Joint ventures (JVs) and strategic alliances are two forms of partnership which have received particular attention. Joint ventures are where two or more businesses jointly own and control an overseas business (Hodgetts and Luthans, 1994, p. 141). A strategic alliance is a co-operative agreement to share resources, capabilities, research and development costs, to provide access to markets, knowledge, etc. There is evidence that both have been increasing (see Table 8.1).

Table 8.1 *Joint ventures and co-operative agreements*

(a) McKinsey study on US international joint ventures

Year	No.
1976	31
1980	94
1987	180

(b) Commission Report on the European Community – co-operative agreements

Year	No.
1983	46
1986	81
1989	129

Source: Dunning (1993), p. 192

Porter (1991) is unequivocal in his views about alliances with firms based in foreign countries. He considers them merely a passing management fashion with serious costs attached. Moreover, he suggests that they may help a firm to achieve a mediocre performance, but they will not bring success in the form of international leadership. If the alliance is created because of specific advantages that may be obtained on a temporary basis, then alliances may be of some usefulness on a selective basis. The implication is that the company contemplating entering a strategic alliance should think twice before risking the creation of a competitor and that other ways should be found to build skills and assets that are central to competitive advantage.

Local responses to global competition

This chapter has been written from the viewpoint of a firm wanting to compete in other countries. It has not addressed strategic responses available to local firms that are experiencing global competition. Cost competitiveness is unlikely to be a satisfactory response as even when transportation and associated costs are taken into account, it is demonstrably clear that local firms have difficulty in matching global firms' prices. Further, it can be argued that not only do local firms came under pressure because of prices but the product quality of the multinational is far superior. For example, the UK motor industry decline in the 1970s was caused by both low price and better quality imports. A strategy that builds upon specific local tastes that are hard to mimic effectively by large multinationals might have more success. Clegg (1990) gives the example of French bread, in France and how this is still produced by small *boulangeries* and not large multinationals. Finding products or services that are still outside the homogeneity of world taste is hard, with MacDonalds becoming a world cuisine. Even in France it might be harder to achieve in the future!

Key points

1 One of the major strategic issues in internationalization appears to be how firms can balance economies of standardization and local preference. This is linked to another issue which needs to be balanced: the division of responsi-

bilities between the multinational centre and the country managers. Much of the thinking in this area agrees that firms move through a multidomestic stage to a truly global strategy stage. The superiority of the global strategy is seen to derive from the way it integrates activities in different countries and makes integrated competitive moves. There is also considerable support for the importance of standardization of products in a global strategy.

2 Multinationals make important changes in their organizations and their culture as they become global. Decision making has to change and the culture (and focus?) becomes polycentric.

3 Joint ventures (JVs) and strategic alliances are two forms of partnership between multinational firms that have received much attention in recent years. There is empirical evidence that both have been increasing. Their benefits, however, have been contested by some influential opinion (Porter, 1991).

4 Local firms may be able to resist global competition by sheltering behind unique local tastes that are hard to duplicate.

References

Ansoff, I. and McDonnell, E. (1990) *Implanting Strategic Management* (Prentice Hall).

Clegg, S.R. (1990) Modern Organisations: *Organisation Studies in the Postmodern World* (Sage).

Dunning, J.H. (1993) *The Globalization of Business* (Routledge).

Hamel, H. and Prahalad, C.K. (1994) *Competing for the Future* (Wiley).

Hodgetts, R.M. and Luthans, F. (1994) *International Management* (McGraw-Hill).

Johansson, H.J., McHugh, P., Pendlebury, A.J. and Wheeler, W.A. (1993) *Business Process Reengineering* (Wiley).

Johansson, J.K. and Yip, G.S. (1994) 'Exploiting Globalization Potential: US and Japanese Strategies', *Strategic Management Journal*, Vol. 15, pp. 579–601.

Levitt, T. (1991) 'The Globalization of Markets' in Montgomery, C.A. and Porter, M.E. (editors) *Strategy: Seeking and Securing Competitive Advantage* (Harvard Business School).

Lorenz, A. (1995) 'Ford Drives to Win World Leadership', *The Sunday Times*, 1 January.

Mitchell, W, Shaver, J.M. and Yeung, B. (1992) 'Getting There in a Global Industry: Impacts on Performance of Changing International Presence', *Strategic Management Journal*, Vol. 13, pp. 419–32.

Mito, S. (1990) *The Honda Book of Management* (The Athlone Press).

Porter, M.E. (1991 'The Competitive Advantage of Nations' in Montgomery, C.A. and Porter, M.E. (editors) *Strategy: Seeking and Securing Competitive Advantage* (Harvard Business School).

Quinn, J.B. (1991) 'Honda Motor Company' in Mintzberg, H. and Quinn J. B. (editors) *The Strategy Process: Concepts, Contexts, Cases* (Prentice Hall).

Yip, G.S. (1991) 'Global Strategy ... In a World of Nations?' in Mintzberg, H. and Quinn, B. (editors) *The Strategy Process: Concepts, Contexts, Cases* (Prentice Hall).

9

Ethical aspects of strategic management

Introduction

It is not known how much time top managers spend on the ethical aspects of strategy. It is difficult to infer it indirectly. On the one hand, the media has on a number of occasions publicized business activities that have been of concern because of the risks, or actuality, of fraud, corruption, moral impropriety and environmental damage. The dumping of toxic wastes, insider trading, bribing of democratically elected officials to win contracts, child labour, low pay, health risks to employees and many other issues have been debated in the press and on television over many years. Major companies and financial institutions have been subjected to the bad publicity caused by scandals and controversies. Famous cases include:

- the escape of poisonous gas from Union Carbide's chemical plant in Bhopal
- the oil spillage by the Amoco Cadiz
- the US's financial scandal involving the case of Ivan Boesky and his use of inside information
- the Guinness and Robert Maxwell financial scandals in the UK
- the controversy over Nestlé's marketing of infant formula in the third world
- accusations of the use of child labour by suppliers to C&A.

And yet, on the other hand, the business sections of newspapers and management books and journals do not seem to give much attention to the subject.

Argenti (1989), who sees corporate conduct as generally important but uncontroversial, is of the opinion that 'it is seldom necessary to spend much time on this aspect of strategy' (Argenti, 1989, p. 78). He suggests that most organizations have one sensitive area and recommends that they include a clear statement on it in what he calls its 'corporate conduct statement'. However, he argues that, apart from this, ethics is not much of an issue for the strategy process.

> Most organizations in most Western nations behave in much the same way. There is a broad consensus as to how one should behave in a civilized society towards employees, customers, the community, and so on. Common sense, custom and practice are often sufficient guide-lines for most organizations.
>
> Argenti, 1989, pp. 78–9

We do not really know much for sure about how ethics relates to the strategic aims of organizations in practice. In abstract terms there has long been a view that ethics are a constraint or limitation on the organization's aims. This is reflected in Argenti's definitions of the corporate objective and corporate conduct: 'the objective describes what the organization is doing for whom; conduct describes how, while achieving this, the organization proposes to behave within society' (Argenti, 1989, p. 78). As a constraint, the ethical aspect can be seen as a burden. When corporate ethics are viewed in this way, the organization that is world class in competitive terms and conducts itself ethically in relation to customers, employees and others is seen as extraordinarily commendable. This view sees ethics as having a price tag and it sees a real conflict, therefore, between the profit motive and ethical conduct. One expression of this conflict is the decision to compromise between corporate objectives and ethical standards by adopting the 'no harm' principle. 'This states that, in pursuing its aims, no organization should cause significant harm to any third party' (Argenti, 1989, p. 82).

An alternative view of the relationship between ethics and strategic aims is that ethics can enrich corporate aims. A number of companies appear to have found being ethical very profitable. Examples may be found in the US computer industry (e.g. Control Data), in the cosmetic industry (e.g. Body Shop) and in banking (e.g. the UK's Co-operative Bank). This view can be incorporated into perspectives on the evolution of business which are essentially rooted in conceptions of postindustrialism. Is there a long-term swing towards the remoralization of business, with consequences for the way in which businesses compete (strategic alliances) and the nature of products and services (environmentally friendly and socially responsible)?

Whilst there may be emergent trends in the ethical aspects of strategy, for the individual manager there has long been a need to balance morality with their business activity.

> There was a notion formerly that a man made money for himself, a purely selfish occupation, in the daytime, and rendered his service to the community by sitting on the school board or some civic committee at night. Or he might spend his early and middle life in business, in getting money, and then do his service by spending his money in ways useful to the community – if he did not die before that stage arrived.
>
> Follett, 1941, p. 133

Quaker businesses have had a reputation for seeking to make moral choices within their business activity. For them, their conscience had to be satisfied within their conduct of business. The way they behaved as business people had to reflect their conception of what was right and good.

The climate for the attempts to make moral choices within business activity may be changing because of the increasing importance of public authority. Nutt and Backoff (1992) suggest that nowadays all organizations – private, voluntary and public sector – have a degree of 'publicness' because they are influenced to some degree by public authority.

> Publicness stems from markets that are made up of authority networks, constraints that limit autonomy and flexibility, the prospect of political interference, coercive means that can be used to fund or force the use of services, many externalities that cue action possibilities, the prospect of scrutiny by outsiders, ubiquitous accountability, vague and argumentative goals, authority limits, shifting performance expectations and ambiguous incentives to coax desirable behaviour.
>
> Nutt and Backoff, 1992, pp. 51–2

If we accept that even private firms have a degree of publicness, we can more readily understand the argument that private businesses are allowed to pursue profit in a political and social environment that expects a certain responsiveness and even active co-operation from businesses in return for a legal framework which protects the activities of businesses (including limited liability, which is a major benefit to business owners conferred by public authority).

There are, however, a wide variety of ways of conceptualizing what is expected of businesses which have some degree of public-ness. One idea is that they should not pursue profits at the expense of the public good. Another is that they should not only meet the legal requirements of society, but should also voluntarily meet the ethical or moral standards of society.

Some commentators, recognizing the power and wealth of businesses, want them to become proactive in the solution of social problems. Chamberlain (1973) was pessimistic about the possibility of this aspect of social responsibility: 'the only initiatives that can be expected even from our largest and financially strongest corporations will necessarily be limited in scope and substance, barely touching the most grievous social problems' (Chamberlain, 1973, p. 4).

It is apparent from the preceding paragraphs that the subject of ethics and business is fertile soil for ideas and opinions. There has been much discussion in recent years of problems regarding ethical issues in auditing practices, share trading, advertising and selling practices, equal opportunities and so on. There clearly is a need for a good theory of individual integrity and honesty within business. In this chapter, however, we want to concentrate on the ethical aspects of strategic management. As much as possible, we will root the discussion of the ethical aspects of strategy in the practicalities of business – rather than in abstract philosophical discussions of ethical principles – and we will pay attention to the processes by which ethics and strategy are combined. We begin by looking at the reasons for being ethical. This is followed by a discussion of three approaches to the incorporation of ethics into strategy. We then look at the specialized areas of ethics within international business and within strategic alliances.

Why be ethical?

There are different arguments about why strategic management should be ethical. One argument is that businesses are threatened by increasing societal expectations of business; therefore, as a matter of enlightened self-interest, businesses must act responsibly or the government will bring in laws to regulate them (Solomon and Hanson, 1985, p. 19).

Hosmer (1994) argued equally pragmatically that companies need to act ethically because of the competitive threats of operating in a global economy. His basic argument for the inclusion of ethical principles in the strategic management process is as follows:

1 Stakeholder groups (suppliers, customers, creditors, investors, industry associations, etc.) can affect the firm's achievement of objectives.
2 These stakeholders can help with competitive innovation which is important for competitive success.
3 These stakeholders need to be motivated to help with competitive innovation by building trust, commitment and effort.
4 Strategic decisions result in harms (moral problems) and benefits to stakeholders.
5 Firms that recognize and resolve moral problems using ethical principles can create trust amongst stakeholders, releasing commitment and effort towards co-operative, innovative and strategically directed results.

In other words, an ethical approach to strategic management is good business in a competitive global economy. Therefore, Hosmer concluded, 'Strategic planning must be both analytical and ethical ... ' (Hosmer, 1994, p. 32).

Uniting strategy and ethics

How can and how do, businesses unite strategic management and business ethics? In recent years there have been at least three positions, or models, on this matter, which for convenience we will call:

- the social responsiveness model
- the moral leadership model
- the stakeholder model.

Social responsiveness model

This is where businesses seek to become responsive to their social environment. It is an essentially modernist approach to building social responsibility into strategic management, as will be seen from the following consideration of the ideas of Frederick, Post and Davis (1992). They provide a particularly clear and coherent statement of the modernist view and confidently suggest that individual businesses need a social strategy.

As with some early conceptions of corporate strategy formulation, they view the overall issue as one of aligning the business with its changing environment to achieve a fit. In this case, the strategy formulation process is seeking a fit between company goals and the 'changing needs, goals, and expectations of the public' (Frederick *et al.*, 1992, p. 102).

Within their modernist perspective, the first step is to understand how the environment is changing. Thus they introduce the idea that the environment is divided up into four separate but interrelated segments: political, economic, social and technological. And they introduce the idea that an analysis of the external environment can be carried out through a process of environmental scanning. They suggest that scanning can be based on trend analysis, issues analysis and stakeholder analysis. For instance, companies may need to understand long-term trends in lifespan; they may need to make assessments of issues such as taxation proposals before legislatures; and they may need to collect information on the concerns of stakeholders through, say, direct discussions with their representatives.

They define environmental analysis as including forecasting as well as identification and monitoring of trends and issues. Some forecasting is seen as dealing with the predictable. 'School enrollments, the number of entry-level jobs, and school dropout or graduation rates can be forecast with a reasonable degree of accuracy because of experience and the ability to double-check past forecasts' (Frederick *et al.*, 1992, p. 111).

There are situations and circumstances that are not predictable on the basis of projected trends, but, in some cases, their possible occurrence may be anticipated on the basis of warning signals. So, whilst recognizing that some forecasting may be problematic, they suggest that most companies see the importance and value of it.

Frederick and his colleagues then move on to the implementation phase in their model of how businesses can become socially responsive. This is broken down into:

- a policy stage
- a learning stage
- an organizational commitment stage.

In the first of these, the *policy stage*, the top management and the board of directors formulate policies which will guide the company's response to social issues. It is, of course, typical of a modernist perspective that the response is conceptualized as guided by explicit and formal decisions made by top management. The next stage of implementation is the company *learning* how to tackle a social problem and learning how to make the top management policy effective. They suggest that experts may be brought in to help at this stage, but say that learning by supervisors and managers is needed to implement the policy. 'Social responsiveness requires the full cooperation and knowledge of line managers as well as staff experts' (Frederick *et al.*, 1992, p. 114). Through this learning, the new policy is translated into new administrative routines. Finally, in the *commitment* stage, the new policy and the new routines are incorporated into standard operating procedures; for the new policies and routines 'should become so well accepted throughout the entire company that they are considered to be a normal part of doing business' (Frederick *et al.*, 1992, p. 115). This implementation of social responsiveness needs to consolidated by organizational changes. Thus, nonexecutive members of the board of directors may be appointed for their broader perspective, appropriate behaviour within the company can be reinforced via rewards and sanctions, the business can include information on their social activities in their annual reports to shareholders and a 'climate of respect for social values and stakeholder interests' can be encouraged by a 'demonstrated personal commitment by top-level managers', by codes of conduct and by training programmes (Frederick *et al.*, 1992, p. 120). (See Figure 9.1.)

Figure 9.1   *Ethics management practices*

Berman, West and Cava (1994) report a study of ethical management practices in the United States. The aim of the study was to
examine public–private differences in ethics management practices.
   The researchers surveyed 427 municipal governments and 209
firms in a range of industries. They found that:

• organizations used four sets of practices to manage ethical standards:

   (a) adopting and implementing codes of ethics
   (b) exemplary moral leadership by corporate leaders or elected offi-
       cials, and by top management
   (c) human resource management (ethics training for employees,
       counselling for ethical issues, protection of employees in whistle
       blowing)
   (d) regulatory practices (e.g. requiring approval of outside activities,
       requiring financial disclosures)

• exemplary moral leadership and regulatory practices had some
  effectiveness in minimizing wrongdoing in both the municipal and
  firm's sectors
• firms were more likely than municipal government to adopt codes of
  ethics, monitor adherence to codes, provide exemplary moral leadership, survey employees' opinions about ethics and to provide
  counselling on ethical issues
• municipal government was more likely than firms to use regulatory
  practices (e.g. requiring financial disclosure) and provide ethics
  training for employees
• human resource management practices in municipal government
  and codes of ethics in the firm's sector also had some effectiveness
  in minimizing wrongdoing
• organizations in both sectors were motivated to manage their ethical
  standards by an aim of promoting good public relations, by concerns
  about litigation and by public complaints.

The message of all this is very reassuring. The ethical and moral
issues arise outside of the business – there are social problems or
new expectations in the business environment – and the individ-

ual business can and should adapt to them. The task of environmental scanning and the technique of forecasting may be difficult but they are feasible and acceptable; thus businesses can know what they need to do. The process of making strategic changes in response to social problems and trends may take time and may involve hard work and commitment, but it can be done in a fairly logical way, developing from policy through to new operating procedures. In this sense, the organization can be reprogrammed – 'reinvented' as Frederick *et al.* (1992, p. 101) put it – to incorporate a concern for social and environmental issues. All it requires is the re-engineering of the strategic management techniques of environmental scanning and the application of the usual management techniques for implementing the consequent new social strategy.

The moral leadership model

We have inferred the moral leadership model from the writings of Peters and Waterman (1982). Its importance lies not only in the popularity of the ideas of Peters and Waterman as such, but also in the intellectual bridge it provides between the social responsiveness model and the stakeholder model.

An ethical dimension within their writing has been noted by Freeman (1991): 'Peters and Waterman's prescription for corporations could be summarized as a modern-day version of Kant's principle: Treat others with respect and dignity' (Freeman, 1991, p. 4). This has also been couched in terms of relationships with stakeholders:

> Peters and Waterman (1982) have argued that being close to the customer leads to success with other stakeholders and that a distinguishing characteristic of some companies that have performed well is their emphasis on the customer. By paying attention to customers' needs, management automatically addresses the needs of suppliers and owners. Moreover, it seems that the ethic of customer service carries over to the community. Almost without fail the 'excellent companies' in Peters and Waterman's study have good reputations in the community. We would argue that Peters and Waterman have found multiple applications of Kant's dictum, 'Treat persons as ends unto themselves,' and it should come as no surprise that persons respond to such respectful treatment, be they

customers, suppliers, owners, employees, or members of the local community.

Evan and Freeman, 1993, pp. 260–1

In fact, much of the work of Peters and Waterman concerned how employees should be treated. They argued that people have a need for self-determination and that excellent companies recognized this and pushed authority down the organization. They reported that excellent companies had 'the apparent absence of a rigidly followed chain of command' (Peters and Waterman, 1982, p. 262). Big companies might be generally perceived to have a low rate of innovation, but the excellent companies, Peters and Waterman claimed, had enviable records of innovation despite being big.

> Perhaps the most important element of their enviable track record is an ability to be big and yet to act small at the same time. A concomitant essential apparently is that that they encourage the entrepreneurial spirit among their people, because they push autonomy remarkably far down the line ... It eventually became clear that all of these companies were making a trade-off. They were creating almost radical decentralization and autonomy, with its attendant overlap, messiness around the edges, lack of co-ordination, internal competition, and somewhat chaotic conditions, in order to breed the entrepreneurial spirit. They had forsworn a measure of tidiness in order to achieve regular innovation.
>
> Peters and Waterman, 1982, p. 201

This emphasis on messiness and chaos was subversive of traditional ideas of how to structure organizations for efficiency. But there were other subversive messages. These companies opposed the rational analytical approach to strategic management. Productivity and innovation were to be obtained by telling those down the line to go ahead and be entrepreneurial, productive and innovative *now*, not to wait for the corporate plan nor to restrict themselves to the behaviour implied by the formal organizational structure. They also criticized popular ideas and practices of strategic management (such as acquisition strategies and matrix structures).

The subversive message was, however, counterbalanced by their insistence on the importance of strong corporate cultures and shared values. Thus they had confidence in the loosening of hierarchical control where organizational leaders provided a moral leadership, where, in other words, the leaders provided 'meaning' for employees through establishing shared values for the organization. In a sense, they were recommending an alternative form of control based on the symbolic integration of all the employees in the organization. The potency of this form of control was based on the need employees had to search for meaning in their lives. Peters and Waterman had some worries about abuses of strong company cultures – they suggested that people might be too willing to yield to authority – but they thought that there were countervailing tendencies which limited abuses.

We can now, building on the ideas of Peters and Waterman, define the moral leadership model as follows. It implies both that strategic planning, in its modernist form, finds it difficult to be responsive to the rapidly changing economic and social environment and that the motivation of people is the key to strategic change. So strategic management must transform itself into a more liberal regime in which decision making is pushed down the line. The ethical treatment of employees is, thus, the act of managers giving them more self-determination, an act which is taken as the basis for the view that employees are being treated with respect. Pragmatically, the provision of self-determination is meant to unleash entrepreneurialism by the employees, with consequent benefits for productivity and innovation. Therefore, ethical management is crucially, at the same time, an expectation that employees will respond positively to decentralization and autonomy. It is the cornerstone of an attempt by those controlling strategic planning to divest themselves of some of the responsibility for strategic planning, based on the proposition that ethical treatment of employees brings about their moral integration into the business organization's traditional economic performance goals.

This model may be criticized for the fact that it ends up denying an autonomous sphere for ethics and social responsibility; they are subsumed within the economic responsibilities of management for productivity and innovation. Questions about irresponsible business behaviour in relation to the community, the environment, etc. are just not an issue within this model. It represents an important divergence from the modernist model in its assumptions about the centralization of decision making and the participation of employees. An important empirical question is: 'Does the ethical management of employees produce the economic gains in terms of productivity and rate of innovation that are suggested by this model?'

The stakeholder model

The stakeholder model assumes that there are a multiplicity of interest groups with separate but related interests in a firm. Evan and Freeman (1993) identify the following stakeholder groups: owners, suppliers, employees, customers, the local community and management. In each case, the stakeholder group can affect or be affected by the business. For example, they remark about the community:

> In return for the provision of local services, the firm is expected to be a good citizen ... The firm cannot expose the community to unreasonable hazards in the form of pollution, toxic waste, and so on. If for some reason the firm must leave a community, it is expected to work with local leaders to make the transition as smooth as possible.
>
> Evan and Freeman, 1993, p. 261

The stakeholder theorists takes a broad view of the interests which managers should attempt to address. Bowie (1995) states:

> A stakeholder theorist argues that a manager should treat employees and customers well because it is the right thing to do; the needs and rights of the corporate stakeholders are the ends the manager should aim at. Profits are the happy results that usually accompany these ends.
>
> Bowie, 1995, p. 601

This is not necessarily easy for management. Evan and Freeman see management as having a responsibility which 'involves balancing the multiple claims of conflicting shareholders' (1993, p. 261).

We would suggest that Wartick and Cochran's (1995) discussion of corporate social performance thinking suggests that 'social issues management' is integral to the stakeholder model. They comment: 'issues analysis, the crucial linkage between issues identification and effective response development, is being significantly enhanced by "stakeholder analysis" (Freeman, 1984)' (Wartick and Cochran, 1995, p. 36). Consequently, whereas in the social responsiveness model corporate planners might be concerned about emerging social trends and changing expectations in the social environment, the strategic management process in the stakeholder model has to deal with an issue agenda which is constituted by the conflicting claims and interests of stakeholders.

Managers, in balancing multiple and conflicting claims, may find it useful to enter into negotiations and dialogue with representatives of the stakeholder groups. It looks as though Frederick *et al.* (1992) had some elements of a stakeholder model in mind when they discussed the socially responsive approach to strategic management. For example, they recognized the possibility of firms influencing their environment. They labelled this an 'interactive strategy', which they commented on as follows:

> An interactive strategy promotes harmonious relations between a firm and the public by reducing the gap between public expectations and business performance. This is often accomplished through a serious management commitment to dialogue with its stakeholders.
>
> Frederick *et al.*, 1992, p. 104

So, the stakeholder model leads to quite specific prescriptions about how ethical and social responsibility are united with strategic management. In general terms, this implies that management has to act so as to enable the firm 'to serve as a vehicle for co-ordinating stakeholder interests' (Evan and Freeman, 1993, p. 262), and that management has a political role in managing conflicts amongst stakeholder groups.

The stakeholder model can be contrasted with both the previous models we have considered. Whereas the social responsiveness model sees the source of strategic social challenges as located in the social environment and as being processed by the senior management's strategic planning process, and the moral leadership model made ethical management an entirely internal matter, the stakeholder model sees the emergence and resolution of strategic social and ethical issues in a more complicated way. This is because the simple distinction between external environment and internal organization is partially broken down by the development of the firm itself as a 'forum of stakeholder interaction' (Evan and Freeman, 1993, p. 263). To put this another way, the organization has become a network of relationships with stakeholders, some internal and some external.

How do managers share decision making with stakeholders and manage the power aspects of the process of decision making? Frederick *et al.* (1992) suggest that the management response to stakeholders depends on the company's stake in maintaining the status quo and management's perceptions of the validity of the stakeholders' concerns. Consequently managers may, variously, resist stakeholder demands, avoid conflict with stakeholders, accommodate them, co-operate with them or collaborate with them. The nature of the management response is likely to be a shifting and evolving one, as issues change over time and the relative importance of different stakeholder groups rises and falls.

Collective strategy

The stakeholder model assumes that the firm has gone some way towards recognizing the right of stakeholders to participate in strategic decision making and so the decisions are not unilaterally made by management. 'The key point about corporate stakeholders is that they may, and frequently do, share decision-making power with a company's managers' (Frederick *et al.*, 1992, p. 9).

This implies a redefinition of the values guiding business decisions. Hosmer (1994), for example, suggested that strategic changes can be measured using applied ethical principles:

> What effect will this proposed change have upon our long-term, rather than merely our short-term, self interests? Is this proposed change open and honest and truthful; and something of which we could all be proud if it were to become widely known? Does it build a sense of community among all our stakeholders, or does it tend to destroy – or even worse, to exploit – that sense of community?
>
> Hosmer, 1994, p. 25

Hosmer's view implies that strategic action must be judged not only by the instrumentality of strategic action, but also by its contribution to a sense of collective strategy on behalf of all the stakeholders. This points towards some aspects of what we would see as a pragmatic view of strategy, one embracing a view that the widest possible consensus is desirable, and a view that consensus should be based on honest and open dialogue of all the participating stakeholders.

Is the stakeholder model feasible?

The stakeholder theory has its critics (Argenti, 1989). The whole formulation can sound very persuasive and attractive because of its pluralist assumptions, but is it realistic? Do many real situations approximate the shared decision making of the model? How many stakeholder groups are really able to take part constructively and fruitfully in the defining and resolving of the strategic issues facing firms?

In our view, the problem with all this discussion of the managers sharing power with stakeholders is that it is far from clear that the current systems and culture of corporate decision making, at least in the US and the UK, are satisfactory in ensuring sufficient involvement of stakeholders in strategic decision making – especially of the general public stakeholder.

And even if stakeholders are given a seat at the decision-making table, the quality and nature of the interaction between management and stakeholders is obviously quite critical to the definition of the stakeholder model. At one extreme, the interaction might be such as to enable the managers to influence the stakeholders in the interests of long-term profitability.

Of course, at the present time there are actually legal barriers in the shape of corporate law in the way of managers conducting affairs to the benefit of the stakeholders. Evan and Freeman (1993), referring to the US, suggest that boards of directors should include representatives of stakeholder groups and that corporate law needs to be amended so that companies can be managed for the benefit of its stakeholders. Such structural changes would have a big impact on the purpose of the firm.

The ethics of international business

Issues in the ethics of international business have been explored by Donaldson (1989, 1991). He claims that business academics have neglected the moral element of international business, whilst having studied the problems of international business, the structure of global markets and the strategies of multinational corporations.

One of Donaldson's contributions to the ethics of international business is a list of ten fundamental human rights, which he offers as 'bottom-line moral considerations for multinational corporations' (Donaldson, 1991, p. 140). His concern is with the rights which should be respected absolutely; in his terms, he is concerned with minimal duties that should be regarded as mandatory, rather

than corporate conduct better than this which would be praise-
worthy.

Of course, to fail in a minimum duty to observe fundamental
human rights would be to harm someone or some group in terms
of their human rights. A right protects something of importance; if
the protection is breached, harm occurs. This identifies Donaldson's
approach to the ethics of international business with the 'no harm
principle' which we associated earlier in this chapter with the view
of ethics as a constraint on business and burdensome. As he puts it,
'Our aim is to inquire, for example, whether a foreign corporation's
minimal duties include refusing to hire children in a Honduran
assembly plant, even if doing so harms the company's competitive
position' (Donaldson, 1991, p. 140).

Donaldson arrived at his statement of the ten fundamental
human rights after a consideration of existing statements such as
the 'Universal Declaration of Human Rights', which includes rights
to social security, employment, health care and education. His own
list of rights consists of items each meeting three criteria: (a) the
right protects something of extreme importance, (b) which is subject
to significant and recurring threats and (c) which generates afford-
able and fairly distributed burdens. The full list is as follows:

1   The right to freedom of physical movement
2   The right to ownership of property
3   The right to freedom from torture
4   The right to a fair trial
5   The right to nondiscriminatory treatment
6   The right to physical security
7   The right to freedom of speech and association
8   The right to minimal education
9   The right to political participation
10 The right to subsistence.

Multinational businesses are seen by Donaldson as having a minimal duty to avoid depriving people of these rights and, in many
cases, a duty to protect people from being deprived of them. So, for
example, the multinational has duties to establish appropriate procedures and to educate lower level managers to protect employees
from being deprived of their right to nondiscriminatory behaviour.
Other duties identified by Donaldson include: providing safety
equipment (right to physical security), not barring the emergence of

trade unions (right to freedom of speech and association), not employing child labour (right to minimal education), not supporting dictatorships and not bribing elected officials (right to political participation).

Donaldson is also concerned about the ethical standards that are not international and the moral dilemma this poses for the multinational corporation in deciding on its business practices. His approach in this case is to develop an ethical algorithm for corporate decision making on permissible business practices. This provides a decision-making route which takes account of the possible violation of human rights, the necessity of the business practice, the level of economic development of the host country and home country moral values. The algorithm does not allow violation of human rights, nor does it allow practices that are permissible because of the host country's level of economic development but would not be regarded as permissible by the home country under relevantly similar conditions. It also requires companies to speak out against practices which are necessary to do business successfully but are not violations of human rights. Our interpretation of Donaldson's algorithm is presented in diagrammatic form in Figure 9.2.

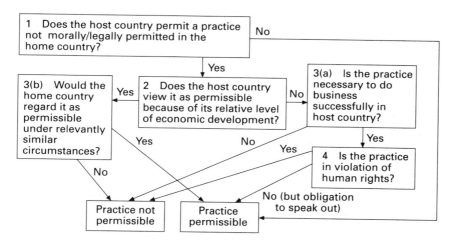

Figure 9.2 *Ethical algorithm for international business. Source: Based on proposals for an algorithm by Thomas Donaldson (1989), The Ethics of International Business (Oxford University Press)*

The implicit framework of Donaldson's thinking is the social responsiveness model. This is evident from his view that the ethical standards within the multinational firm (assumed to reflect the standards of the home country) may not match those in its environment (that is, the host country); consequently, there is a moral or ethical challenge offered by the environment and there is a requirement for a response which will adapt the multinational firm to its context. His proposals for a decision-making algorithm to handle the decision making about this ethical challenge also marks his work as framed within a modernist strategic planning model.

Intercompany ethics

Ethical conduct by firms within a strategic network is essential: it might be said that it is itself a source of competitive advantage for the network of firms.

Strategic networks, which are made up of a number of formally independent companies that co-operate as suppliers and buyers in the production of a good or service, can be seen as a special case of the stakeholder model. This is because the strategic network appears to be co-ordinated for the benefit of all the constituent firms. The 'hub' firm in a strategic network develops win–win relationships with its suppliers and buyers. This can be contrasted with the more competitive pattern posited in the 'competitive advantage' model of Michael Porter. Jarillo (1993) characterizes Porter's thinking as follows:

> the profits that a company can expect to make are determined, first by the profit potential of its industry, and second by its position within it. And the profit potential of the industry is dependent on how easy it is for suppliers and customers to capture the value being created by the industry. Thus, in order to prosper, a company has to compete not only with its current competitors but also with all potential ones, with its suppliers and with its clients.
>
> Jarillo, 1993, p. 128

In contrast to these win–lose relationships with customers and suppliers, a network of suppliers and buyers in a strategic network cultivate co-operative relationships and invest in specialization which adapts each to the other. Jarillo suggests that strategic networks have self-reinforcing characteristics:

> every characteristic of the network builds on the others: adaptation, specialization, trust, long-term outlook, internal consistency vis-à-vis the outside world, etc., which provide efficiency and flexibility. Those deliver a good competitive position, justifying the existence of the network and reinforcing its characteristics.
>
> Jarillo, 1993, p. 143

The emphasis on trust is important because the firms become dependent on each other – and thus can be exploited. The co-operation and adaptation which leads to greater efficiency and flexibility create the problem of individual firms being taken advantage of because they have become specialized in a way which locks them into the alliance; this specialization and adaptation is of no value outside the network of firms. There is also the issue of who benefits from the greater efficiency. So, trust and a belief in the fairness of those involved are essential to this successful form of business organization, and ethical treatment of suppliers and buyers is integral to these win–win business transactions within the network – it is not a limitation on the transactions. And it can be contrasted with the ethic of 'everybody for himself' which could be said to characterize other forms of interbusiness relationship (Jarillo, 1993, p. 127).

Key points

1 Business ethics is a fertile ground for opinion and argument. The view that ethics are a constraint or limitation on the organization's aims seems to imply that the ethical aspect is a burden and may predispose firms to adopt the 'no harm' principle such that they have an ethical duty not to cause significant harm to customers, the community, employees and so on. An alternative view of the relationship between ethics and strategic aims is that ethics can enrich corporate aims.

2 The climate for attempts to make moral choices within business activity may be changing because of the increasing

importance of public authority. Private businesses are allowed to pursue profit in a political and social environment that expects a certain responsiveness and even active co-operation from businesses in return for a legal framework that protects their activities.

3 Businesses are urged to conduct themselves ethically as a matter of enlightened self-interest; if businesses do not act responsibly, the government will bring in laws to regulate them (Solomon and Hanson, 1985). More recently it has been argued that companies need to act ethically because of the competitive threats of operating in a global economy.

4 There are different models of how organizations unite strategic management and ethical conduct. The social responsiveness model sees the source of strategic social challenges as located in the social environment and as being processed by the senior management's strategic planning process. The moral leadership model makes ethical management an entirely internal matter and, in effect, plays down the centralized strategic planning process by top management. The stakeholder model sees the emergence and resolution of strategic social and ethical issues as taking place through stakeholder interaction, with management working with a network of relationships with stakeholders and sharing decision-making power with the stakeholders.

5 An influential contribution to the ethics of international business has been made by Donaldson (1989, 1991). One of his concerns is with minimal duties that should be regarded as mandatory. His approach to the ethics of international business is consistent with the 'no harm principle'. He also provides a decision-making algorithm which will enable firms to adapt to the ethical and moral climate of the host country without transgressing moral considerations.

6 Ethical conduct within a strategic network is essential: it might be said that it is itself a source of competitive advantage for the network of firms. The key ethical features of the strategic network appear to be trust and fairness.

References

Argenti, J. (1989) *Practical Corporate Planning* (Routledge).

Berman, E., West, J. and Cava, A. (1994) 'Ethics Management in Municipal Governments and Large Firms: Exploring Similarities and Differences', *Administration and Society*, Vol. 26, No. 2, August, pp. 185–204.

Bowie, N. (1995) 'New Directions in Corporate Social Responsibility' in Hoffman, V.W. and Frederick, R.E. (editors) *Business Ethics: Readings and Cases in Corporate Morality* (McGraw-Hill), pp. 597–607.

Chamberlain, N.W. (1973) *The Limits of Corporate Responsibility* (Basic Books).

Donaldson, T. (1989) *The Ethics of International Business* (Oxford University Press).

Donaldson, T.J. (1991) 'Rights in the Global Market' in Freeman, R.E. (editor) *Business Ethics: The State of the Art* (Oxford University Press).

Evan, W.M. and Freeman, R.E. (1993) 'A Stakeholder Theory of the Modern Corporation: Kantian Capitalism' in Chryssides, G.D. and Kaler, J.H. (editors) *An Introduction to Business Ethics* (Chapman & Hall), pp. 254–66.

Follett, M.P. (1941) *Dynamic Administration: The Collected Papers of Mary Parker Follett* (Management Publications Trust Ltd).

Frederick, W.C., Post, J.E. and Davis, K. (1992) *Business and Society: Corporate Strategy, Public Policy, Ethics* (McGraw-Hill).

Freeman, R.E. (1991) 'Introduction' in Freeman, R.E. (editor) *Business Ethics: The State of the Art* (Oxford University Press).

Hosmer, L.T. (1994) 'Strategic Planning as if Ethics Mattered', *Strategic Management Journal*, Vol. 15, pp. 17–35.

Jarillo, J.C. (1993) *Strategic Networks: Creating the Borderless Organization* (Butterworth-Heinemann).

Nutt, P.C. and Backoff, R.W. (1992) *Strategic Management of Public and Third Sector Organizations* (Jossey-Bass).

Peters, T.J. and Waterman, R. H. (1982) *In Search of Excellence* (Harper Collins).

Solomon, R.C. and Hanson, K. (1985) *It's Good Business* (Harper & Row).

Wartick, S.L. and Cochran, P.L. (1995) 'The Evolution of the Corporate Social Performance Model' in Brooks, L.J. (1995) *Professional Ethics for Accountants* (West Publishing).

10

Managing strategic change

Introduction

The literature on the management of change is large and unruly. It has been written from a variety of perspectives, taking many different starting points. There is a need to place the existing theories and concepts into some kind of framework and check this against academic research on the processes, variations and consequences of the management of strategic change. Such a framework needs to be academically adequate, but it should also have clear practical implications for managing in real situations.

Each set of ideas on managing strategic change implicitly offers answers to questions. The assumption made here will be that the following questions are the critical ones.

1 What makes strategic change difficult?
2 How willing and committed are members of an organization to making strategic changes?
3 What processes or types of intervention can be used to effect strategic changes successfully?

We have selected for closer examination three models of the management of change – the implementation model, the problem solving model and the political model – seeing in them a cumulative attempt to come to grips with strategic change. Each contributes important insights into what makes strategic change difficult and what needs to be done. The first model concentrates on the formal organizational systems, the second introduces the importance of the cultural component and the third introduces the importance of the power structure within the organization. Consequently, they end up being offered here not as alternatives but as complementary theories which can be drawn on in devising effective strategies for managing strategic change.

Strategy implementation

When managing strategic change is seen as identical to the process of strategy implementation, the main concern is likely to be seen as translating corporate goals and strategy into effective functional operations (production, marketing, finance and human resource management), including allocating resources to enable strategies to be implemented. In each functional area, targets may be set (e.g. target sales volumes, target rates of return on investment, target levels of liquidity) and appropriate policies established (e.g. policies on the selection of markets and segments, policies on funding) (McNamee, 1992).

The implicit assumptions of this model are that achieving strategic change has to confront the difficulty of connecting strategic management and operational management, that there is no particular problem of motivating organizational members to implement strategy and that formal procedures and systems may be used successfully to set targets, allocate resources, etc.

The difficulty of connecting strategic management and operational management can be a simple lack of ability by managers to take abstract plans and work out the implications for operational activity. This may be a widespread difficulty. Ohmae (1982) suggests: 'Too many companies try to short-circuit the necessary steps between the identification of critical issues and line implementation of solutions by skipping the intermediate steps: planning for operational improvement and organizing for concrete actions' (Ohmae, 1982, p. 21). This may occur because firms have not developed the requisite management skills for implementing strategy amongst their strategic and operating managers. Thus, strategy documents may gather dust and remain in the realm of ideas rather than action.

Another difficulty arises because of the limitations of managerial capacity. This occurs where the total demand on management time due to existing operating problems and the time required to implement new strategies reaches the point where the management systems are overloaded. Ansoff and McDonnell (1990) have put forward the proposition that whenever 'both operating and strategic work compete for management attention, the former drives out the latter' (Ansoff and McDonnell, 1990, p. 419). Consequently, making the necessary changes and improvements in operational activities required by a new strategy may prove difficult because line managers are busy meeting the ongoing problems of operational management. Delays and patchy implementation may be the result.

In the face of these difficulties, top management may apply strong pressures on departments and line managers to implement strategy through the formal procedures of budget allocation and the formal control systems. Such pressure can bring compliance, even where management systems are overloaded.

Extending the implementation model

When some of the implicit assumptions of the implementation model are evidently dubious – for example, when there are motivational problems or top managers oppose the changes – then the implementation model must be widened in its scope. Consequently, implementation may be seen as also requiring adjustments and changes in organizational leadership, culture and company structure (McNamee, 1992, p. 218). Thus, major changes in strategy may require a change of leadership, or the top managers may require management development. New strategies may require new cultures. And, perhaps more obviously, a company's organizational structure may need changing to help implement a new strategy more successfully; the fit and relationship between strategy and structure has been highlighted in the strategic management literature, and is illustrated in Figure 10.1.

Implementation problems

In practice, many of the problems experienced by companies in implementing strategic decisions are as expected (see Figure 10.2). For example, the limits of management skills in planning and managing change may be exposed by the need to move from the abstract strategic decision to the concrete details of the changes

Figure 10.1 *Managing change – the strategy implementation framework*

needed; this may show up as insufficient detail in management specifications of key implementation tasks and actions, and poor co-ordination of implementation activities. And there are signs that management systems may often be overloaded since there are frequent reports that competing activities and crises cause implementation to be neglected.

Figure 10.2 *Strategic implementation problems – Alexander (1989)*

Alexander's survey of private businesses identified a number of important problems which occur at the implementation stage. Perhaps surprisingly, relatively few of his respondents considered that organizational structure changes were a problem, relatively few thought that financial resources were insufficient and relatively few said that rewards and incentives had been insufficient to get employee acceptance of the changes.

The sample comprised ninety-three strategic business units belonging to private sector firms in the United States, most of which were included in Fortune's list of 1000 leading industrial companies. Data collection was based on a questionnaire, followed up by in-depth telephone interviews with twenty-one chief executives. The study also drew on another study involving twenty-five interviews with heads of governmental agencies.

Respondents to the questionnaire were asked to select a recently implemented strategic decision about which they had personal knowledge. This produced evidence on the implementation of decisions to introduce new products or services, opening and starting up a new plant or facility, entering new markets, discontinuing products, withdrawing from markets, acquiring or merging with other firms and so on. The most common of the substantial or major problems are shown in Table 10.1.

Table 10.1   *Implementation problems*

Problem	% *saying it* was *sub-stantial/major problem*
Implementation took more time than originally allocated	28
Major problems surfaced during implementation that had not been identified beforehand	26
Competing activities and crises distracted attention from implementing this decision	20
Capabilities of employees involved were not sufficient	20
Co-ordination of implementation activities was not effective enough	18
Uncontrollable factors in the external situation had an adverse impact on implementation	17
Leadership and direction provided by depart-mental managers were not adequate enough	17
Key implementation tasks and activities were not defined in enough detail	17

Base: 93 strategic business units.

Based on his interview data, Alexander recommended the following as ingredients in successful strategic implementation:

- communication (two-way ideally)
- a well-formulated strategic decision
- sufficient resources (money, human, technical expertise and time)
- an implementation plan with an adequate level of detail and responses for possible problems worked out.

But some of the other implementation problems experienced by firms may be indicating the shortcomings of the implementation model. First, frequent reports that implementation has suffered because there is inadequate leadership and direction by lower level managers may show that there has been insufficient strategic leadership of a kind which generates shared values and commitment – in other words, the managers at an operational level may often have not been motivated to use their initiative appropriately. Second, the frequent reports of implementation taking longer than expected may be caused by problems of resistance to change. Third, perhaps the frequency of reports of unforeseen problems, competing crises and adverse environmental impacts on implementation all testify to the limited ability of managers to think and plan rationally, suggesting that change always calls for a degree of creativity and experimentation and cannot be completely programmed.

The Peters and Waterman model

The problem of managing strategic change is discussed by Peters and Waterman (1982) as an aspect of their concern for developing organizations that have a bias for action, a bias for getting things done. This concern is grounded in a critique of the formal bureaucratic structures which deliver the routine activities of businesses but are not good at making changes. This concern is expressed as follows: 'ideas about cost efficiency and economies of scale are leading us into building big bureaucracies that simply cannot act' (Peters and Waterman, 1982, p. 134). The problem of change in the bureaucracy seems to spring from the difficulty of mobilizing both commitment and the momentum for strategic change:

Most organizations, when confronted with an overwhelming strategic problem, either give it to planning staffs or tack it onto the objectives of numerous otherwise busy line managers. If staff is supposed to solve the problem, commitment never develops. If the usual line organization is supposed to solve it, momentum never develops.
Peters and Waterman, 1982, p. 133

Peters and Waterman use an anecdote about an Exxon Asian affiliate, and its reported success on the strategy front, to imply that strategic improvements are composed of continuous pragmatic problem solving rather than 'shrewd foresight and bold strategic moves' (1982, p. 125). Elsewhere they claim:

The excellent companies are not really 'long-term thinkers.' They don't have better five-year plans. Indeed, the formal plans at the excellent companies are often marked by little detail, or don't exist at all (recall the complete absence of corporate level planners in many of them).

1992, p. 324

So, if planning specialists, formal plans and bold strategic moves are not the answer and the line managers who occupy the bureaucratic positions of the formal structure cannot generate the necessary momentum, what is to be done?

Their answer is essentially to get line managers to operate outside of the formal bureaucratic structures. Consequently, their model of change puts its faith in informality, temporary structures and pragmatic problem solving. Let us look at each of these points in turn.

Informality

Their message is that organizations need to encourage informal networks. Why? Because 'rich informal communication leads to more action, more experiments, more learning' (Peters and Waterman, 1982, p. 124). Management can promote informal communication in a variety of ways; for example, by requiring employees to wear name tags with first names on them, by adopting open door policies, by the practice of MBWA (management by walking about) and by designing physical layouts that promote face-to-face contacts.

Temporary structures

Task forces and project teams are temporary structures, both of which can be effective in solving and managing problems. Peters and Waterman describe the task force (when not perverted by bureaucratic contexts) as a remarkably effective problem-solving tool and as suitable for multifunctional problem solving. The task forces have to be properly designed. They are thought to work best:

- when they have small memberships
- when members comprise people with appropriate seniority in the light of the problem being confronted
- when membership is voluntary

- when pulled together quickly
- when they have to complete their work in a short timescale (say six months at most)
- when follow-up is swift.

Task forces should not have 'staff' persons permanently assigned and should not produce long formal reports.

Problem solving

The key word in connection with their view of problem solving is probably the word 'pragmatic'. Pragmatic problem-solving implies getting on and doing something, rather than getting stuck in analysis and debate. Pragmatic problem-solving also means adjusting decisions in the light of experience of acting in the situation. So, changes emerge as attempted solutions to problems, attempted solutions which test out the organization's understanding of the situation. In other words, change proceeds by experimentation to solve problems. These experiments, which Peters and Waterman label as 'doing things', build up into strategies: ' ... our excellent companies appear to do their way into strategies, not vice versa' (1982, p. 74).

The organizational leaders take the experimental actions and orchestrate and label them 'into lasting commitments to a new strategic direction' (1982, p. 75). And so strategic change takes on the form of an accumulation of successful experiments within a company, with early successful experiments providing a basis for building a momentum for change and specific successful experiments providing a platform for company-wide change on the basis of diffusion.

Leadership and social change

But why should informality, temporary structures and pragmatic problem-solving work for the organization; why don't they produce conflicts with the formal and permanent structure or chaos and disruption? Peters and Waterman believe that autonomy works for the business because there is a discipline based on shared values:

the free-wheeling environments in which *ad-hoc* behaviour flourishes are only superficially unstructured and chaotic. Underlying the absence of formality lie shared purposes, as well as an internal tension and a competitiveness that makes these cultures as tough as nails.

1982, p. 134

So, their approach posits some essential qualities to the successful organization – namely the existence of shared purposes (values) throughout the organization and a culture of competitiveness which together constitute an internal rather than an external discipline to achieve corporate goals. How can these be created?

Peters and Waterman identify the role of top managers as responsible for shaping and managing shared values and suggest that effective top managers provide visions and values which they implant by being visible and persistent. The values that appear to have been critical in the value systems of the excellent companies include:

- the importance of quality and service
- attention to detail
- treating people as individuals
- informality
- innovation by rank and file employees.

This top management role could be seen, but is not seen, as requiring top managers with charismatic personalities. Instead it is seen as requiring a style of management behaviour and, because it is a style, this behaviour can be developed by the individuals concerned. We will be examining this in more detail in the next chapter.

There is also a tactical dimension to creating the right environment for pragmatic problem solving and experimentation. The top managers need a tactical sense in building up the momentum for change. This involves selecting the right initial problems for solution: these are problems which are easier to solve and where there is organizational support for doing something about them. Early success, in other words, is a tactical requirement for continued attempts to experiment. And when there is some momentum for change it is important, tactically, that management celebrates successful experiments and tolerates modest failures so as not to suppress risk taking. This tactical sense can, and probably should, be distinguished from the work the top managers do in orchestrating and labelling action into a strategic change of direction: tactics keep the experiments flowing; the orchestrating and labelling transform the stream of experiments into a definite strategic direction.

The management of change via problem solving

So, the ideas of Peters and Waterman seem to suggest a fairly simple model of managing strategic changes, at least when looked at in outline terms. It is assumed that big bureaucracy makes change difficult, that organizational members are willing and committed to change providing the leadership establishes the right shared values and that informal processes and temporary structures are needed to bring about successful strategic change. Further, their model equates strategic change with an accumulation of experiments conducted in a spirit of pragmatic problem solving, but orchestrated and labelled into a commitment to a new strategic direction. This is shown in Figure 10.3.

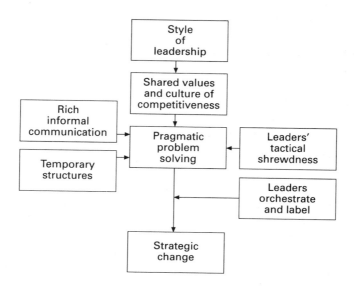

Figure 10.3 *Strategic change as an accumulation of experiments*

Contradictions

There has been a growing interest in the 'contradictions' found within organizations. Peters and Waterman (1982) touched on this in their seminal work:

> Any business is always an amalgam of important contradictions – cost versus service, operations versus innovation, formality versus informality, a 'control' orientation versus a 'people' orientation, and the like.
>
> Peters and Waterman, 1982, pp. 284–5

As we saw in the previous section, they recommended that organizations choose the use of informality and temporary structures rather than formality and the permanent structures of the bureaucracy if they want to bring about change. Indeed, they suggested that excellent companies had value systems identifying with 'one side of these apparent contradictions' (1982, p. 285). In other words, they decided in the end that these are not real contradictions because choosing one side delivers the other anyway. Take the cost versus service contradiction noted above. Late in their book they conclude: 'Cost and efficiency, over the long run, follow from the emphasis on quality, service, innovativeness … ' (1982, p. 321).

Mintzberg (1995) has in recent years taken up the issue of contradiction, which he sees as a characteristic of the 'system of forces' centred on any organization. The seven most fundamental forces he identifies are:

* direction
* efficiency
* proficiency
* concentration
* innovation
* co-operation
* competition.

The nature and origin of these forces is unclear from Mintzberg's analysis, but he links the dominance of individual forces to coherent organizational forms. Thus what he terms a 'machine organization' (found in mass production firms) is the result of the force for efficiency dominating the others. Likewise, 'entrepreneurial organization' results from the dominance of the force for direction, the 'professional organization' is the result of the dominance of proficiency, 'adhocracy' is the result of the dominance of innovation and the 'diversified organization' results from the dominance of concentration. When no single force dominates, then hybrid organizational forms develop. So, the picture he constructs is one of a tug of war between these forces, with the form of the organization being determined by those that are dominant (see Figure 10.4).

Organization form	Force
Entrepreneurial	Direction
Machine	Efficiency
Diversified	Concentration
Professional	Proficiency
Adhocracy	Innovation
	Co-operation Competition

Figure 10.4 *Mintzberg's forms and forces*

The forces are never really elucidated, but we wonder if it is assumed implicitly that they are really the effects of culture. For at one point Mintzberg refers to the effects of a *dominant* culture (p. 742). He also says that an organizational form (configuration in his language) is not merely a structure and a power system; each is also a culture in its own right (p. 742).

Mintzberg advances two propositions about the relationships between these forces. First, a dominating force can debilitate the other forces. This can be a problem when the organization requires these other forces in order to respond to the need for change; and in consequence of this weakness of the other forces, the organization fails to adapt and, in Mintzberg's words, 'goes out of control'. For example, a machine organization may suffer from a weakness in its force for direction and may not be able to develop a new strategy because the drive for efficiency has suppressed its capacity to be entrepreneurial. Second, an organization can become paralysed when two or more forces are rivals for the dominant position.

These propositions emerge from Mintzberg's particular understanding of the concept of contradiction. We understand him to mean that contradictions are formed by the *oppositions* of the forces within the system, and that the system either gets out of control because one force is too dominant relative to the rest, or the opposing forces are so even that there is paralysis.

Conflicts between groups

These contradictions in the system of forces are related to the conflicts between groups inside the organization. Thus, Mintzberg suggests that the paralysis created by two opposing forces is illustrated by 'the battles between the R&D people who promote new product innovation and the production people in favour of stabilizing manufacturing for operating efficiency' (Mintzberg, 1995, p. 745). In this example, departmental rivalry is directly linked to two opposing forces; departments are therefore the agents of the forces in Mintzberg's analysis. The conflicts between groups within the organization appear to follow a structural logic because, as Mintzberg says, the 'forces tend to infiltrate parts of an organization (for example, direction in senior management, efficiency in accounting)' (1995, p. 747).

Mintzberg is interested in what happens when external changes (e.g. new inventions, changes in market conditions) cause the needs of organizations to alter and they are, in consequence, required to change their organizational form. Obviously, from what has already been said, sometimes such change is inhibited by the debilitating effects of one of the forces being too dominant and in other cases the organization may be paralysed by two or more very strong and opposing forces. The inhibition of change due to systemic contradictions, is manifested through the resistance of people. 'Two sides battle, usually an "old guard" committed to the status quo challenged by a group of "Young Turks" in favour of the change' (1995, pp. 746–7). Even where change is accomplished, the period of transition in organizational form may be experienced as difficult and conflictual. So Mintzberg approaches the management of change as an aspect of managing contradictory forces.

Co-operation and competition

Mintzberg suggests that two forces – co-operation and competition

– have a special role in managing contradictory forces, but are themselves contradictory.

Co-operation is identified with ideology, which is 'a rich culture in an organization, the uniqueness and attractiveness of which binds the members tightly to it' (1995, p. 747). Ideology, which may be created by charismatic leaders, helps the different forces within the organization to work together instead of dominating or opposing each other and thus helps the organization to adapt. This is explained at the behavioural level by Mintzberg positing a growth of respect: 'People behind these different forces develop a grudging respect for one another: when it matters, they actively cooperate for the common good' (1995, p. 748). So, ideology is a reconciler of contradiction. However, ideologies are themselves hard to create and change and can make organizational change difficult by becoming a force for maintaining the status quo.

Mintzberg identifies competition with politics in an organization. Politics can seem petty and a waste of resources: some people 'lord their power over everyone else' and block changes in the interests of the status quo; those behind opposing forces fight skirmishes and battles; and political manoeuvring can be spurred by the pursuit of personal ends. But politics can also be a positive force for change since challenges to the status quo may be necessary: 'In the absence of entrepreneurial or intrapreneurial capabilities, and sometimes despite them, politics may be the only force available to stimulate change' (1995, p. 751).

Mintzberg favours a balanced combination of ideology and politics to achieve organizational effectiveness in the long run. By balancing these two forces secondary forces are assisted to challenge the dominant one, the organization is prevented from being too insular and excessive divisiveness is kept under control. He sees this happening in such a way that most of the time the organization is in a co-operative mode (tempered by healthy internal competition), but with occasional vigorous politics to assist more fundamental change to take place.

The political model

In what we call the political model, strategic change becomes difficult when an organization is no longer managing the contradiction between ideology and politics and when, in consequence, contradictions between fundamental forces lead to debilitating weaknesses or paralysis.

The importance of the willingness and commitment of organizational members to make strategic changes is somewhat ambiguous in this model: are they merely a structural artefact of the balance of forces or are they the very essence of the forces themselves?

In terms of intervention, the political model stresses the critical importance of political processes in conjunction with ideology, whereas the problem-solving model puts the primary focus on ideology (shared values) alone.

Empirical studies

It is difficult to validate the various models we have considered. There is a major UK study which looked at the management of strategic change as a contributory factor in competitive success (Pettigrew and Whipp, 1993 – see Figure 10.5), but its level of abstraction is such as to make it difficult to choose between the three models we have just been discussing. Indeed, there were signs that all three models might have some validity. For example, some of Pettigrew and Whipp's analysis draws attention to the need to link the strategic and operational levels properly. Consequently, they suggest:

- breaking down strategic intentions into actionable components
- the allocation of responsibility for these components
- setting clear and exacting targets
- rethinking communication and reward systems.

These remarks are consistent with the implementation model.

Figure 10.5   *Pettigrew and Whipp's (1993) study of strategic change and competitive success*

Pettigrew and Whipp (1993), in Managing Change for Competitive Success, reported the results of a study of seven firms in four sectors (automobile manufacture, book publishing, merchant banking and life assurance). The study began in 1985 and was finished in

1989. They carried out more than 350 interviews in the firms.

Their answer on why firms differ in performance is couched in terms of a discussion of two abilities:

1 the ability to identify and understand competitive forces
2 the ability to mobilize and manage the resources required for a strategic response.

Assessing the environment

'The need for management to assess environment, make choices and mount the necessary alterations is vital to explaining contrasting performances between firms' (1993, p. 28). They suggest that organizations need to become open learning systems and that environmental analysis can not be left to technical specialists. All levels of an organization have to take part in analysing and interpreting information about the environment.

Mobilizing and managing the firm's resources

They argue with respect to the firm's resources that a competitive strength is based, usually, on a collection of abilities, which have been created over time as layers of competences and advantages. In their analysis, they place considerable emphasis on human resources. The logical implication is that there should be a focus on human resource management (HRM) within firms which are good at strategic change. And this is what Pettigrew and Whipp argue. An HRM approach, they say, cannot be created quickly. They suggest that it is a long-term process, a learning process, brought about by 'positive spirals of development' (1993, p. 283).

They assume that the firm's strategy cannot just concern senior management – the whole organization has to be mobilized for strategic change. The organization's leaders have to challenge, raise energy levels and foster leadership at all levels.

Adaptation and adjustment

They say that the strategic and operational levels need to be linked. However, they talk in terms of interpretation and adaptation rather than simple translation of strategic intentions into actions. And they suggest that change is marked by 'continual assessments, repeated choices and multiple adjustments' (1993, p. 31). The repeated choices and adjustments they refer to can be taken as a characterization of strategy as 'emergent'. This means, amongst other things, that the

'hen implemented may turn out differently from what was
indeed the additive effect of otherwise separate decisions
acts of implementation may be so powerful that they overwhelm
the original intention and even help create an entirely new context for
future strategic decision making' (1993, pp. 281–2).

On the other hand, Pettigrew and Whipp also say that it is possible to convert short-run adjustments into a strategic posture (1993, p. 282).

Strategic coherence

Coherence is defined as concerned with 'the ability to hold the business together as a totality while simultaneously changing it, often over lengthy periods of time' (1993, p. 283). They seem to say, in effect, that a firm can engineer coherence by designing a feasible, sensible and plausible strategy. So, the strategy must:

- have consistent goals
- be an adaptive response to its environment
- provide for the maintenance of competitive advantage
- not over-tax resources
- not create unsolvable problems.

The strategy process

Their view of how strategic change is managed rejects the notion that strategy is structured in 'neat, successive stages of analysis, choice and implementation' (1993, p. 31). For a start, the competitive conditions are unstable, dynamic and require continuous strategic change. They see knowing the competitive environment and strategic management (mobilizing and managing resources for change) as two processes which take place continuously and simultaneously.

Improving strategic change

They suggest various kinds of practical action to improve the capacity for strategic change, including:

- networks that link the firm with stakeholders
- the use of specialist task forces or teams to contribute to the assessment process
- articulation of successful outcomes to build confidence
- breaking down strategic intentions into actionable components
- allocation of responsibility for these components

- setting clear and exacting targets
- rethinking communication and reward systems
- ensuring a coherence of belief and purpose among the senior managers
- HRM initiatives which produce apposite knowledge
- ensuring interorganizational coherence (customers, suppliers, distributors and collaborators)
- fostering the ability to manage interrelated and emergent changes.

Comments on Pettigrew and Whipp's ideas

1 In many ways their ideas relate to the work of Quinn (1991) on logical incrementalism.
2 Their work seems to fit into a new modernist paradigm. Thus, Pettigrew and Whipp say that the ability to compete depends on the ability of the organization to know its competitive environment and to control (i.e. mobilize and manage) its resources for organizational change. But they stress that being strategic is a hard process and emphasize the internal operation of the firm. New modernists assume that there are limits to what is knowable about the environment and so an experimental approach to change is required; they assume that organizational control is limited and so change is brought in opportunistically. By stressing a processual theory Pettigrew and Whipp suggest that there is a battle against these limits, especially the organizational ones, and thus they highlight the role of adaptation rather than simple implementation in strategic management.

Their specific points about open learning organizations and leadership suggest both that you cannot rely on staff specialists for environmental assessment, and that the organization cannot easily or routinely generate the momentum for change. Thus, briefly, when they talk about open learning organizations, in which they say people at all levels are involved in analysing and interpreting the environment, it reminds us of the Peters and Waterman view that strategy cannot be left to staff specialists. When discussing the role of leadership it is clear that they think the organization has to be lifted out of its usual mode of existence. So, they emphasize the leader's responsibility for building the right kind of climate and setting out new directions for the organization and, they say, the leader has to raise energy levels, suggesting that line management in the usual state lacks the energy required. These assumptions are very compatible with those made in the problem-solving model of Peters and Waterman.

There is also a strong concern in their work for the political dimension. They lay stress on the following: the divisions within the organization, saying that the firm consists of individuals and groups, who differ in motivation, information and frames of reference; the contradictory forces during periods of change, when they discuss the need to change organizations while holding them together; some of the political practices of top management, when they refer to the importance of ensuring a coherence of belief and purpose among the senior managers.

A single model?

The three models are quite different (see Table 10.2). Perhaps then, all three models provide parts of the jigsaw puzzle of managing major strategic changes? We believe they do. The question then becomes how can they be brought together as a useful framework for thinking about the practice of managing strategic change.

The modernist model of strategic management implies the implementation model of strategic change. It sequences strategic analysis

Table 10.2   *Three models of strategic change*

Model	Main concern	Organizational assumption
Implementation model	How to translate corporate goals and strategy into effective functional operations	Use existing structures and procedures to translate strategy into operational activity
Problem-solving model	How to overcome bureaucratic inertia	Use informal communication and temporary structures to get action
Political model	How to overcome resistance to change	Use ideology and politics to manage the organization's systemic contradictions

and strategy choice prior to implementation. The question of selecting a structure suited to the strategy is placed within the analysis
required for the implementation stage. A broadened view of the
implementation model sees the need to consider questions of
power (leadership) and culture as issues alongside other implementation issues. In other words, strategy choice determines (and
precedes) changes in operational activity, organizational structure,
culture and leadership.

The problem-solving model indicates that there is a need to take
involvement in strategy formulation and implementation deeper
down organizational structures but within a discipline created by
the cultural or value system of the organization. Thus cultural
change needs to precede the changes in the organization's operational activities.

The insights of the political model are that the cultural framework cannot be successfully established in a vacuum and that politics are needed to update the cultural values which define the organization's value system. This implies that the political processes
need to be got right before the changes in the operating systems.

Arguing inductively from a consideration of these models, managing strategic change ought to proceed from developing an appropriate political context within the firm, to developing a suitable cultural or value system, and finally to more formally planned strategic change. Of course, firms may go through approximately this
sequence without it being formally announced that this is what
they are doing. For example, firms that have been through a turn-
around process may have started off with such poor profitability
and cash flow that they had to rationalize and cut the organization
to bring costs under control. This could also destabilize the existing
power structures within the firm and allow senior management to
operate in an autocratic way for a period of time. Formal programmes of cultural change may then be launched to counter the
poor morale and pessimism created by the poor company performance and the rationalization. Where the programmes have
involved delayering and breaking down functional hierarchies,
there will be further impacts on the political context. Perhaps, formal strategic planning processes take over the shaping of change
when the political and cultural changes have created sufficient consensus around which it is possible to formulate a clear strategy. In
this way, the process of change could move through overlapping
but sequencial political, cultural and formal strategy phases.

Key points

1 There are different perspectives on managing strategic change. We have looked at these in terms of three models: the implementation model, the problem-solving model and the political model. At the heart of each of these are different underlying concerns. For example, how can this strategy be made the basis of a new set of operations? How can the dead-hand of bureaucracy be overcome to generate change and produce turned-on employees? How can resistance to change be managed? It is also clear that different models posit different management measures to get the requisite organizational changes.

2 The one major UK study which looked at the management of change as a contributory factor in competitive success (Pettigrew and Whipp, 1993) seemed to validate some of the assumptions and ideas of the three models we have been discussing.

3 All three models possibly provide parts of the jigsaw puzzle of managing major strategic changes. They need to be brought together to form a useful framework for thinking about the practice of managing strategic change. Arguing inductively from a consideration of these models, managing strategic change ought to proceed from developing an appropriate political context within the firm, to developing a suitable cultural or value system, and finally to strategic change. This would be subject to contingent circumstances and their impact in terms of urgency and opportunity.

4 Organizations can improve their capacity for successful strategic change by means of a wide range of measures, such as: networking with stakeholders; using participative methods for carrying out strategic assessments; an active role by senior management (praising and publicizing successes, ensuring strategic coherence); effective management of implementation (identifying actionable components of strategy, allocation of responsibility for implementation, setting clear and exacting targets, etc.); appropriately designed communication, reward and HRM systems; and entering into partnerships with customers, suppliers, distributors and collaborators.

References

Alexander, L.D. (1989) 'Successfully Implementing Strategic Decisions' in Asch, D. and Bowman, C. (editors) *Readings in Strategic Management* (Macmillan).

Ansoff, I. and McDonnell, E. (1990) *Implanting Strategic Management* (Prentice Hall).

McNamee, P. (1992) *Strategic Management* (Butterworth-Heinemann).

Mintzberg, H. (1995) 'Beyond Configuration: Forces and Forms in Effective Organizations' in Mintzberg, H., Quinn, J.B. and Ghoshal, S. (editors) *The Strategy Process* (Prentice Hall).

Ohmae, K. (1982) The Mind of the Strategist (McGraw-Hill).

Peters, T. and Waterman, R. (1982) *In Search of Excellence* (Harper Collins).

Pettigrew, A. and Whipp, R. (1993) *Managing Change for Competitive Success* (Blackwell).

Quinn, J.B. (1991) 'Strategic Change: "Logical Incrementalism"' in Mintzberg, H. and Quinn, J.B. (editors) *The Strategy Process* (Prentice Hall).

The strategic manager

Introduction

In the twentieth century, as firms grew larger and the numbers of managers increased, there was a trend towards specialization which produced the familiar pattern of organizational units based on functions (production, marketing, R&D, etc.). Consequently, the concept of general management can be seen as a necessary management activity to integrate and co-ordinate the work of the separate functions. In more recent times the general manager's role in co-ordinating the functional activities of the organization has been subsumed within the role of strategic manager. This transition from general manager to strategic manager meant that co-ordination involved more than conflict resolution or arbitration between the different functions; the top managers had now also to provide a strategic competence which synthesized the contributions of the functions to achieve an optimal performance in relation to organizational objectives. Exactly what this strategic competence involves is much debated. Is it a technical competence for strategy analysis and strategy formulation? Is it a leadership competence that endows organizations with vision and meaning, requiring skills in change management and a personal quality of charisma? Is it a competence for creative crafting of strategic change? Is it an intellectual competence for pragmatic and rational problem solving of strategic issues?

In this chapter we focus on the strategic manager as an individual and look at how his or her activities and competences have been conceptualized; we are especially interested in the implications of this for the education and training of strategic managers.

The issue of the education of top managers has been receiving more and more attention within Europe over the last decade. Prior to this, the main dispute in the approach to education of the general manager was between those who maintained that there was no substitute for practical experience and those who considered that education produced a superior approach. This decades-old argument received a new lease of life in the 1980s, when it was argued that business schools were harmful because they taught a narrow and exclusive concern for financial ratios and analytical techniques. In addition, some theorists of strategic management were critical of the assumptions that lay behind the forecasting techniques of long-range and strategic planning. Their arguments seemed to be urging a number of shifts: from analysis-driven to value-driven organizations, from rational decision making to the excitement and commitment of spontaneity and intuition, from management by numbers to the search for innovation and creativity, and from formal planning and hierarchy to informality and learning.

Before this 1980s backlash can be appreciated properly, we need to characterize what had come to signify the dominant mode of strategic thinking. This was the view of strategic management as a technical competence. It was a view which defined strategic managers as technocrats. We will look at this technocratic style of leader and then look at some other styles – transforming, passive-learner and pragmatic – which all contain implicit criticisms of the technocratic style. These four management styles are illustrated in Figure 11.1.

The technocratic leader

The thinking emerging in the 1960s seemed to imply that the organizational leaders' role centred on setting clear corporate objectives, and on allocating organizational resources based on decisions made in the light of the results of analytical techniques and the calculation of key financial ratios. It can be called technocratic because it was preoccupied with technical proficiency in the use of these techniques and was concerned with the allocation of financial resources in the technically most rational way possible.

Considerable attention is paid by the technocratic leader to the

Figure 11.1   *Four strategic management styles*

discipline of setting clear objectives, which may then be expressed as financial targets in private sector companies. Clear objectives and targets are essential for the leader to make judgements about the organization. But it is probably more than that. These objectives are the organization's mandate. Argenti (1989), who has written extensively on the proper determination of objectives, has, for instance, warned about the dangers of corporate perversion, which occurs when the organization's resources are used by interest groups or pressure groups for their own ends (Argenti, 1989, p. 57). He argues that it is more difficult to pervert the organization the more accurately its objectives are stated. So, close attention to stating objectives is critical.

Once the objectives are set, and before the strategies are selected and implemented, that is, before action, there must be strategic analysis. This emphasis on analysis first – before action – justifies the characterization of the technocratic leader as steeped in a rationalist ethic: it is assumed that the keys to the truest strategic action are rational analysis and judgement, not that action and experimentation are the keys to sound strategic knowledge.

Business schools have a strong tendency to teach a curriculum suited to technocrats. However, in their educational programmes, the use of analytical techniques such as SWOT analysis and PEST analysis (see Chapter 4) looms larger than the emphasis on setting clear objectives and calculating financial ratios. Since these particular techniques can end up just as methods for making lists, there is some justification for the description of the dominant methodology of strategy as the construction of lists (Kay, 1993, p. 360). In the texts used in business schools there is a subsidiary interest in the specification of algorithms for decision making, giving the impression that decision making is a matter of processing information rather than solving difficult dilemmas. At their worst, educational programmes have emphasized skills in listing and classifying, rather than in investigating and reasoning.

The technocratic model of strategic management, by putting the emphasis on analysis and choices, may have facilitated the development of specialist planning staffs, who could draw up analyses that could then be adopted by the executive. This is another reason for labelling the thinking as technocratic – i.e. it is suited to the needs of the technocracy advising the business executives.

The 1980s critics of this style of strategic thinking argued that intuition and creativity were missing from the strategic planning orthodoxy of the 1960s and 1970s. 'Great strategies, like great works of art or great scientific discoveries, call for technical mastery in the working out, but originate in insights that are beyond the reach of conscious analysis' (Ohmae, 1982, p. 4).

The critics had a point. Moreover, the critics' more measured remarks did not completely reject the rational approach. Ohmae warned: 'Intuition or gut-feel alone does not ensure secure business plans' (1982, p. 35). Analysis was an essential activity for strategists. It could help to stimulate the creative process, to test out ideas, to work out implications and so on. It was the balance they were really concerned about. The key was to combine the creative and intuitive quality, which Ohmae also referred to as mental elasticity, with the analytical method. Both reinforced the other: analysis could stimulate and lead on to creativity, and the creative and inquisitive mind was best able to pose the most fruitful questions for the analysis stage.

The transforming leader

In the 1980s, books on corporate strategies emphasized the role of top managers as motivators of organizational members (Pascale and Athos, 1981; Peters and Waterman, 1982). Their job was to supply meanings, not objectives and analysis. The label of 'transforming leader' was coined by Burns (1978).

As we saw in the previous chapter, Peters and Waterman (1982) argued that their sample of excellent companies did not carry out strategic analysis, make a choice and then implement new strategic options. Instead, the leaders of these companies created a favourable context for problem-solving experiments, sustained it and then transformed the experiments into new strategic directions. The 'making of meanings' appears to have been intertwined with these processes in different ways. First, the leaders were responsible for the shared values, or culture, which provided the internal discipline that made it safe to encourage problem solving and experiments. Strong cultures directed towards the market place made the para-phernalia of formal organizational controls less necessary and enabled an informal context to prevail. Second, the leaders sustained experimental actions and then transformed them into strategies through the management of the after-the-fact labelling process.

Peters and Waterman suggest that transforming leaders create the cultures of top companies by consistently promoting one or two values over long periods of time. The values are promoted by the personal attention of the leader, who is said to be concerned with the 'tricks' of the pedagogue, the mentor and the linguist. The leader uses every opportunity, even very small ones, to put across these values. If the first step in the creation of culture is down to the personal action of the leader, the second step is the diffusion of the shared values through the organization by means of the telling of stories, myths and legends. The end result is the instilling of a common purpose in the organization.

It might seem that the shared values created by the transforming leader are equivalent to the objectives and financial targets prized within the technocratic leadership style. However, Peters and Waterman did not find that they produced equivalent results. They refer to the results of a study which preceded their own study of excellent companies, and which compared organizations with financial targets and those with well defined guiding beliefs:

> Ironically, the companies that seemed the most focused – those with the most quantified statements of mission, with the most precise financial targets – had done less well financially than those with broader, less precise, more qualitative statements of corporate purpose.
>
> Peters and Waterman, 1982, p. 281

However, the excellent companies with their strong cultures motivated employees to act in a disciplined way; the technocratic leadership, logically speaking, use objectives and financial targets as a way of judging their organization, which leads to quite a different ethos of discipline.

> The top companies, on the other hand, always seem to recognize what the companies that only set financial targets don't know or don't deem important. The excellent companies seem to understand that every man seeks meaning (not just the top fifty who are 'in the bonus pool').
>
> Peters and Waterman, 1982, p. 76

So, transforming leaders emphasize the need for values to educate the members of the organization, whereas the clear objectives and the financial targets of the technocratic leaders merely measure the organization's performance.

Arguably, this style of transforming leadership is in some sense the opposite of the technocratic one. In place of the neutral and *technical* planning of resources to achieve organizational objectives, this transforming leadership welds the members of an organization into an effective and creative *social* unit. As Hamel and Prahalad (1994, p. 71) put it, the senior management have the responsibility of building 'an intellectually compelling and emotionally enticing view of the future', establishing a sense of purpose and helping everyone to understand their role in bringing about success in competing for the future. When managers achieve this focusing of the organization's intellectual and emotional energy, they have constructed a cohesive social unit.

Crafting strategy

Mintzberg (1995), who has come to occupy a very distinctive position within the literature of strategic management because of his strong focus on organizational matters, developed the conception of the strategist as engaged in crafting strategy. The statement of the essence of this 'crafting' concept by Mintzberg probably cannot be bettered:

What springs to mind is not so much thinking and reason as involvement, a feeling of intimacy and harmony with the materials at hand, developed through long experience and commitment. Formulation and implementation merge into a fluid process of learning through which creative activities evolve.

Mintzberg, 1995, p. 114

Like transforming leadership this seems to be a rejection of the technocratic model. In the very word 'crafting' we have a rival view of proficiency – not a proficiency in terms of analytical techniques, but proficiency based on learning from experience.

In effect, Mintzberg is saying that learning takes place in a complex relationship between thinking and action. Analysis does not simply precede strategic action (i.e. the assumption of the technocratic style), but is mixed up with it dynamically. Strategists can take advantage of learning by 'allowing their strategies to develop gradually' (1995 , p. 117). They can allow the actions to converge into emergent strategic patterns and then become a deliberate strategy through recognition by senior management.

The emergent strategies can develop in very unexpected ways because of errors. They can be surprising for other reasons – for example, when experiments affect the emergent strategies. However, Mintzberg is not advocating totally unplanned or uncontrolled strategies. He sees the process of turning emergent strategies into deliberate ones as important. It is desirable for the strategists to learn from actions and then incorporate the lessons into formal strategy. In this sense, learning is enriching control.

Passive learning

It is important to distinguish this view from that of transforming leadership. Both bring out a processual view of strategy. But whereas transforming leaders are active in 'shaping' a strategy from experimental action, Mintzberg conceptualizes the leaders as learning in a passive way. That is, top management do not create or shape the emergent strategy; they intervene after the fact to bestow official recognition on a pattern which has formed. Consequently, learning is conceptualized as 'pattern recognition' and thus learning is about discovering strategies rather than actively creating them. We would say that these are leaders who discover rather than experiment (see Chapter 2 on paradigms where discovery and experimentation are discussed).

Mintzberg argues that crafting strategy produces better strategies than planning strategy does. 'Some strategists appreciate that they cannot always be smart enough to think through everything in advance' (1987, p. 117). We have labelled this the passive-learner style.

The pragmatic leader

There is a final view of the requirements of top managers as strategists. This is the hardest to spell out because it has not become a widespread assumption in the literature; nor has it been much evangelized in guru books. In one respect it is a return to the technocratic leadership model, because it is a return to the rational theme. However, instead of stressing objective setting, analytical techniques and decision-making routines, it looks for a pragmatic assessment of the opportunities of specific situations, learning and participative planning processes (Thurley and Wirdenius, 1989). It is a pragmatic leadership – and we would see it as an embodiment of a scientific approach in a business setting.

A scientific approach

Whilst they had a point, the critics of the technocratic approach did not go far enough in their assessment of this thinking of the 1960s and 1970s. They were so busy suggesting that rationality had been overdone (see for example, Peters and Waterman, 1982, pp. 53–4) that they overlooked a way in which the technocratic approach was deficient in rationality. Rationality is more than just using analytical techniques and working out financial ratios.

The fullest expression of rationality over the last 300 years has been the scientific frame of mind, the essence of which has been described as an interest in detailed facts combined with a devotion to abstract generalizations (Whitehead, 1938, p. 13). On the one hand this means the development of a sceptical or doubting posture until a thing has been proved to be a fact; and on the other, a desire to show how a bewildering and massive number of facts can be made intelligible, perhaps as determined by scientific laws (as in the laws of physics). This scientific mind is underpinned by the assumption that all occurrences can be studied and causes found: everything is susceptible to causal explanation. (As with other areas, we are aware that this view of science may be contested, and not just by the post-modernists with their new paradigms of science.)

The scientific mind has already had a major impact on management, as in the development of 'scientific management' in the early part of the twentieth century, when science was being applied chiefly to the operational effectiveness of organizations. The point we wish to raise, however, is: could there be a scientific strategic management?

The plea for a scientific approach to strategic management has been made most persuasively in recent times by Kay (1993). He has stated his belief in the benefits of building up empirical knowledge of business strategy. While noting that the subject of management has far to go before it can claim, like medicine, to be a science, he argued that the study of business, to develop scientifically, needed to base its statements on deductions from stated premises or to make potentially verifiable claims about the empirical world (Kay, 1993, p. 360).

This seems to argue for the relevance of a scientific approach for the study of strategic management. What about the practitioner of strategic management? Can a scientific approach be recommended for them as well? We think the answer is yes, providing an appropriate view of a scientific approach to strategic management is adopted.

The overall model of a scientific approach for management practitioners has been articulated by Mary Parker Follett (1941). She defined science as 'knowledge gained by systematic observation, experiment and reasoning; knowledge co-ordinated, arranged and systematized' (Follett, 1941, p. 123).

Follett (1941) urged a focus on the growth of the capacity for organized thinking in the development of top managers:

> If you wish to train yourself for higher executive positions, the first thing for you to decide is what you are training for? Ability to dominate or manipulate others? ... But I am convinced that the first essential of business success is the capacity for organized *thinking*.
>
> Follett, 1941, p. 131 (our italics)

The characteristics of the pragmatic strategist

A pragmatic and scientifically inclined strategic management has a general commitment to rational and scientific decision making, but it distinguishes itself in its insistence on specificity in designing strategies to suit situations (Follett, 1941; Thurley and Wirdenius, 1989). This is based on a commitment to studying the facts of the situation, and on a rejection of knee-jerk responses which fail to investigate situations for integrative solutions that optimize the organization's results. It is certainly unimpressed by the blind implementation of strategies recommended by strategic management gurus. In general, this style is opposed to ideological decision making, being always concerned to find or evolve what will work in the specific situation the organization finds itself in.

It entails devising strategies which specifically meet the requirements of the internal social situation as well as the external business situation. Consequently, a scientific approach to strategic management posits the capacity of this approach to develop strategies which are effective for the social relationships within the organization. This means that consent should be sought by developing objectives and strategies that are widely supported within the organization (Thurley and Wirdenius, 1989) and that are effective because they are simultaneously designed for the external business situation. It is in the last sense that Follett recommended top managers to seek creative and integrative solutions to situations rather than compromises.

The result of a pragmatic and scientifically inclined strategic management would be greater *conscious* control of strategic action and greater ability by top managers to solve problems by means of investigation and *thinking*. There is also implicitly contained within this approach a management commitment to open discussion and debate within the organization – because strategy decisions are based on rational and scientific appraisals of the situational requirements.

The all-round strategic manager

Ansoff and McDonnell (1990) say that the strategic manager

must be a divergent, creative solver of ill-structured problems, and whose skills should include sensitivity to the environment, and skills in strategy analysis and in design of strategically responsive structures. His leadership skills and style should be, in part, those of the entrepreneur: vision, risk-taking, change management, charisma and, in part, those of a political statesman.

Ansoff and McDonnell, 1990, p. 261

This is almost a composite picture of the strategic manager, reflecting the accumulation of thinking about the styles and expected impacts of the strategic manager.

Perhaps even better for its comprehensiveness is the prescription to be found in Thurley and Wirdenius's (1989) suggestion of six values for managerial action within a European context. The six values are as follows:

1 Decisions should be the result of scientific, rational thinking.
2 Specific strategies should be evolved pragmatically to work in specific situations and strategies should not be based on ideologies or following universalistic theories.
3 Management should show an emotional commitment to successful change with consequent implications for inspiring employees to regard future possibilities seriously.
4 Rational thinking should make use of managerial and technical experience, in the context of open debate and a scientific philosophy.
5 Management should act to achieve commitment to organizational goals and to ensure broadly consensual decisions (i.e. management should act democratically).
6 There should be a continuous process of creative learning by managers, through and with other colleagues, and a continuous process of self-development within organizational life.

This statement of a value system for European managers gets to the heart of a scientifically inclined strategic management with its emphasis on scientific, rational decision making, specific strategies for specific situations and the requirements for commitment to organizational goals and for consensual decisions. But it also encompasses other notions of the strategic leadership role, such as the need for emotional commitment in order to inspire employees (*cf.* transforming leaders) and the importance of creative learning and making use of managerial and technical experience (*cf.* the passive learner style).

Consequently, it seems that the all-round strategist has to have a bit of all the styles (probably including the technocratic one), even though specific situations may require them in different proportions.

Empirical research

One of the most interesting studies of management in recent years was that by Boyatzis (1982). He was particularly interested in the link between personal competencies and management effectiveness.

His sample included some executive managers in a small number of US companies. The numbers of executive managers for whom he had skill level data was quite small (n = 75), but the results were curiously reflective of the ideas discussed in the first part of this chapter. Comparisons of poor and superior performing executive managers suggested six critical difference in skills. These were:

1 efficiency orientation
2 self-confidence
3 use of oral presentations
4 conceptualization
5 diagnostic use of concepts
6 proactivity.

These are shown in Figure 11.2, where they have been placed in the appropriate quadrant of the figure for strategic management style.

Boyatzis defined the competency that he identified as the 'efficiency orientation' in terms of managers wanting to do things better. However, the compatibility with the technocratic leadership style becomes clear when it is noted that managers with this orientation demonstrate skills in goal setting, planning and organizing resources efficiently.

Then we can suggest the correspondence of the transforming style of strategic leadership with two of the competencies identified by Boyatzis: namely, 'self-confidence' – with its associated self-presentation skills – and 'use of oral presentations'. The rationale in

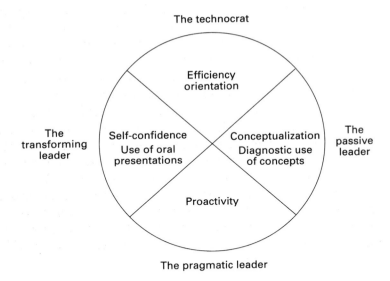

Figure 11.2   *Personal competencies*

this case is that Peters and Waterman suggested that these leaders were concerned with the 'tricks' of the pedagogue, the mentor and the linguist. Boyatzis comes quite close to making a similar type of connection when he suggests that managers in executive-level jobs have some of their power based partly 'in the stimulation of commitment of personnel through inspiration (i.e., self-confidence and the use of oral presentations)' (1982, p. 222).

Another two of Boyatzis's competencies, 'conceptualization' and 'diagnostic use of concepts', seem to fit quite logically the passive learner style. Mintzberg, as we saw above, conceptualizes effective strategists as learning in a passive way by intervening after the fact to bestow official recognition on a strategic pattern that has formed. He specifically refers to this type of learning as 'pattern recognition'. So, it is very striking that conceptualization is described by Boyatzis as a thought process in which patterns in information or events are identified or recognized through the development of concepts. The second competence – the diagnostic use of concepts – also fits the passive learner style since this is where existing concepts are applied to situations in order to interpret and explain them.

Finally, the Boyatzis concept of the 'proactivity' competence shows obvious affinities with the scientifically inclined pragmatic style of strategic leadership. The scientific approach to strategic management is defined in part as a pragmatic concern with the facts of the situation and a rejection of doctrinaire or ideological decision making. Boyatzis defined proactive managers as demonstrating skills in information seeking and problem solving. These seem highly relevant skills for the pragmatic strategic leader.

This study (see Figure 11.3) provides evidence not only of the kinds of skill that executive managers need in order to perform well, but also evidence that good strategists in top management need to have a mix of the four styles we have reviewed above – the technocrat, the transforming leader, the passive learner and the pragmatic leader. It appears that the literature on strategic management (Argenti, Peters and Waterman, Mintzberg, and Thurley and Wirdenius) has been slowly accumulating the ideas of the profile of the all-round strategic leader.

Figure 11.3   *Boyatzis (1982) and personal competencies of executive-level managers*

Boyatzis (1982) looked at the relationship between the personal competencies of managers and their management performance using a sample of US managers in a small number of organizations. The managers were located at different levels in management structures (namely, in entry level, middle level and executive-level jobs).

The managers were classified into performance groups – poor, average or superior performers.

The skill levels of 253 managers in their sample, drawn from ten of the organizations, were assessed using behavioural event interviews (a form of critical incident interview) which produced qualitative data on the manager's actual behaviour. Each manager was asked to describe three incidents in which he or she had felt themselves to be effective and three in which he or she felt ineffective. This method is said to be most useful in assessing skill-level competencies (as opposed to competencies at the level of traits, motives, etc.). The interviews were coded for frequency of occurrence of nineteen different characteristics. It was hypothesized that better performing managers would demonstrate more of these characteristics than poorer performing managers.

The study found twelve competencies to be important in explaining managerial effectiveness across the three levels of management. Ten competencies were used in a discriminant analysis technique to correctly classify 51 per cent of the sample in terms of their performance group, i.e. they achieved a moderate amount of success in explaining the variation in management performance. The ten competencies were:

- self-control
- spontaneity
- perceptual objectivity
- diagnostic use of concepts
- developing others
- concern with impact
- use of unilateral power
- use of socialized power
- use of oral presentations
- concern with close relationships.

The rest of the variation might be explained by other competencies not investigated or other kinds of variables (e.g. environmental and job variables).

For the executive managers (n = 75), six skill-level competencies are worth noting. The mean skill levels for each of the six are shown for poor, average and superior executive managers in Table 11.1. In each case there was a significant difference between the mean skill level of the superior group and the poor group.

Table 11.1   *Skill levels*

Competencies test	Mean skill level			Significance level of T-test (poor vs superior)
	Poor (n = 19)	Average (n = 15)	Superior (n = 41)	
Efficiency orientation	0.58	0.80	1.20	0.013
Self-confidence	0.11	0.53	0.44	0.001
Use of oral presentations	0.05	0.13	0.20	0.044
Conceptualization	0.11	0.27	0.42	0.007
Diagnostic use of concepts	0.58	1.07	1.22	0.002
Proactivity	0.95	1.07	1.42	0.041

Sample: 75 executive managers.

The definition of these competencies was as follows.

Efficiency orientation – The manager with this orientation wants to do things better and demonstrates skills in goal setting, planning and organizing resources efficiently. It is associated by Boyatzis with the role of innovator.

Self-confidence – This is concerned with self-presentation skills.

Use of oral presentations – This is, as the name suggests, skill in verbal presentation.

Conceptualization – Managers with this skill are able to develop new concepts to describe, understand and interpret events and information; it is a useful creative skill and facilitates communication about issues or problems to others. It has been described by Boyatzis as a 'thought process in which the person identifies or recognises patterns in an assortment of information' (Boyatzis, 1982, p. 111).

Diagnostic use of concepts – This is where existing concepts are applied to situations in order to interpret and explain them.

Proactivity – Proactive managers demonstrate skills in information seeking and problem solving.

The development of strategic managers

Much of the training and education for strategic managers has been limited in its effectiveness and limited in its applicability to contemporary conditions. Training within organizations has been insufficient and education has lagged behind developments in industry.

The amount of training for top managers has been modest. Most UK directors appear to have had no formal preparation for board positions (Coulson-Thomas, 1993, p. 82).

Such training as there has been has also evolved. An old idea of training was to rotate the individual manager through functional assignments, so that the manager gains an all-round perspective. Another idea was to place individuals in assistant positions where they could learn top management skills. But as strategic management gained in credibility, these old methods of training general managers have proved insufficient. Ansoff and McDonnell (1990) suggest that it 'has been common to introduce strategic planning by means of one-day seminars during which general managers were converted into "instant" strategic planners' (Ansoff and

McDonnell, 1990, p. 264). It has also been evident that managers have turned to books to undertake their own individual development. The phenomenal success of books like Peters and Waterman's *In Search of Excellence*, and the active experimentation with their ideas, shows that some books can inspire managers to adopt strategic management methods.

But the effectiveness of most of these modest attempts at developing strategic management competence must be doubted. Can one-day seminars or guru books have deep enough impacts? Follett, long ago, warned that training involves changing habits and skills.

> Managerial skill cannot be painted on the outside of executives; it has to go deeper than that … managerial workers have to acquire certain habits and attitudes … for the acquisition of these habits and attitudes three conditions must be given: (1) detailed information in regard to a new method; (2) the stimulus to adopt this method; and (3) the opportunity to practise it so that it may become a habit.
>
> Follett, 1941, p. 130

The growth of training for competence-based management qualifications in the UK has been slow and a very serious weakness is that the intellectual dimension – the capacity for organized thinking – in developing managers has been (temporarily at least) eclipsed by the emphasis on assessing performance against statements of role requirements, which are assumed to be universally and absolutely true.

Business schools are to some extent still caught up in the old model of general management. This means that, in part, they are still inclined to view the top managers as co-ordinators and integrators of the separate functions. On this basis, the student of business policy needs to be introduced to the theory and techniques of each of the main functional areas (production, finance, marketing, human resource management and information management) and then helped to integrate these separate disciplines. This very point has been made by Ansoff and McDonnell (1990).

> A student was first exposed to the theory and practice of the respective functional skills and then to a series of integrative general management cases. Later, when computers emerged, instead of (or in addition to) the cases, the student participated in complex computer-assisted marketing-production-finance integrative games.
>
> Ansoff and McDonnell, 1990, p. 261

This general management model for the curriculum has begun to give way to a strategic management model but, as we have seen, strategic management itself has evolved. The business school curriculum and academic textbooks tend to reflect this evolution of strategic management, although many reflect its earlier rather than its later phases. Thus there are many textbooks written in the technocratic genre, showing more interest in strategic analysis and strategic choices and only residual concern for implementation. This has served to entrench pseudo-scientific techniques and algorithms as the core of strategic thinking and has marginalized the contributions of experience, investigation and reasoning within the curriculum. There have been some textbooks, adopting positions antithetical to the technocratic ethos, that have attempted to put across a postmodernist curriculum, but these are quite rare.

Our own view is that business schools should be developing pragmatic (scientific) strategic management. Practical experience and intuition are important, but urging people to turn their back on the rational dimension, urging them to be intuitive managers, in which hunches rather than thinking win the day, is unlikely to produce any long-term improvement in strategic management. This is not to say that subjectivity can be eliminated from strategic management, nor the creativity which accompanies it. But subjectivity, experience and intuition are not enough: they need a scientific outlook to enable subjectivity to be tested, experience to be enriched by learning and intuition to be supplemented by scientifically inclined problem solving.

There are practical implications from these remarks for the use of case studies in business education. The technocratic obsession with analytical concepts and financial ratios makes case studies a vehicle for students to practise the deployment of analytical techniques and to practise calculating financial ratios. In other words, the case study can be a rehearsal of technocratic approaches to strategic management. They can, however, also be opportunities to develop scientifically inclined modes of thinking, in which individuals learn to make observations and investigate experience, discuss and compare experiences, and develop knowledge on a systematic and logical basis.

So far we have discussed the development of strategic managers in terms of the separate spheres of training and education. We must finish by noting the importance of trying to link these two spheres together. The development of approaches to strategic management that involve participative planning and creative learning could be a continuation of the educational process for managers. If we turn this around, the educational process within business schools needs to be a platform which enables the continuation of lifelong learning for managers and for others, within organizations. Greater thought needs to be given, therefore, to how experience and training in organizations can influence and be influenced by, the educational processes that are being evolved in business schools. Boyatzis's work on the personal competencies of effective executive managers provides some strong indications of the objectives and content for educational programmes for strategic managers.

Key points

1 Major contributions to the literature on strategic management (Argenti, Peters and Waterman, Mintzberg, and Thurley and Wirdenius) have been presenting ideas, implicitly as well as explicitly, of the profile of the strategic leader. These have been reviewed in this chapter as four styles – the technocrat, the transforming leader, the passive learner and the pragmatic leader.

2 These four styles may each be contributing some of the fundamental ingredients of the all-round good strategist. There is certainly empirical evidence from the work of Boyatzis (1982) which suggests not only the kinds of skill that executive managers need in order to perform well, but also that superior performing executives have skills which might be associated with all four styles.

3 This chapter has very briefly considered the record on training and education for strategic managers. We have suggested that the development of approaches to strategic management that involve participative planning and creative learning could be a continuation of the educational process for managers, and that business schools need to provide an educational platform that enables the continuation of lifelong learning for managers and for others within organizations.

References

Ansoff, I. and McDonnell, E. (1990) *Implanting Strategic Management* (Prentice Hall).

Argenti, J. (1989) *Practical Corporate Planning* (Routledge).

Boyatzis, R.E. (1982) *The Competent Manager* (Wiley).

Burns, J.M. (1978) *Leadership* (Harper & Row).

Coulson-Thomas, C. (1993) *Developing Directors* (McGraw-Hill).

Follett, M.P. (1941) *Dynamic Administration: The Collected Papers of Mary Parker Follett* (Management Publications Trust Ltd).

Hamel, G. and Prahalad, C.K. (1994) *Competing for the Future* (Wiley).

Kay, J. (1993) *Foundations of Corporate Success* (Oxford University Press).

Mintzberg, H. (1995) 'Crafting Strategy' in Mintzberg, H., Quinn, J.B. and Ghoshal, S. (editors) *The Strategy Process* (Prentice Hall).

Ohmae, K. (1982) *The Mind of the Strategist* (McGraw-Hill).

Pascale, R.T. and Athos, A.G. (1981) *The Art of Japanese Management* (Simon & Schuster).

Peters, T. and Waterman, R.H. (1982) *In Search of Excellence* (Harper Collins).

Thurley, K. and Wirdenius, H. (1989) *Towards European Management* (Pitman).

Whitehead, A. N. (1938) *Science and the Modern World* (Penguin).

Appendix

Strategic planning worksheets

The worksheets that are provided here are designed to support a strategy planning process and the use of the analytical techniques discussed in Chapters 3 and 4.

Process steps and worksheets

Step		Worksheets
Step 1	Trend analysis	Worksheet 1: Trend analysis
Step 2	Environmental and resource analysis	Worksheet 2: PEST analysis
		Worksheet 3: Skill mapping
Step 3	Target setting	Worksheet 4: Scenario analysis
Step 4	SWOT analysis	Worksheet 5: SWOT analysis
Step 5	Identification of strategic issue(s)	Worksheet 6: Key problems
Step 6	Formulation of strategic actions	Worksheet 7: Strategy brainstorming
Step 7	Evaluation of actions	Worksheet 8: Appraisal of strategy proposals
Step 8	Planning implementation	Worksheet 9: Stakeholder analysis
		Worksheet 10: Resources analysis

Worksheet 1: Trend analysis

Briefly describe (using a short phrase) the trends affecting the whole organization over the last three to five years.

Will these same trends continue impacting over the next three to five years (encircle Yes or No)?

(Checklist: level of demand for organization's products or services, customer/client needs, organization's skills, its resources, structural developments, communications, managers and management practices, and other major organizational changes.)

In my view, the trends over the last three to five years have been?	Will these continue over the next three to five years?
1..	Yes/No
....	
2..	Yes/No
....	
3..	Yes/No
....	
4..	Yes/No
....	
5..	Yes/No
....	
6..	Yes/No
....	
7..	Yes/No
....	
8..	Yes/No
....	
9..	Yes/No
....	
10..	Yes/No

Worksheet 2: PEST analysis

What specific events and trends do you think will impact on the organization over the next three to five years? Please consider political, economic, social and technological events and trends. Please bear in mind that some events and trends may not have occurred in the past.

Rate their probability of occurring using a 0–10 scale. Rate events or trends you think will definitely occur as 10, and those you think are improbable as 0. A rating of 5 implies a 50:50 chance of the event or trend occurring.

Rate the *importance* of the events or trends, again using a 0–10 scale. Rate those which are of critical importance as 10, and those which are of negligible importance as 0. A rating of 5 implies a moderately important event or trend.

Political/economic/social/ technological events/trends (over next three to five years)	Probability	Importance
1..	....	....
2..	....	....
3..	....	....
4..	....	....
5..	....	....
6..	....	....
7..	....	....
8..	....	....
9..	....	....
10..	....	....
11..	....	....
12..	....	....

Worksheet 3: Skill mapping

What specific skills does the organization have? List the skills below, aiming at the identification of at least five or six. The list may be based on what organizational members claim, what customers say and may be inferred from organizational charts and the organization's products or services.

For each specific skill, rate the *infrastructural support* for the skill. For example, does the organization have good or the best machinery and equipment to exploit this skill? Does the management value and help to sustain and develop this skill? Is the use of this skill adequately rewarded? Rate the infrastructural support for the skill using a 0–10 scale. Rate specific skills that are well supported as 10 and those you think are neglected as 0. A rating of 5 implies a moderate level of infrastructural support.

Also rate each specific skill for its *contribution to the value of the product or service* as perceived by customers/clients/consumers. Use a 0–10 scale, with 10 representing a critical contribution to the value of the product or service and 0 representing a negligible contribution.

Specific skill	Infrastructural support for skill	Contribution to value of product/service
1..	....	....
2..	....	....
3..	....	....
4..	....	....
5..	....	....
6..	....	....
7..	....	....
8..	....	....
9..	....	....
10..	....	....

Worksheet 4: Scenario analysis (for target setting)

This worksheet helps you to carry out a scenario analysis in order to produce a statement of the future desired state of the organization. This is not a conventional scenario analysis because it does not focus exclusively on the external environment. A statement of the desired future state of the organization in three to ten years from now can be used as a target in the strategy planning process – a strategy for the organization can be planned to achieve this desired future state.

First list, using short phrases, the components of the future situation if everything developed in a perfect way. For example: How would customer/clients/consumers perceive the organization's products and services? What products or services would be marketed/distributed? Who would the customers/clients/consumers be? What would be happening to sales/market share/profitability/income, etc.? What skills would the organization have and be developing? What levels of efficiency/quality/innovation would the organization be achieving?

Components of a future state if everything developed in a perfect way:

1...

....

2...

....

3...

....

4...

....

5...

....

6...

Second, include these components (in a short statement of one to three sentences) in your scenario of the future desired state of the organization in three to ten years:

Scenario of the organization's future state:

....

....

....

....

....

....

....

....

....

....

....

....

....

....

....

You can produce a counterpart statement of an undesired future state, resulting from all the developments impacting negatively on the organization.

Worksheet 5: SWOT analysis

What are the strengths and weaknesses of the organization? What opportunities and threats are coming up?

Note: a *strength,* e.g. a skill or resource, can be used by the organization to do something successfully; a weakness make successful action less likely; *opportunities* require action to be taken by the organization before benefits result; and *threats* will cause harm to the organization unless action is taken.

1 List below the organization's strengths, weaknesses, opportunities and threats.
2 Review the lists, noting any evidence that the items listed really exist. For example, what evidence is there that a particular threat to the organization really exists? Revise the lists by deleting any items you no longer think need be included.
3 Rank in order of importance the strengths you have listed. Indicate each item's ranking in the appropriate column (1 = most important, 2 = second most important, etc.). Rank weaknesses, opportunities and threats in the same way.

Strengths	Importance ranking
1..	....
....	....
2..	....
....	....
3..	....
....	....
4..	....
....	....
5..	....
....	....
6..	....

Weaknesses	Importance ranking
1..	....
....	....
2..	....
....	....
3..	....
....	....
4..	....
....	....
5..	....
....	....
6..	....

Opportunities	Importance ranking
1..	....
....	....
2..	....
....	....
3..	....
....	....
4..	....
....	....
5..	....
....	....
6..	....

Threats	Importance ranking
1..	....
....	....
2..	....
....	....
3..	....
....	....
4..	....
....	....
5..	....
....	....
6..	....

Worksheet 6: Key problems

1 What are the key *problems* concerning the organization's managers? List these below, briefly identifying each problem in a short phrase.
2 Provide an explanation of, and evidence of, how these problems are impacting on any of the following:

- the organization's objectives and targets
- the organization's vision of its ideal or desired future state
- the organization's core values or beliefs.

   Note these in the *Impact* column.

3 Finally, *rank* the key problems, showing the ranking in the last column.

Problem	Impact	Ranking
1		
2		
3		
4		

Problem	Impact	Ranking
5		
6		
7		
8		
9		
10		

Worksheet 7: Strategy brainstorming

The key problems that have been identified by managers in Worksheet 6 and that can be demonstrated as having an impact on the organization's objectives and targets, or the vision of its ideal or desired future state or its core values or beliefs may be regarded as strategic issues. Take the issue ranked as most important on Worksheet 6 and use this worksheet to decide some possible strategic actions.

If you use a brainstorming approach, concentrate on generating as many as possible strategic actions without worrying too much about their feasibility.

You can cue this brainstorming by answering the question: How can the organization deal with the most important strategic issue – can it make use of one its strengths, can it act to remedy or overcome one of its weaknesses in a way that deals with the issue, can it use one of its opportunities, can it take an action to counter a threat that will deal with the issue?

....

....

....

....

....

....

....

A brainstormed list of proposals for strategic action may need to be refined before the individual ideas are ready for evaluation. For instance, many of the ideas may be essentially the same and thus the list can be reduced. Some items on the list may be connected with others on the list and could thus be grouped together under a broader proposal for strategic action. This will also lead to a shorter list.

Worksheet 8: Appraisal of strategy proposals

Each item on a list of proposals for strategic change (see Worksheet 7) needs to be evaluated. (If the list is too long, some screening criteria may be needed to bring the list down to a manageable length.)

The first step is to decide the criteria to be used in appraising each proposal. The selection of criteria may be influenced by the need to devise a strategy to suit the specific situation, but commonly used criteria are:

- feasibility – can the strategic action be made to happen?
- suitability – will the strategic action solve the strategic issue?
- acceptability – will the strategic action produce results that will be perceived as satisfactory by important stakeholders (e.g. will profitability be sufficient)?
- timeliness – will the strategic action have its beneficial impact in the required timescale?

Each proposal for strategic action is appraised using one of the tables below. The selected *criteria* are entered in the left-hand column. A weighting is decided for each criterion: a *weighting* between 1 and 10 is used, with 10 indicating that the criterion is very critical.

Each proposal is assessed on a scale of 1–4 to assess how well it meets each criterion, with 1 = fails criterion, 2 = just meets criterion, 3 = meets it comfortably, and 4 = ideal. This is then multiplied by the weighting to give the score on this criterion.

Proposal:...

Criteria	Weighting (1–10)	Assessment of proposal (1–4)	Score (W x A)
1................................	....	....	....
2................................	....	....	....
3................................	....	....	....
4................................	....	....	....
		Total =	

Proposal:..

Criteria	Weighting (1–10)	Assessment of proposal (1–4)	Score (W x A)
1....................................	....	....	....
2....................................	....	....	....
3....................................	....	....	....
4....................................	....	....	....
		Total =	

Proposal:..

Criteria	Weighting (1–10)	Assessment of proposal (1–4)	Score (W x A)
1....................................	....	....	....
2....................................	....	....	....
3....................................	....	....	....
4....................................	....	....	....
		Total =	

Proposal:..

Criteria	Weighting (1–10)	Assessment of proposal (1–4)	Score (W x A)
1....................................	....	....	....
2....................................	....	....	....
3....................................	....	....	....
4....................................	....	....	....
		Total =	

Worksheet 9: Stakeholder analysis

When an organization has decided on a strategic action to resolve its strategic issues, it needs to decide how it will implement it. This involves assessing the likely reactions of stakeholders to the implementation of the strategy. There are three steps.

1 *The stakeholders* – individuals, groups or organizations who affect or are affected by the organization – are listed.
2 Then rate the stakeholders' likely *reactions* on a scale of –5 to +5. Those who are likely to welcome or support the strategy are rated as +5; those who are most likely to be strongly opposed are rated –5. Stakeholders who are unlikely to react either positively or negatively, are rated as 0.
3 Finally, rate the *power* of the stakeholders on a scale of 1–10 (with 10 being high).

Stakeholder	Reaction to strategy (–5 – + 5)	Power (1–10)
....	....	....
....	....	....
....	....	....
....	....	....
....	....	....
....	....	....

This analysis is used both to identify stakeholder groups in terms of their likely reaction to the chosen strategic action, and to assess their power. The organization then needs to plan its strategy taking into account these factors.

Worksheet 10: Resources analysis

A resources analysis is also useful in planning the implementation of strategy. A careful assessment needs to be made of the resources required for the strategic action and how they can be mobilized. The basic approach is to identify the resources needed, who controls or owns those resources, their availability and their criticality to the implementation of change.

The most obvious resources needed to implement strategic changes include money, skills, legitimacy, power, time, commitment, etc.

In the table below list each *resource* and its *owner*, and rate the availability of each resource on a scale of 1–10. Resources with uncertain availability are 10; resources that are definitely available are rated as 1. Rate the *criticality* of resources from 1–10, with 1 representing resources that are not important and 10 representing essential resources.

Resource required	Owner, supplier or controller of the resource	Availability of resource (1–10)	Criticality of resource (1–10)
....	....	....	....
....	....	....	....
....	....	....	....
....	....	....	....
....	....	....	....
....	....	....	....
....	....	....	....
....	....	....	....

This table helps you to identify systematically those resources needing most attention (i.e. those that are not available but are highly critical), and draws attention to where those resources are currently located. This is important information for planning strategy implementation.

Index